www.EZmethods.com

SAT®

TEST PREPARATION MODULE
MATH TEST TAKING STRATEGIES

2007 EDITION

EZ SIMPLIFIED SOLUTIONS – THE BREAKTHROUGH IN TEST PREP!

LEADERS IN TEST PREP SOLUTIONS – WE MAKE IT EZ FOR YOU!

AUTHOR: PUNIT RAJA SURYA CHANDRA

EZ Solutions
P O Box 10755
Silver Spring, MD 20914
USA

EZ SOLUTIONS
P.O. Box 10755
Silver Spring, MD 20914

Conceived, conceptualized, written, and edited by:
Punit Raja Surya Chandra, EZ Solutions

November 2006

International Standard Book Number:
10-digit ISBN: 0-9727790-1-9
13-digit ISBN: 978-0-9727790-1-2

PRINTED AND MANUFACTURED IN THE UNITED STATES OF AMERICA

10 9 8 7 6 5 4 3 2 1

TABLE OF CONTENTS

INTRODUCTION

▪ ABOUT EZ SOLUTIONS

EZ Solutions – *the breakthrough in test-preparation*!

EZ Solutions is an organization formed to provide *simplified solutions* for test-preparation and tutoring. Although EZ Solutions is a fairly new name in the publication industry, it has quickly become a respected publisher of test-prep books, study guides, study aids, handbooks, and other reference works. EZ publications and educational materials are highly respected, and they continue to receive an unprecedented amount of praise from professionals, instructors, librarians, parents, and students.

OBJECTIVE: Our ultimate objective is to help you *achieve academic and scholastic excellence*. We possess the right blend and matrix of skills and expertise that are required to not only do justice to our programs and publications, but also to handle them most effectively and efficiently. We are confident that our state-of-the-art programs and publications will give you a completely *new dimension* by enhancing your skill set and improving your overall performance.

MISSION: Our mission is to foster continuous knowledge to develop and enhance each student's skills through innovative and methodical programs/publications coupled with our add-on services – leading to a better career and life for our students.

OUR PHILOSOPHY: We subscribe to the traditional philosophy that everyone is equally capable of learning and that the natural, though sometimes unfulfilled and unexplored impetus of people is towards growth and development. We know that the human brain is undoubtedly a very powerful and efficient problem-solving tool, and every individual is much more capable than they realize. We strive to implement this philosophy throughout our books by helping our students explore their *potential* so that they can *perform at their optimum level*.

OUR COMMITMENT TOWARDS YOUR SATISFACTION: Reinventing, Redesigning, and Redefining Success: We are committed to providing total customer satisfaction that exceeds your expectations! Your satisfaction is extremely important to us, and your approval is one of the most important indicators that we have done our job correctly.

Long-Term Alliance: We, at EZ, look forward to forming a long-term alliance with all our readers who buy our book(s), for the days, months, and years to come. Moreover, our commitment to client service is one of our most important and distinguished characteristics. We also encourage our readers to contact us for any further assistance, feedback, suggestions, or inquiries.

EZ Solutions publishing series include books for the following major standardized tests:
- GMAT
- SAT
- PSAT
- ASVAB
- PRAXIS & PARA PRO
- GRE
- ACT
- CLEP
- TOEFL
- Other (national and state) Standardized Tests

EZ Solutions aims to provide good quality study aides in a wide variety of disciplines to the following:
- Students who have not yet completed high school
- High School students preparing to enter college
- College students preparing to enter graduate or post-graduate school
- Anyone else who is simply looking to improve their skills

Students from every walk of life, of any background, at any level, in any field, with any ambition, can find what they are looking for among EZ Solutions' publications.

FOREIGN STUDENTS: All of our books are designed, keeping in mind the unique needs of students from North and South America, U.K., Europe, Middle East, Far East, and Asia. Foreign students from countries around the world seeking to obtain education in the United States will find the assistance they need in EZ Solutions' publications.

CONTACT US: Feel free to contact us, and one of our friendly specialists will be more than happy to assist you with your queries, or feel free to browse through our website for lots of useful information.
E-Mail: info@EZmethods.com
Phone: (301) 622-9597
Mail: EZ Solutions, P.O. Box 10755, Silver Spring, MD 20914
Website: www.EZmethods.com   or   www.ezTestPrep.com

FEEDBACK: The staff of EZ Solutions hopes that you find our books helpful and easy to use. If you have any specific suggestions, comments, or feedback, please email us at: feedback@EZmethods.com

BUSINESS DEVELOPMENT: If you are interested in exploring business development opportunities, including forming a partnership alliance with us, kindly email us at: partners@EZmethods.com.

PRODUCT REGISTRATION: In order to get the most up-to-date information about this and our other books, you must register your purchase with EZ solutions by visiting our website www.EZmethods.com.

ERRORS AND INACCURACIES: We are not responsible for any typographical errors or inaccuracies contained in this publication. The information, prices, and discounts given in this book are subject to change without prior notice. To report any kind of errors or inaccuracies in this publication, kindly email us at: errors@EZmethods.com.

▪ABOUT OUR AUTHOR

The name of the man behind EZ publication series is Punit Raja Surya Chandra, who is also the founder of our company. He holds a Bachelors in Business and an MBA. It took him many years to write and publish these unique books. He researched every single book available in the market for test-preparation, and actually realized there is not even one book that is truly complete with all the content and concepts. This was the single most important reason that prompted him to write these books, and hence our ***EZ prep guidebooks were born***. He has made every effort to make these books as comprehensive and as complete as possible. His expertise and experience are as diverse as the subjects that are represented in our books. He has the breadth and depth of experience required to write books of this magnitude and intensity. Without his unparalleled and unmatched skills and determination, none of this would have been possible.

In developing these books, his primary goal has been to give everyone the same advantages as the students we tutor privately or students who take our classes. Our tutoring and classroom solutions are only available to a limited number of students; however, with these books, any student in any corner of the world can benefit the same level of service at a fraction of the cost. Therefore, you should take this book as your personal EZ tutor or instructor, because that's precisely how it has been designed.

ACKNOWLEDGEMENTS:
Our author would like to extend his vote of appreciation and gratitude to all his family members for their unconditional and continuous support, to all his close friends for their trust and confidence in him, and to all his colleagues for their helpful consultation and generous advice.

Our EZ books have benefited from dedicated efforts and labors of our author and other members of the editorial staff. Here at EZ, we all wish you the best as you get comfortable, and settle down with your EZ tutor to start working on preparing for your test. In pursuing an educational dream, you have a wonderful and an exciting opportunity ahead of you. All of us at EZ Solutions wish you the very best!

▪ABOUT EZ BOOKS

THE EZ NAME:
All our books have been written in a very easy to read manner, and in a very easy to understand fashion, so that students of any background, of any aptitude, of any capacity, of any skill-set, of any level, can benefit from them. These books are not specifically written for the **"dummies"** or for the **"geniuses"**; instead, they are written for students who fit into any category of intellectual acumen. This is how we acquired the name **"EZ Solutions"** for our publications – and as the name itself suggests, **we make everything EZ for you**!

THE EZ TUTOR:
Like any good tutor, EZ Tutor will work with you **individually and privately**, providing you with all the tools needed to improve your testing skills. It will assist you in recognizing your weaknesses, and enlighten you on how to improve upon them while transforming them into strengths. Of course, it will also point out your strengths as well, so that you can make them even stronger. By employing innovative techniques, EZ tutor will **stimulate, activate, and accelerate your learning process**. Soon after you start working with your EZ tutor, you will see **remarkable and noticeable improvement** in your performance by utilizing your newly acquired learning skills.

Whenever, Wherever, and However: EZ tutor also has the **flexibility** to work with you whenever you like – day or night, wherever you like – indoors or outdoors, and however you like – for as long or as short. While working with your EZ tutor, you can work at your own pace, you can go as fast or as slow as you like, repeat sections as many times as you need, and skip over sections you already know well. Your EZ tutor will also give you explanations, not just correct answers, and it will be **infinitely patient and adaptable**. Hence, our EZ Tutor will make you a more intelligent and smarter test-taker, and will help you maximize your score!

ADD-ON OPTIONS: *Turn your EZ Virtual Tutor into a Real Tutor!*

EZ TUTORING OVER THE PHONE:
Along with buying the entire series of our modules, students can also add on services like email/online support and/or telephone support. In fact, you can get the best preparation for your test by blending our professional 1-on-1 tutoring with our state-of-the-art books. The most important feature of our add-on features is our individualized and personalized approach that works toward building your self-confidence, and enhancing your ability to learn and perform better. This will also invigorate your motivational, organizational, as well as your learning skills. Our phone specialists are highly qualified, experienced, innovative, and well trained. You can do all this in the exclusivity and comfort of your home. Students can get in touch with one of our specialists anytime they need help – we'll be there for you, whenever you need us! We offer several packages with different levels, features, and customizations for tutoring over the phone to suit your individualized needs. Contact us for more details.

EZ 1-ON-1 TEST-TAKING & ADMISSION CONSULTATION:
We understand that standardized tests and school/college admissions can sometimes become very stressful. Our 1-on-1 Test-Taking & Admission Consulting Program can dramatically reduce your stress and anxiety. One of our consultants can personally guide you through the entire process, starting from familiarizing you with a test to getting you successfully admitted into a school/college of your choice. Again, you can do all this in the exclusivity and comfort of your home. We offer several packages with different levels, features, and customizations for test-taking and admission consultation over the phone to suit your individualized needs. Contact us for more details.
The following are some of the features of our EZ 1-on-1 Test-Taking & Admission Consulting Program:
- Familiarize you with a particular test
- Equip you with test-taking skills for each section of your test
- Reduce test-taking anxiety, stress, nervousness, and test-fever with personal counseling
- Draft and edit your essays
- Re-design your resume
- Prepare you for a telephone or personal interview
- Select the right school/college & help with admission application procedures
- Presentation Skills – how to present and market yourself

EZ UNIQUE FEATURES:

Your EZ Tutor offers you the following unique features that will highlight important information, and will let you find them quickly as and when you need to review them.

EZ STRATEGIES: It provides you with many powerful, effective, proven, and time tested strategies for various concepts, and shows you exactly how to use them to attack different question types. Many of these test-taking strategies cannot be found in any other books!

EZ SHORTCUTS: It gives you many time-saving shortcuts you can apply to save yourself some very valuable testing-time while solving a question on your actual test.

EZ TACTICS: It shows you several important tactics to use so that you can solve problems in the smartest way.

EZ DEFINITIONS: It defines all the key definitions in an easy to understand manner so that you get a clear description and concise understanding of all the key terms.

EZ RULES: It presents all the important rules in an orderly manner so that you can learn the basic rules of all the concepts.

EZ STEPS: It walks you through hundreds of concepts, showing you how to tackle every question type in an organized user-friendly step-by-step easy-to-understand methodology that adapts to your understanding and needs so that you get the best procedural knowledge.

EZ MULTIPLE/ALTERNATE METHODS: It gives you a choice of multiple methods of answering the same question so that you can choose the method that seems easiest to you.

EZ SUMMARIES: It lists a complete summary of all the important concepts in an ordered and organized manner so that you will never have to hunt for them.

EZ FACTS: It provides you with numerous key facts about various principles so that you know all the facts-and-figures of the material you are reviewing.

EZ HINTS: It supplies you with innumerable hints and clues so that you can use them to become a smarter and wiser test-taker.

EZ TIPS: It also presents you with many tips and pointers that will prevent you from making any careless mistakes or falling into traps.

EZ NOTES: It reminds you to make notes of some important points that will come handy while answering a question.

EZ WARNINGS/CAUTIONS: It warns you of some obvious mistakes that will prevent you from making them while answering a question.

EZ EXCEPTIONS: It makes you aware of the exceptions and exclusions that apply to any particular rule.

EZ REFERENCES: It gives you references of related materials that you may want to refer to in other parts of the same or different modules, while learning a specific concept.

EZ SPOTS: It lists buzzwords and phrases that will help you easily spot some specific question types.

EZ SOLVED EXAMPLES: It also throws several realistic solved examples with easy to understand detailed explanations for each and every question type explained so that you can understand and learn how to apply the concepts.

EZ PRACTICE EXERCISES: Last but not the least; it also includes intensive realistic practice exercises with easy to understand detailed explanations for each and every question type explained so that you can put to practice what you learned in an actual test question – solved examples will help you understand the concepts & practice will make you perfect!

GUESS WHAT!! No other book offers you so much. Your EZ tutor strives to provide you with the **best possible training** for your test, and **best value for your time and money**; and it is infinitely committed to providing you with **state-of-the-art** material.

Amazing Results: Most people will see amazing results in the first few days of the program!

Disadvantages: The only disadvantage is if you don't make use of our programs and publications!

THE EZ ADVANTAGE:

EZ TEST-PREP PROGRAM BROKEN INTO MODULES:
Instead of having a "*big fat ugly scary all-in-one gigantic book*," we have broken our entire test-prep program into "*small easy-to-use modules*".
- **Exclusivity:** Each module is exclusively dedicated to covering one major content area in extensive depth and breadth, allowing you to master each topic by getting an in-depth review.
- **More Content:** You will find many more topics and many more pages per topic than what you can find in all other books combined.
- **Tailored and Customized:** Separated modules offer test-takers of all levels with a more tailored and customized approach towards building specific foundational and advanced skills, and successfully preparing for the test.

EZ TO READ, CARRY, AND MANAGE:
EZ Modules are convenient – they are **easier to read, carry, and manage**.
- **EZ to Read:** EZ Modules are easier to read with text in spacious pages with a bigger font size than those other books with overcrowded pages with a small print.
- **EZ to Carry:** EZ Modules are easier to carry and hold than those other big fat bulky gigantic books.
- **EZ to Manage:** EZ Modules are overall easier to manage than those other all-in-one books.

BUY ONE MODULE OR THE ENTIRE SERIES:
The individually separated modules give you the flexibility to buy only those modules that cover the areas you think you need to work on; nevertheless, we strongly suggest you buy our entire series of modules. In fact, the most efficient and effective way to get the most out of our publications is to use our entire set of modules in conjunction with each other, and not just a few. Each module can be independently bought and studied; however, the modules are somehow connected with and complement the other modules. Therefore, if you are serious about getting a good score on your test, we sincerely recommend you purchase our entire series of modules. Contact us to order, or go to www.EZmethods.com, or check your local bookstore (look at the EZ Book Store on the last page for more information).

NO NEED TO REFER TO ANY OTHER BOOK:
Almost all other test-prep books contain a small disclaimer in some corner. They themselves spell it out very loud and clear, and admit that their book is only a brief review of some important topics; hence, it should not be considered to be an overall review of all the concepts. Most other test-preparation guides only include information for you to get familiar with the kind of topics that may appear on the test, and they suggest that you refer to additional textbooks, or consult other reference books if you want more detailed information and to get an in-depth knowledge of all the concepts. These books are not designed to be a one-stop book to learn everything you must know; instead, they are more like a summary of some important points. Moreover, they assume that you already know everything, or at least most of the concepts.

However, if you are using our EZ modules to prepare for your test, it's the opposite case, you don't need to refer or consult any other book or text or any other source for assistance. On the contrary, we, in fact, discourage you from referring to any other book, just because there is absolutely no reason to. Our EZ modules contain everything that you need to know in order to do well on your test. We haven't left anything out, and we don't assume anything. Even if you don't know anything, you will find everything in our modules from topics that are frequently tested to topics that are rarely tested, and everything in between. The only topics that you won't find in our books are the topics that will probably never appear on your test!

Frequently Tested:	Included in our review – topics that are repeatedly tested on your test, on a regularly basis
Occasionally Tested:	Included in our review – topics that are sometimes tested on your test, every now and then
Rarely Tested:	Included in our review – topics that are seldom tested on your test, very infrequently
Never Tested:	Not included in our review – since these topics are never tested on your test, we don't even mention them anywhere in our review

The bottom line is, if something *can be* on your test, you'll find it in our modules; and if something is *not going to be* on your test, it's not going to be in our modules. Each and every math concept that even has the slightest possibility to be on the test can be found in our modules.

THE OFFICIAL REAL PRACTICE TESTS:
Although we don't suggest you refer to any other book, the only time we recommend using other books is for practicing previously administered tests to exercise your skills. The best resources for actual practice tests are the official guides published by the test makers that have several actual previously administered tests. One can **replicate** these tests as closely as one can, but no one other than the test administrators can **duplicate** them, and have the ability to reproduce or publish them. Therefore, to get the maximum effect of our approach, you must practice the actual tests from the official guide. You can also take a free online practice test by going to their website. EZ's practice tests are also based upon the most recently administered tests, and include every type of question that can be expected on the actual exam.

Disclaimer: Throughout this book, you may sometimes find repetitive information. The reason for this redundancy is that we often need to emphasize and sometimes re-emphasize a few concepts and rules over-and-over again, and that too at the right places at the right time, to ensure you understand them, and are able to apply them correctly.

HOW OUR BOOKS CAN HELP YOU:
Our books are designed to help you identify your strengths and the areas which you need to work on. If you study all our modules, you will be fully equipped with all the tools needed to take your test head-on. Moreover, you'll also have the satisfaction that you did all you possibly could do to prepare yourself for the test, and you didn't leave any stone unturned. The amount of content covered in our books is far more than what you would learn by studying all the other test-prep books that are out there, put together, or by even taking an online or an actual prep course, and of course, spending thousands of dollars in the process. This will give you an idea of how material we have covered in our books.

STRUCTURE OF OUR MODULES:
All our modules are *structured in a highly organized and systematic manner*. The review is divided into different modules. Each module is divided into units. Each unit is further subdivided into chapters. Each chapter covers various topics, and in each specific topic, you are given all that you need to solve questions on that topic in detail – explaining key concepts, rules, and other EZ unique features. Also included in some topics are test-taking strategies specific to the topics discussed. Following each topic are solved sample examples with comprehensive explanations, which are exclusively based on that topic, and utilizing the concepts covered in that topic and section. Finally, there are practice exercises with thorough explanations containing real test-like questions for each topic and section, which are very similar to actual test questions. All units, chapters, and topics are chronologically numbered for easy reference.

Moreover, the modules, units, chapters, and topics are all arranged in sequence so that later modules, units, chapters, and topics assume familiarity with the material covered in earlier modules, units, chapters, and topics. Therefore, the best way to review is to work through from the beginning to the end.

MODULES > UNITS > CHAPTERS > TOPICS > SOLVED EXAMPLES > PRACTICE EXERCISES

THE EZ DIFFERENCE:

DIFFERENCE BETWEEN EZ SOLUTIONS' PUBLICATIONS AND OTHER BOOKS:

Most of the other test-prep books suggest that your exam only tests your ability to take the test, and it does not test any actual content knowledge. In other words, they claim that your test is all about knowing the test-taking strategies, and it has very little to do with the actual knowledge of content; others claim that your test is all about knowing a few most commonly tested topics. While we have great respect for these books and the people who write or publish them, all these books have one thing in common: they all want to give their readers a quick shortcut to success. They actually want their readers to believe that just by learning a few strategies and memorizing some key formulas, they'll be able to ace their test. We are not sure if it's the fault of the people who write these books or the people who use them; but someone is definitely trying to fool someone – either those test-prep books for making the readers believe it, or the readers for actually believing it (no pun intended).

With a test as vast as this, it's simply not possible to cover the entire content in just a few pages. We all wish; however, in life, there really aren't any shortcuts to success, and your test is no exception to this rule. Nothing comes easy in life, and that is also precisely the case with your test. You have to do it the hard way by working your way through. Unfortunately, there is no magic potion, which we can give you to succeed in math! Therefore, if you want to do well on your test – be mentally, physically, and psychologically prepared to do some hard work. In this case, efforts and results are directly proportional, that is, greater the efforts you make, better your results are going to be.

While most test-preparation books present materials that stand very little resemblance to the actual tests, EZ's publication series present tests that accurately depict the official tests in both, degree of difficulty and types of questions.

Our EZ books are like no other books you have ever seen or even heard of. We have a completely different concept, and our books are structured using a totally different model. We have *re-defined the way test-prep books should be*.

STRATEGIES SEPARATED FROM CONTENT:
What we have done in our modules is, *separated the actual content-knowledge from the test-taking strategies*. We truly believe that a test-prep program should be more than just a *cheat-sheet of tricks, tips, and traps*. The test you are preparing for is not a simple game that you can master by learning these quick tactics. What you really need to do well on your test is a program that builds true understanding and knowledge of the content.

PERFECT EQUILIBRIUM BETWEEN STRATEGIES AND CONTENT:
In our modules, we've tried our best to present a *truly unique equilibrium* between two competing and challenging skills: test-taking strategies and comprehensive content-knowledge. We have *blended* the two most important ingredients that are essential for your success on your test. We have enhanced the old traditional approach to some of the most advanced forms of test-taking strategies. To top all this, we have refined our solved examples with detailed explanations to give you hands-on experience to real test-like questions before you take your actual test.

Other Books: Most of the other test-prep books primarily concentrate on teaching their readers how to *"guess"* and *"use the process of elimination,"* and they get so obsessed with the tactics that in the process they completely ignore the actual content. Majority of the content of these books consists of pages of guessing techniques.

EZ Books: With our EZ Content-Knowledge Modules, you'll find *100% pure content* that has a highly organized and structured approach to all the content areas, which actually teaches you the content you need to know to do well on your test. *Therefore, if you are looking to learn more than just "guessing by process of elimination" and if you are serious about developing your skills and confidence level for your exam, then our highly organized and structured test-prep modules are the solution.* By studying our books, you'll learn a systematic approach to any question that you may see on your test, and acquire the tools that will help you get there.

EZ Solutions' publications are packed with important information, sophisticated strategies, useful tips, and extensive practice that the experts know will help you do your best on your test.

You should use whichever concept, fact, or tip from that section that you think is appropriate to answer the question correctly in the least possible time. If you've mastered the material in our review modules and strategy modules, you should be able to answer almost all (99.99%) of the questions.

LEARN BACKWARDS AND MOVE FORWARD: Smart students are the ones who make an honest attempt to learn what they read, and also learn from their mistakes, but at the same time, who moves ahead. Therefore, you should learn backwards, that is, learn from your past experiences, and move forward, that is, keep moving ahead without looking back!

ONE CONCEPT, EZ MULTIPLE METHODS:
Our books often give you a *choice of multiple methods* of answering the same question – you can pick the method that seems easiest to you. Our goal is not to *prescribe* any *hard-and-fast* method for taking the test, but instead, to give you the *flexibility and tools you can use to approach your test with confidence and optimism*.

STRATEGIES OR CONTENT?

In order to do well on your test, it is absolutely essential that you have a pretty good grasp of all the concepts laid out in our review modules. Our review modules contain everything you need to know, or must know to crack your test. They cover everything from basic arithmetic to logical reasoning, and everything in between. Nonetheless, that's not enough. You should be able to use these concepts in ways that may not be so familiar or well known to you. This is where our EZ Strategies kick in.

CONTENT VERSUS STRATEGIES:

There is a *succinct* difference between knowing the math content and knowing the math strategies.

Hypothetically speaking, let's assume there is a student named Alex, who learns only the test-taking strategies; and there is another student named Andria, who learns only the math-content. Now when the test time comes, Andria who learns only the math-content is extremely likely to do a lot better than Alex, who learns only the test-taking strategies.

The truth is that someone who has the knowledge of all the math content, but doesn't know anything about the strategies, will almost always do better on the test than someone who knows all the strategies but doesn't know the content properly.

Now let's assume there is another student named Alexandria, who learns both, the test-taking strategies and the math-content. Yes, now we are talking! This student, Alexandria, who knows both the strategies and the content, is guaranteed to do a lot better than Alex, who only knows the strategies, or Andria who only knows the content.

This brings us to our conclusion on this topic: don't just study the strategies, or just the content; you need to know both simultaneously – the strategies and the content, in order to do well on your test. How quickly and accurately you can answer the math questions will depend on your knowledge of the content and the strategies, and that will have an overall effect on your success on the test.

Hence, the equation to succeed on your test is: **Strategies + Content = Success!**

We are confident that if you study our books on test-taking strategies along with our books on content-knowledge, you'll have everything you possibly need to know in order to do well on your test, in fact, to ace your test, and come out with flying colors!

The good thing is that you made the smart decision to buy this book, or if you are reading this online, or in a bookstore, or in a library, you are going to buy one soon!

CONTENT-KNOWLEDGE REVIEW MODULES:

THOROUGH IN-DEPTH REVIEW:
Most other test-prep books briefly touch upon some of the concepts sporadically. On the other hand, our books start from the basics, but unlike other books, they do not end there – **we go deep inside, beyond just touching up the surface** – all the way from fundamental skills to some of the most advanced content that many other prep books choose to ignore. **Each concept is first explained in detail, and then analyzed for most effective understanding** – each and every concept is covered, and we haven't left any stone unturned. Overall, our program is more challenging – you simply get the **best-of-the-best**, and you get more of everything!

COMPREHENSIVE REVIEW:
Our Content-Knowledge Review Modules provide the **most comprehensive and complete review** of all the concepts, which you need to know to excel in your test. Each module is devoted to one of the main subject areas so that you can focus on the most relevant material.

The ideal way to review our modules is to go through each and every topic thoroughly, understand all the solved examples, and work out all of the practice exercises. You must not rush it; instead give yourself enough time to review everything.

If you are not able to spend enough time, you may not have the time to review each topic, understand every solved example, and work out all of the practice exercises. In this case, you may skip over the topics that you're already familiar with or good at. Just glimpse through a section. If you feel comfortable with it, move on to something else that may potentially give you more trouble. If you feel uncomfortable with it, review that topic more thoroughly.

Moreover, if you carefully work through our review, you will probably find some topics that you already know, but you may also find some topics that you need to review more closely. You should have a good sense of areas with which you are most comfortable, and in which areas you feel you have a deficiency. Work on any weaknesses you believe you have in those areas. This should help you organize your review more efficiently. Try to give yourself plenty of time and make sure to review the skills and master the concepts that you are required and expected to know to do well on your test. Of course, the more time you invest preparing for your test and more familiar you are with these fundamental principles, the better you will do on your test.

While doing your review, it may be worthwhile to keep the following in mind:

(A) Extensive Content: There is a whole lot of content reviewed in these modules. Although the amount of material presented in our books may appear to be overwhelming, it's the most complete review to get prepared for your test. To some of you, this may seem like a great deal of information to assimilate; however, when you start reviewing, you'll probably realize that you are already comfortable with many concepts discussed in our review modules. We also suggest that you spread your use of our modules over several weeks, and study different modules at your own pace.

Even if you are sure you know the basic concepts, our review will help to warm you up so that you can go into your test with crisp and sharp skills. Hence, we strongly suggest that you at least touch up on each and every concept. However, depending on your strengths and weaknesses, you may be able to move quickly through some areas, and focus more on the others that seem to be troublesome to you. You should develop a plan of attack for your review of the wide range of content.

(B) Using EZ Test-Taking Strategies: In our content review modules, there may be some instances when the test-taking strategies will come into play. So get comfortable using our EZ strategies to the fullest. Work on your weaknesses, and be ready to take advantage of your strengths.

Nevertheless, our main objective in the content review modules is to refresh your knowledge of key concepts on the test and we attempt to keep things as concrete and concise as possible.

▪ABOUT THIS BOOK

It's important to get a hold of the mathematical fundamentals and principles; nevertheless, it's equally important to learn the art of tackling the questions you'll see on the test. Apparently it's not enough to only know the types of math questions you will get on your test, and how to solve them. If that were the case, we wouldn't have this book at all. This book is exclusively dedicated to the **Overall Math Test-Taking Strategies and Shortcuts** that apply to the math section of your test.

WHAT'S COVERED IN THIS BOOK: In this book, you will learn several important strategies and shortcuts that can be used on different types of questions throughout the math section. Mastering these tactics will not only improve your performance on the math section, but will also make you a smarter and wiser test-taker. In this module, you'll learn all the test-taking strategies, as well as how to solve the problem quickly, correctly, and more efficiently. In fact, test-taking strategies, shortcuts, and alternative approaches to problem solving are the key to success on the math section.

WHAT'S NOT COVERED IN THIS BOOK: This book does not cover any topic-specific strategies for tackling specific types of questions or any actual content-knowledge – for that, you must buy our modules on math content-knowledge.

PRE-REQUISITES FOR THIS BOOK: The pre-requisite for this module is your familiarity with all the basic mathematical principles and concepts. Hence, when you go through this book, you are already expected to know all the content-knowledge covered in our other content-knowledge modules.

RELATED MODULES FOR THIS BOOK: You will get the best out of this book if you use it in conjunction with some of our other modules listed below.

List of related modules for this book:
▪ EZ SAT Math Content Knowledge Review Module – Arithmetic
▪ EZ SAT Math Content Knowledge Review Module – Algebra
▪ EZ SAT Math Content Knowledge Review Module – Geometry
▪ EZ SAT Math Content Knowledge Review Module – Word Problems
▪ EZ SAT Math Content Knowledge Review Module – Algebra Applications
Note: Look at the back of the book for a complete list of EZ books

CHAPTER 1.0: EZ NUTS & BOLTS OF MATH

HIGHLIGHTS:
1.1 Basics About Standardized Tests
1.2 Basics About Math Section

1.1   BASICS ABOUT STANDARDIZED TESTS

REGULAR TESTS VERSUS STANDARDIZED TESTS:

There is a huge difference between standardized math and regular math, which you studied in school. In fact, taking a standardized math test is a completely different ball game than taking any other regular test. Generally speaking, the basic difference is that *regular math tests are more tough than tricky*; on the other hand, *standardized math tests are more tricky than tough*.

Success on standardized math tests requires learning to avoid careless errors, and realizing the fact that these errors are often the result of traps that are *seamlessly* built into the questions. We'll show you a different approach to test-taking, one that takes advantage of, instead of falling prey to the nature of standardized tests.

Full-Credit vs. Partial-Credit: On a regular math test, if you work out the steps in a problem but don't get the correct answer, you would still get partial credit even if you accidentally made a silly mistake, or did something wrong. However, on a standardized test – it's either right or wrong – there is nothing in between. If your chosen answer is correct – you'll get full credit, and if it's wrong – you'll get no credit.

Standardized Math Tests are all about Results: On most regular tests, you are expected to show your work and demonstrate your ability to work step-by-step from the information given to the correct answer. In fact, you'll lose points if you don't work out the problem properly or don't show the proper steps. They test whether or not you know how to approach a problem and the process of solving it rather than just finding the answer. However, on a standardized math test, it really doesn't matter how you come up with the correct answer as long as you get to the correct answer, even if you randomly guessed it. Instead of asking you to show your work and demonstrate your knowledge of mathematical concepts or ability to solve a problem correctly, standardized test is all about results. So all that matters is that you get to the correct answer, and get there quickly. While taking a standardized test, you are at liberty to use all different types of shortcuts, and you can even guess the answer. In fact, solving problems the correct way can sometimes slow you down or get you into trouble. Some of the math questions are more hypothetical and imaginary in nature; however, many of the questions also reflect real-life situations. Therefore, solving a problem the way you've been taught in school is a lot different from solving a problem for standardized tests.

Standardized Math Tests require more Interpretative than Calculative Skills: The test administrators are not interested in testing your basic arithmetic calculative skills. For instance, they are not testing whether you know how to calculate the average of given numbers, find the area of a square, use the Pythagorean Theorem, or read a table. They assume that you already know all this. Most questions involve a little bit more than just the basics. You may get a problem that requires you to calculate the average, but you may have to find out a missing term. You may get a problem that requires you to find the area of a square, but in order to do that you may first have to find the measure of its side. You may be required to apply the Pythagorean Theorem, but you may first have to calculate the hypotenuse, or prove that it's a right triangle. You may be required to read a table in order to determine something else from it. Therefore, most of the questions require you to apply more interpretative skills rather than computational skills; that is, they test your understanding of mathematical concepts and systems as opposed to your ability to do arithmetic.

Standardized Math Tests are more about the Application than Memorization: Additionally, they are not even interested in testing your memory. There are only a few formulas that you must memorize, and you'll realize most of these formulas are easier to remember if you understand the logic behind them. Merely memorizing the formulas will not help you in applying them correctly in the questions. In order to apply these formulas successfully in the questions, it's important to have their fundamental understanding.

Standardized Math Tests don't contain Advanced Math: Your standardized test does not contain any advanced math similar to what you see in high school mathematics. Well, now you must be thinking if your test has no advanced mathematics, then why so many students find some of the questions so difficult. The answer is quite simple – *your test is designed to be a test of general "reasoning ability" and "aptitude" – it tries to use basic concepts of arithmetic, algebra, and geometry as a means of testing your ability to think logically, critically, and analytically*.

Therefore, the objective or purpose of your test is to use your familiarity with numbers, algebraic concepts, and geometric figures as a way of testing your logical, critical, and analytical thinking skills.

RECORD YOUR WORK:

Yes, this is a standardized test, and by no means are you required to show your work for getting any credit, and yes, it doesn't matter how you get the answer as long as you get the correct answer to receive credit. Of course, we are completely aware of this fact; nevertheless, contrary to popular belief, it is still a good idea to record your work in the empty space of your test booklet.

Obviously, you're not going to have time during the test to write down neatly and systematically every step for every problem, at least not the way you might on a homework assignment or final exam, and no one even expects you to do that either. However, writing down at least some of what you are thinking and doing as you solve a problem will be worth the time it takes. Think of this as a way of record keeping, to write down numbers that you used in your calculations, and the intermediate results it gives you in the process of solving a problem.

In case you don't record anything down, and you think you arrived at the wrong answer, or if your answer doesn't match any of the answer choices, your only alternative is to start all over again almost from scratch. However, if you have at least something written down, you may be able to go back over your work, find the mistakes, and correct some minor errors instead of re-doing the whole problem. Remember, *it's always easier to fix the wheel than to re-invent it!* Moreover, if you want to go back to check your solution, having something written down will enable you to check over your work quickly and easily. Working out a problem in the empty space of your test booklet may even help you avoid errors, as *steps will be more visible and errors more noticeable*.

USING EMPTY SPACE OF TEST BOOKLET ON MATH SECTIONS:
On the math questions, make sure to use the empty space of your test booklet as your scratch paper to your advantage. You might be tempted to visualize and do a lot of work in your head; however, never make this mistake. If you do the calculations in your head, you'd be open to all sorts of careless errors. It's very important that you actually use the empty space on your test booklet as scratch paper!
On the mathematics questions, use your test booklet as scratch paper to do the following:
- all of your calculations, and
- drawing diagrams or redrawing and labeling given diagrams, and
- writing down anything that will help you reason through the problem
When you practice questions from our books, you should do all of your calculations and other work by writing on the problems on the book itself instead of writing on a separate sheet of scratch paper. It's better to get used to this practice of working out your problem in the empty space, the same way you would do when you take the actual test.

TWO TYPES OF PEOPLE:

For some strange reason, it's an established fact that not everyone is neutral or feels the same way when it comes to the subject of Mathematics. Almost like a rule of thumb, you either love it or hate it. Either you get a kick out of it, or it bores you to death. Either it becomes almost like your hobby, or it becomes a source of distress. Either you derive a secret thrill out of solving a challenging math problem, or your elementary math teacher traumatized you to an extent where the very sight of numbers and math symbols induces so much panic that you feel nauseated with accelerated heartbeat.

Whichever side of the great **math-split** you inhabit, we have some great news for you regarding standardized math tests. In general, we can divide people who take the standardized math tests into two categories:
- the **Math Wizards**, who are the math lovers, and
- the **Math Paranoiacs**, who are the math haters

FIRST CATEGORY OF PEOPLE: THE MATH WIZARDS:

The first category of people is the **"Math Wizards"** – the ones who are **"supposedly"** experts in math.
Well, if you really are a good math student, then you should ace the math test. However, many students who are very good in math somehow don't always do very well on standardized tests. Now you must be wondering what the reasons could be for this mystery. We'll explain why this happens.

Most Math Wizards think that they probably don't need us – **you are both, right and wrong**.

You are right, because you do have the instincts and the mind that is required to be good in math. You are equipped with the knowledge of all the concepts and formulas.

You are wrong, because, although you are good in math, however, that may not necessarily mean you are good in taking standardized tests or that you are a good test-taker. So be careful, acing the math test takes more than just knowing math. Most of you are under the misconception that the same skills that lead to success on other school or college math tests necessarily translate to success on standardized math tests. Apparently, taking standardized math tests is a lot different from your regular math tests.

SECOND CATEGORY OF PEOPLE: THE MATH PARANOIACS:

The second category of people is the **"Math Paranoiacs"** – the ones who are **"paranoid"** about math.
Well, if you are not a good math student, then you should give yourself a moment and think why some students are good in math and why you are not.

Like anything else in life, it's hard to do well on something you hate or fear.

The first thing you should do is take the fear of math out of your mind. Math is not as horrible or as terrifying as you think. For most of you, all this fear probably started when you were in elementary or middle school. You probably were never taught math the right way, and hence you could never develop an interest in the subject of mathematics.

Secondly, transform the hatred you have for math to at least "liking" if not "love". The best way to do so is by trying to develop a genuine interest in solving math problems.

Take this as an opportunity to prove to yourself that you can also do it. This is when you can take revenge on that math teacher who made your life miserable, and for the most part, the one who is responsible for the way you feel about math. Also, to take revenge on all your friends who probably laughed at you for not even being able to calculate a simple percent discount while shopping. Well, **success is the best way to take revenge**. This is the perfect time to show to the whole world, and most importantly to yourself, that you too can do well on math tests.

In our books, we'll show you how to do well on standardized math tests. You'll learn how to avoid making careless mistakes, manage your time, and all that is required to succeed on your test. By taking advantage of our EZ methods, test-taking strategies, shortcuts, and other techniques, **you'll soon be able to erase two words from your vocabulary: hate and fear** (for math, of course).

So don't let all the big numbers intimidate you. Big numbers are like big marshmallows – gigantic in looks but much easier to melt. Likewise, big numbers are only bigger in looks but much easier to crack! In fact, the bigger the numbers, the easier they are to tackle.

FIRST CATEGORY: MATH WIZARDS OR SECOND CATEGORY: MATH PARANOIACS – IT DOESN'T MATTER:

It doesn't matter which of the two categories you belong to, the truth is that you need us either way, much more than you even realize. Our books have been designed for people with both categories in mind.

Both historically and statistically, there are far more students who fear the math sections much more than they fear any of the verbal sections. But, guess what? There is absolutely no reason to feel this way. For all sections, there are proven EZ strategies and tested EZ tactics for approaching the different kinds of questions.

If you ever get stuck, you can always use the various guessing and alternative strategies that you will learn in our strategy module. Nevertheless, you should make sure that you understand the correct mathematical way to answer the questions. In our review modules, major emphasis is made on doing the mathematics properly; however, a few references are given to our other strategies.

Our module on Test-Taking Strategies attacks the math test-taking strategies, tactics, and traps. It covers all the strategies, tactics, favorite math traps, and how to recognize them and avoid falling for them on the test. Our Content-Knowledge Modules are specifically structured around the different math concepts you will encounter on the test, and provide content-specific strategies for solving different types of math problems.

GMAT/GRE MATH VS SAT/ACT MATH:

Concepts: The GMAT/GRE tests the same type of mathematical concepts, skills, and knowledge, as the SAT/ACT tests. In fact, the math that appears on the GMAT/GRE is almost similar to the math on the SAT/ACT.

Amount of Time & Number of Questions: GMAT/GRE consists of fewer numbers of math questions, and it gives more time to answer them than on the SAT/ACT.

Special Format: In addition to regular multiple-choice problem-solving questions: GMAT consists of math questions in a completely different format known as "Data Sufficiency" questions. GRE consists of math questions in a completely different format known as "Quantitative Comparison" questions. SAT also consists of math questions in a completely different format known as "Grid-In Response: questions. ACT does not consist of math questions in any special format.

Use of Calculator: On the GMAT/GRE, you are not allowed to use a calculator, whereas, on the SAT/ACT, you are. This may appear as a big drawback; however, in reality it's not as bad as it sounds. The GMAT/GRE math questions don't involve a lot of calculations. Actually, if a question seems to involve many ugly calculations, you should look at it again – there ought to be a shortcut that exists which will allow you to avoid crunching the numbers. You'll see many shortcuts in our books. Nevertheless, since it's a math test, you will need to use arithmetic, so you must review and practice your computational skills.

Accuracy of Diagrams: On the SAT, diagrams are always drawn to scale, unless a note underneath the diagram specifies that the diagram is not drawn to scale. Whereas, on the GMAT, diagrams are not necessarily drawn to scale, except when a note underneath the diagram specifies that the diagram is drawn to scale.
This implies that on the GMAT, unlike on the SAT, just by the way a figure looks, you can't make solid assumptions. Instead, you have to depend on the information given in the question. It is recommended that in most cases you should redraw the diagram to get a better idea. Moreover, this also means that on the GMAT, unlike on the SAT, generally, the diagrams cannot be used to estimate angle measures and length segments. For instance, just because a figure looks like a square or an equilateral triangle, you cannot assume that it indeed is a square or an equilateral triangle; the square can also be a rectangle, and the equilateral triangle can also be a right triangle.

SAT MATH VS ACT MATH:
The SAT and the ACT test the same type of mathematical concepts, skills, and knowledge. In many ways, the math that appears on the SAT is almost identical to the math on the ACT. However, the emphasis is somewhat different between the two tests. Some test-takers rate the math on the new SAT to be slightly more challenging than the math on ACT.

1.2 BASICS ABOUT MATH SECTIONS

RANGE OF MATH TOPICS TESTED:

Math is a very vast subject and there are many topics; thus, it's very difficult to pinpoint or predict which specific topic may appear on your test. Although the math section covers a wide range of topics, it does not go too deeply into these subject areas. All you need is a basic understanding without any complicated formulas.

Good News: The good news is that no single test can cover all of the topics listed here; instead, only a few of the topics will be included on your test.

Bad News: The bad news is that no one knows what topics will be covered in the next test you take, or what types of questions are going to show up. Nevertheless, your test is somewhat predictable. About half or more of the test consists of limited numbers of topics that consistently pop-up on every test in more or less the same way, while the other half or less consists of topics that show up sporadically. You can never be sure what will show up in which test. Therefore, you must review all the topics and get a good understanding of all the concepts. But there is nothing to worry about, no matter how much math you already know, you can review all the topics by going through our modules.

STANDARD OF MATH TESTED:

Much of the math content that appears on your test corresponds to the math you came across in middle and high school grade math classes. All or most of you, at some point, already learned the math that's going to be covered on your test. None of the concepts is more advanced than what you learned in high school math classes. There aren't going to be any major surprises – these mathematical concepts are the ones with which you are already familiar or have at least seen before. Therefore, you really won't have to learn a lot of new material – all you have to do is refresh your memory and skills.

Good News: For some of you, this is good news because maybe you are a recent graduate, and you are still good and confident at it.

Bad News: While for others, this may be bad news because it has been a long time since you graduated, and you have forgotten most of it. Moreover, you are probably accustomed to using a calculator or computer software to do most of your number crunching work, or to handle any other math that comes your way. As a result, you haven't really used your math skills lately, and you have not even used any of these concepts for a long time. Like they say, *"If you don't use it, you'll lose it!"* So for those of you who haven't looked at or used the concepts covered in high school math classes, which may have been quite a while ago, it's all the more important that you take some time to review the basics, and learn how they are tested. Again, there is nothing to worry about, no matter how much your math memories have faded, you can refresh them by going through our modules.

EZ NOTE: Remember, you don't need to identify the concept, definition, or terminology in a question; you simply need to locate the correct answer from the given answer choices. Although you will not be required to identify the types of questions being asked, however, being aware of different types of questions as you prepare for the test will probably help you succeed in understanding and answering the questions correctly.

WHAT YOU DON'T NEED TO KNOW:

It's easier to tell what you don't need to know, so let's start with that. The following are some topics that are not tested on the math sections, and you do not need to know them for your test:

✘ Calculus	✘ Trigonometry	✘ Logarithms	✘ Complex Numbers
✘ Advanced Statistics	✘ Truth Table	✘ Matrices	✘ Imaginary Numbers

You will not be required to do the following:

✘ Write a geometry proof   ✘ Prove a trigonometric identity

✘ Do any complex graphing   ✘ Do a compass and straightedge construction

WHAT YOU DO NEED TO KNOW:

Well, essentially, you need to know everything other than what is listed above that you learnt up to your high school level. The math topics that are going to be covered on your test start all the way, from what you learned in elementary school, to middle school, and even some of what you were taught in high school.

- Elementary School Level – basic arithmetic
- Middle School Level – more arithmetic and introduction to algebra and geometry
- High School Level – algebra and geometry

MATH TOPICS: Most math questions fall into five broad areas of arithmetic, algebra, geometry, word problems, and logical reasoning & data interpretation. Some questions, however, may not clearly fall into one of these areas, and those questions are categorized as miscellaneous questions.
About 85% of the test questions are approximately divided evenly among the following topics:

✓ Arithmetic   ✓ Algebra   ✓ Geometry   ✓ Word Problems

The remaining 15% of the questions represent a few miscellaneous topics, such as:

✓ Logical Reasoning   ✓ Interpretation of Data

NO TOPIC REALLY BELONGS EXCLUSIVELY TO ONLY ONE CATEGORY:

There are different topics in math; however, no topic really belongs exclusively to only one category. For instance, arithmetic-mean problems are discussed in averages, but on your test, you may also be asked to find the arithmetic-mean of fractions, decimals, exponents, radicals, algebraic expressions, measures of the angles of a polygon, etc. Similarly, ratios are discussed in ratios and proportions, but on your test, you may also be asked to find the ratio of two angles in a triangle in a geometry problem, ratio of the age of two people in a word problem, ratio of the price of two stocks in a data interpretation problem, etc. Therefore, *in one way or the other, most math topics are inter-related and inter-connected with one another*.

STUDY MATH AREAS IN THE CORRECT ORDER: Similarities between Learning Math & Building a House:

Learning Math is similar to building a house. For instance, if you were building a house, you wouldn't start from building the roof, and then the walls, and then the flooring. Similarly, if you were preparing for your math test, you shouldn't start with word problems, and then the geometry, and then the algebra, and then the arithmetic.

The correct way would be to first start with the foundation of the house, which are the arithmetic principles, and then build the walls, which are the fundamentals of algebra and geometry, and then finally build the roof, which are the word problems. Of course, the next step would be to build the second floor, which is comparable to logical reasoning and data interpretation problems. Fortunately enough, anything beyond this is out of the scope of this book and your test, and you don't need to go any further.

It's not advisable that you start your review with word problems, because most word problems require the use of fundamentals of arithmetic and algebra, without which you are going to run into trouble. Most algebra problems involve the use of arithmetic, many geometry problems involve the use of algebra and arithmetic, and many word problems involve the use of geometry, algebra, and arithmetic. Moreover, there are some other problems in the miscellaneous section, which involve the use and knowledge of arithmetic, algebra, geometry, and word problems.

Once you become an expert in building the foundation, walls, and roof of the house, you can look for ways that can help you build the same house in a shorter amount of time. Likewise, once you become proficient in arithmetic, algebra, and geometry, you can then learn shortcuts that may help you solve the problem much more quickly and easily.

Small Things Lead to Big Things: Some of the most basic concepts are very important, not only because they appear on every test, but also because you need to know how to perform most of these simpler operations in order to carry out some of the more complicated tasks. Many of these math operations are pretty basic, nevertheless, it's imperative that you understand them. So don't ignore the basics, in fact, that's where you should start your prep program. For instance, it's difficult to find the shaded area formed by an overlapping circle and a rectangle, if you don't know how to find the area of a circle and a rectangle.

By now you may have guessed correctly, *Math is a subject that works best if you treat it more like a building block*. You shouldn't just start reading any topic randomly; instead, you must follow the proper order.

CORRECT ORDER:
ARITHMETIC >> ALGEBRA >> GEOMETRY >> WORD PROBLEMS >> DATA INTERPRETATION >> LOGICAL REASONING

CHAPTER 2.0: EZ METHODS TO SOLVE MATH PROBLEMS

HIGHLIGHTS:
2.1 EZ 4-Step Method for Success on Math
2.2 EZ Systematic Method to Solve Math Problems
2.3 EZ Method to Check and Select Your Answer
2.4 EZ Long Term Strategies for Math

2.1 EZ 4-STEP METHOD FOR SUCCESS ON MATH

EZ 4-STEP METHOD FOR SUCCESS ON MATH: UNDERSTANDING – MEMORIZING – APPLYING – USING STRATEGIES:
The right approach towards preparing for the math section of your test is to first understand the content, then memorize the key rules and formulas, then learn how to apply these concepts – all this in conjunction with utilizing test-taking strategies – and yes, in that specific order. Your success on the math section depends on your ability to determine which approach to adopt to solve which problem, and at the same time, being able to apply the test-taking strategies simultaneously.

STEP 1: UNDERSTANDING OF CONCEPTS AND FORMULAS:
First, you must understand all the concepts and formulas. All formulas are logical and are based upon common sense. You can understand most of them by simple observation and deductions. Understanding how the formulas are derived will help you remember them quickly and retain them for a longer period of time. Therefore, make sure you have a crystal clear understanding of all the fundamentals of mathematical concepts and formulas.

STEP 2: MEMORIZATION OF CONCEPTS AND FORMULAS:
After understanding the concepts and formulas, it's now time to memorize all the concepts and formulas that you need to know for the math section. Understanding the concepts first will facilitate your memorization process. It's usually a lot easier to memorize something you understand than memorizing something you don't understand. Memorizing these concepts and formulas will help you save time and let you apply them instantly as and when needed. Besides, once you have a good understanding of the concepts, you wouldn't even need to memorize anything; then you'll see that everything will happen automatically. At that point, you'll develop an instinct to solve these questions and you'll immediately know what needs to be done.

STEP 3: APPLICATION OF CONCEPTS AND FORMULAS:
After understanding and memorizing the concepts and formulas, learn how to apply them effectively. Understanding and memorizing the concepts and formulas is very important, but knowing how to apply them or which formula to apply where is equally important. It's pointless to memorize formulas if you do not know how to apply them, or do not know which one to apply where. Therefore, make sure you review the math section thoroughly, and do enough practice in order to have adequate experience with applying these concepts and formulas in test questions so you know how, when, where, and which principle to apply.

STEP 4: UTILIZATION OF TEST-TAKING STRATEGIES:
The last but not the least, in conjunction with understanding, memorizing, and applying the math concepts and formulas, it is almost essential to use test-taking strategies, shortcuts, and other techniques to be successful on your math test.

EZ REFERENCE: For in-depth knowledge about all the math concepts and formulas, refer to our content-knowledge review-modules. For in-depth knowledge of math test-taking strategies, refer to our module of math test taking strategies.

2.2 EZ SYSTEMATIC METHOD TO SOLVE MATH PROBLEMS

In order to maximize your performance on the math section, it's essential that you work systematically. By adopting our EZ Systematic Method approach in solving any type of math problem, you will have a **clear and concise technique** for thinking your way to a response. You won't waste time by attacking a problem in a haphazard or disorganized manner. A systematic approach will also ensure that you find the most efficient solution to the problem, and will help you save time by adopting the shortest way in solving a problem with as few careless and avoidable errors as possible. The key is to take the question one step at a time, and apply our EZ systematic step-by-step approach.

HATCH A ROAD-MAP:

EZ Systematic Method will help you hatch a **roadmap** for tackling all math problems. By using the roadmap, not only will the problem become more manageable and solvable, but you will also be able to use your time more efficiently and productively. Formulate a different game plan to solve each problem. Decide how to answer the question from the information given, and choose the fastest approach with which you feel most comfortable.

SKETCH A FIGURE:

There are many questions, where drawing a figure or a diagram may help. Nonetheless, drawing should not be limited only to geometry problems. It's always difficult to imagine a problem just in your head. It often becomes easier to solve with the help of a figure where you can visualize the problem instead of just making verbal sense out of the words. Moreover, with a figure, you will have a clear vision about how to get from point A to point B, and which is the shortest way to get there. Always remember, **the shortest distance between any two points is a straight line, and not a curved one**.

PULL-OUT ALL INFO:

Assimilate and "Pull-Out" All the Information that is Given Before Answering: Before you begin to attack the problem and start solving, it is always a good idea to **"pull-out"** all the information that is already **"given"** in the problem, and list it systematically in your own way, and not the way it's given in the problem. Translating words to numbers, that is, converting the words into numbers can make the question easier to solve. **Think about what you need to know in order to answer the question, and use what you know to figure out what you need to know**.

- By pulling-out the facts-and-figures given in the problem, you'll be able to manipulate them easily and solve the problem quickly.
- By pulling-out all the information, you can see what all is given, what needs to be figured out, and what you need to do in order to find out what has been asked in the problem.

THINK BEFORE YOU ACT:

Think, think, and think! Always think before you act upon anything. You must think before you jump in and begin working on any problem. If you follow our EZ Systematic Method to Problem Solving, you will have the correct thinking process, and your thought process will always put you on the right track, which in turn will almost always lead you to the correct answer.

Occasionally, you may suddenly blank-out on a certain procedure to solve a problem or to apply some formula, and if that ever happens, don't panic – there might be another way to solve the problem that will work as well. For instance, while solving a word problem, you don't necessarily always have to translate it into a bunch of equations to solve it. For all you know, you may just be able to reason through the problem and get to the correct answer by some other means without using any equations, such as, by using simple logic, or even plugging-in the answer choices in the question-stem.

Therefore, sometimes it's best to let your logical thinking, analytical reasoning, basic instinct, and common sense about numbers take over.

Fortunately or unfortunately, there are several methods for working through the same math problem. The EZ Methods explained in this book and in our other books will help you save time by adopting the shortest way to solve a problem.

EZ STEP-BY-STEP SYSTEMATIC METHOD:

Apply the following EZ Step-by-Step Systematic Method and formulate your own Road-Map to answer the math questions:

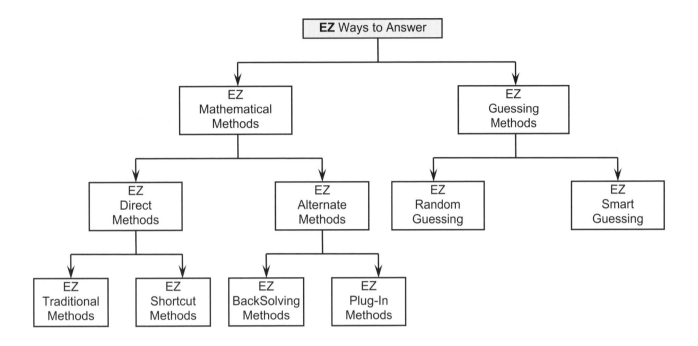

FIRST: EZ Ways to Answer: There are generally two main approaches to answer a question – Choose either EZ Mathematical Methods or EZ Guessing Methods.

SECOND: **(A)** If you pick EZ Guessing Methods, there are generally two options: Choose either EZ Random Guessing or EZ Smart Guessing by using Process of Elimination.

             (B) If you pick EZ Mathematical Methods, there are generally two options: Choose either EZ Direct Methods or EZ Alternate Methods.

THIRD: **(A)** If you pick EZ Direct Methods, there are generally two options: Choose either EZ Traditional Methods or EZ Shortcut Methods.

             (B) If you pick EZ Alternative Methods, there are generally two options: Choose either EZ Back-Solving Methods or EZ Plug-In Methods.

EZ TIP: The key to working systematically on math questions is to think about the question before you try to solve the problem or look for the answer.

2.3   EZ METHOD TO CHECK AND SELECT YOUR ANSWER

PICK – CHECK – RE-CHECK – SELECT YOUR FINAL ANSWER:
After you solve a question and pick your answer – you must try your best to check your solution – if possible try to re-check your solution – and then finally select one of the answer choices as your final answer.

❶ PICK YOUR ANSWER:
After you finish solving a question and you think that you have found the correct answer, pick the appropriate answer-choice.

❷ CHECK YOUR ANSWER:
After solving a question, and before selecting your answer, check your work quickly (if time permits) as this will help you avoid silly and obvious mistakes. Think carefully about the following:

(A) Answered Correct Question: Make sure your response actually answers what's being asked in the question.
   For instance: if a problem about oranges and apples asks for the number of apples, make sure your answer doesn't give the number of oranges by mistake; or if a problem asks for the altitude of a right triangle, make sure your answer doesn't give the hypotenuse instead.

(B) Makes Sense: Make sure that your answer makes sense. In many questions, you can catch an obvious error by simply asking if your answer makes sense or analyzing an easy case of the problem.
   For instance: if you are supposed to find less than 100 percent of a certain number, then you should know that your answer must be less than that certain number.
   For instance: if the original price of an item is $100, and you find the discounted price to be $110; check back, and you will realize that it does not make sense, the discounted price cannot be higher than the original price.

(C) Apply Different Methods: If you have time to check your work, redo your calculations and check your work from the beginning. If possible, use a different approach or method from the one you used the first time to get the answer. If you use the same method, you may again make the same mistake.
   - If you get the same answer using two different methods, your answer is probably correct.
   - If you get two different answers using two different methods, one of your answers is probably incorrect, and the other is correct. Redo the whole problem and figure out which one of the two answers is the correct one.
   For instance: if you have to convert a percent into a fraction, you can do that by either converting the percent directly into a fraction, or you can first convert the percent into a decimal and then convert that decimal into a fraction. By using both methods, you can be sure to find out if you actually got the correct answer.
   Note: While applying this strategy, make sure you don't waste too much time on any one question.

(D) Plug-In Answer into the Question: Plug your answer into the question-stem and determine if it makes logical sense.
   For instance: if you are asked to solve an equation, check your answer by plugging it into the given equation, and see whether it actually satisfies the given equation, and if it holds true.

(E) Approximation and Estimation: Use approximation and estimation as a means of quickly checking your work.

❸ RECHECK YOUR ANSWER: (only if you have extra time):
It's always a good idea to go back and re-check your solution; however, due to limited time on the test, indulge yourself in this process only if:
   - you found a mistake when you checked your solution, i.e., you got two different answers, and
   - you have extra time
Otherwise, you may end up missing-out on other questions and be short on time. Your time is precious on the test, so use it sensibly and wisely.

❹ SELECT YOUR ANSWER:
After you check/re-check your response, select the appropriate answer-choice. Now quickly move on to the next question.

This process of picking, checking, re-checking, and selecting your answers will help you in your entire career, and not just on this test!

2.4 EZ LONG-TERM STRATEGIES FOR MATH

Following are some of the skills that you must try to practice during your entire test-prep period. They will help you a great deal in improving your overall mathematical skills, not only for your test but also in your everyday life, both personally and professionally.

(A) ARITHMETIC SKILLS:

While your test is more about knowledge of concepts and problem analysis than arithmetical skills, it will still involve some calculative skills. Moreover, since we are talking about the math section, it is almost impossible not to deal with some arithmetic while solving the math problems. In fact, most problem solving sections contain at least a couple of basic computational questions, such as multiplying or dividing two decimals, or finding the largest number in a set of fractions, etc. Even if the problem were not purely an arithmetic computational type of a problem, it would still require some form of computational skills. Hence, either way, you are going to do a considerable amount of computations during your test. However, if you are too obsessed with using a calculator for every little calculation, you are asking for trouble. Some of the easiest questions on the test can turn into some of the most difficult ones for you.

Calculator addiction can be detrimental to your performance on the math section of your test. You are probably used to doing most of your calculations with the help of a calculator or a computer program, and it must have been a while since you last did a long division or decimal multiplication by hand. Even though you are allowed to use a calculator on your test, it is a good idea to hide all your calculators at a place where you can't find them, at least until your test is over. It is absolutely essential that you practice your arithmetic before you take the test. You should make sure that your number computation and manipulation skills are crisp and sharp so that you don't make careless mistakes and/or waste your precious time struggling with the calculations. You must already be conversant with the rules and know how to do basic computations – all you need is some hands-on practice to improve your speed and accuracy with the calculations. So make a serious attempt to stretch those math muscles.

We have also mentioned several computational shortcuts and strategies for calculations throughout our math modules. Make sure to put them to good use. Remember, ***all it takes is practice***!

(B) THINK QUANTITATIVELY:

Just like if you want to be a good reader, you should read a lot, if you want to be a good writer, you should write a lot; similarly, if you want to improve your quantitative skills, you should exercise them as frequently as possible. By exercising, we don't mean practicing math problems; that is something you are going to do regardless. What we mean is you must try to think mathematically even when you are not studying math. You should try to do all your day-to-day math without resorting to a calculator. Of course, it's always a good idea to check your results with a calculator, just to make sure. Always remember, to be successful on your math test, you should also be able to apply mathematics to real-life situations.

For instance, following are some real life situations where you can apply and exercise your math skills:
(i)   When you go to the mall for shopping during a sale next time, try to figure out the price after the discount to see how much you would have to pay, or try to figure out the price before the discount to find how much you will save.
(ii)   When you go to the supermarket for grocery shopping next time, try to figure out whether the giant size is cheaper per ounce than the economy size.
(iii) When you go to your favorite restaurant next time, try to figure out the 15-percent gratuity on your bill.
(iv)   When you watch your favorite team play softball next time, try to figure out the batting averages.
(v)   When you get your bank statement next time, try to balance your checkbook.
(vi)   When you look at random statistical figures in the newspaper or television, try to analyze those figures and make comparisons.
(vii) When you look at three-dimensional figures, such as a rectangular box or your living room, try to figure out its approximate surface area and volume.

If you get used to thinking quantitatively, not only will the math sections seem much easier, but you will also feel more confident about your overall exam. Therefore, at least for a few days, ***"live life the mathematical way!"***

CHAPTER 3.0: EZ SHORT & SMART METHODS

EZ OPTIONS: To solve most math problems that are going to be on your test, following are the two ways to approach it:
Either: Solve it by using Long Traditional Methods
Or: Solve it by using EZ Short-n-Smart Methods

3.1   ABOUT EZ SHORT-N-SMART METHODS

MANY QUESTIONS, LIMITED TIME:
Since your test is a time-bound test, what you are being tested on is not whether you can answer the given questions correctly; instead, what you are actually being tested on is whether you can answer the given questions correctly in the given amount of time. Therefore, *you not only have to answer the questions correctly, but you also have to answer them within the stipulated amount of time*. Clearly, time is of the essence. In fact, time is the single most important factor that can determine your performance on your test.

If there are two students of equal skills in math, but one is given a few more minutes than the other is, on a math section, obviously the one with a few extra minutes will do better. In other words, all things being equal, if you are given some more time, you are more likely to get a better score.

Hypothetically speaking, let's assume there is a student named Al, who likes to take short-cuts, that is, solve the problem with a non-traditional approach; and there is another student named Alexandria, who likes to take the long way, that is, solve the problem with a more traditional and direct approach. Now when the test time comes, Al who likes to take the shortcuts is almost always likely to do a lot better than Alexandria, who likes to take the long way.

Although Al and Alexandria know the same amount of math, since Al likes to take the shorter and hence the faster approach, he gives himself more time to work on other questions, a clear advantage over Alexandria who likes to take the longer and hence the slower approach. Both, Al and Alexandria, get to the same correct answer; however, Al can do this in a shorter time than Alexandria. Essentially, what Al does is find shortcuts to answer the question quickly. This doesn't make Al better at math, but it does make him a little bit better and smarter at test taking. Even with a few questions where shortcuts can be applied, Al will score considerably higher than Alexandria, even though the two of them know the same amount of math. Hence, you should try to learn to be more like Al and less like Alexandria.

Less time on one question means, more time for others. While everyone is given an equal amount of time on any math section, there is only one person who can give you at least a few extra minutes, and that person is you – and the way you can do that is by applying the shortcuts!

The secret mantra to more points on your test is: **SHORTER > SMARTER > FASTER > QUICKER**
MORE SHORTCUTS ⟹ LESS TIME ON SOME QUESTIONS ⟹ MORE TIME FOR OTHER QUESTIONS ⟹ HIGHER SCORE

SOLVE THE QUESTIONS USING THE SHORTEST & SMARTEST METHOD:
The amount of time you spend on a problem depends not only on how much math you know, but also on how you approach the problem. Once you have decided to solve a question, it's now time to decide how to tackle it. There are often multiple ways of solving the same problem, you must try to *adopt the fastest and easiest way*. Sometimes the most "obvious" or "direct" way to solve the problem is not necessarily the fastest way to solve it. If the method you select involves lots of calculations, look for another way to solve it. There's usually a shortcut you can use that is maybe easier and quicker, and that won't involve a lot of math. Always look for the fastest, shortest, and smartest way to solve a problem.

NO PROBLEM REQUIRES LENGTHY/COMPLICATED COMPUTATIONS:

Always remember that none of the math problems requires lengthy or complicated calculations. If you ever get into any lengthy or complicated calculations, stop, go back, reread the question, and check if you are answering the question that's being asked, and if you are on the right track. There is almost always a shorter way of solving the same problem.

3.2 HOW TO APPLY EZ SHORT-N-SMART METHODS

Acquire the Content Knowledge: In order to find a "short-cut," which is the indirect way to solve a problem, it's essential that you first know the "long-way," which is the direct way to solve the problem. It's difficult to find the shortcut from Washington DC to New York City, unless you know how to go the long direct way. Your ability to find a shortcut to solve a math problem is a function of how good you are with the math involved, and to solve it the old long traditional way. Your familiarity with the required math knowledge will lead you to shortcuts. Additionally, the more questions you practice, the more likely you are to find shortcuts. So don't be under the wrong impression that you can just learn the shortcuts without studying the long or direct way of solving a problem.

Hunt for Shortcuts: Once you know the direct way of solving a problem, the only way to look for a shortcut is to simply look at the problem and think about the fastest way of solving it. Then it will be more like an act of nature, you'll automatically see the shortcuts. Not all, but most of the math questions that you see on your test have shortcuts. So there is almost always some shortcut that already exists, the point is if you are able to find it within a reasonable amount of time.

Don't Dwell on Finding Shortcuts: By no means are we suggesting that you should be hunting for shortcuts in each and every question that you come across in the math section. As a rule of thumb, after you look at a problem, if you are not able to pinpoint a shortcut within a few seconds, don't bother, probably there isn't one, so just go ahead and solve the problem the way you know. Firstly, not all questions have shortcuts. Secondly, if you make it more like a "search for a shortcut" kind of a game than to actually "solve the problem" and get the answer, you may end up wasting time and may even take longer than the long direct way of solving the problem.

In general, math shortcuts are more common or susceptible to more test-like math questions. All general math shortcuts are explained in this book. All topic-specific shortcuts are explained in our other math content modules.

HOW TO APPLY EZ SHORT-N-SMART METHOD STRATEGY:

Generally, a math problem can often be solved in more than one way. You should **always look for the shortest, easiest, and quickest method for solving the problem**. You must keep your mind open towards the idea that a problem can often be answered without actually solving it in the traditional way. By doing so, not only will you have a higher chance of getting the correct answer, but you will also be able to save some valuable time. Moreover, if it seems like you have a lot of calculations to do, don't waste time on superfluous computations, most likely there's ought to be a shortcut. Therefore, solve the math problem using EZ Short-Cuts, and don't do more work than you have to.

EZ TIP: There is always a long traditional way of solving a problem, and a short and smart way of solving a problem – make sure to always choose the EZ Short-n-Smart Method Strategy.

Following examples are solved using the traditional method and our EZ Short-n-Smart Method so that you can see the difference between the two approaches.

Example #1: A man had $800. He used 25% of it to pay his phone bill, 20% of it to pay his electricity bill, 15% of it to pay his credit card bill, 10% of it to pay his cable bill, 7.5% of it to pay his gas bill, and 7.5% of it to pay his water bill. How much did he spend paying his bills?
(A) $120   (B) $620   (C) $660   (D) $680   (E) $860

Solution A: **Using Long and Time Consuming Direct Method:**
Phone Bill $\Rightarrow$ 25% of 800   = $200
Electricity Bills $\Rightarrow$ 20% of 800   = $160
Credit Card Bill $\Rightarrow$ 15% of 800   = $120
Cable Bill $\Rightarrow$ 10% of 800   = $80
Gas Bill $\Rightarrow$ 7.5% of 800   = $60

Water Bill	$\Rightarrow$ 7.5% of 800 = $60
Total Payment	$\Rightarrow$ $200 + $160 + $120 + $80 + $60 + $60 = $680

Therefore, the man spent $680 paying his bills, and the correct answer is (D).

Solution B: **Using EZ Short-Cut Method:**
The man spent 25% + 20% + 15% + 10% + 7.5% + 7.5% = 85% of his money paying the bills.
$\Rightarrow$ 85% of $800 = $680

Example #2:   Monika had $150. She used 75% of it to pay her electricity bill and 15% of it to pay her phone bill. How much was she left with after paying her bills?
(A) $10`          (B) $15          (C) $25`   (D) $75   (E) $135

Solution A: **Using Long and Time Consuming Direct Method:**

Electricity Bill	$\Rightarrow$ $150 × 75% = $112.50
Phone Bill	$\Rightarrow$ $150 × 15% = $22.50
Total Payment	$\Rightarrow$ $112.50 + $22.50 = $135
Amount Remaining	$\Rightarrow$ $150 – $135 = $15

Therefore, Monika was left with $15 after paying her bills, and the correct answer is (B).

Solution B: **Using EZ Short-Cut Method:**
Monika spent 75% + 15% = 90% of her money paying the bills.
After paying her bills, she was left with 100% – 90% = 10% of her money.
$\Rightarrow$ 10% of $150 = $15

Example #3:   A couple goes to a Mexican restaurant, the man orders three burritos and one taco, and was charged $2.50. The woman orders two burritos and one taco, and was charged $1.95. What is the price of two burritos?
(A) $0.55   (B) $1.05   (C) $1.10   (D) $1.25   (E) $2.20

Solution A: **Using Long and Time Consuming Direct Method:**
The cost of a burrito and taco can be translated into two distinct equations using the variable B for burritos and T for tacos. We can then solve the two resulting equations simultaneously.
Since three burritos and one taco cost $2.50: $\Rightarrow 3B + 1T = \$2.50$ $\Rightarrow$ Equation #1
Since two burritos and one taco cost $1.95: $\Rightarrow 2B + 1T = \$1.95$ $\Rightarrow$ Equation #2
Now let's solve the two equations simultaneously (subtract Equation #2 from Equation #1):

$\Rightarrow \quad 3B \quad + 1T \quad = \quad \$2.50 \qquad \Rightarrow$ Equation #1
$\Rightarrow \underline{-2B \quad - 1T \quad = -\$1.95} \qquad \Rightarrow$ Equation #2
$\qquad 1B \qquad\qquad = \$0.55$
$\qquad 2B \qquad\qquad = \$0.55 × 2 = \$1.10$

Therefore, two burritos cost $1.10, and the correct answer is (C).

Solution B: **Using EZ Short-Cut Method:**
If you read the problem carefully and think smartly, there's an easier and shorter way of solving this problem. You'll realize that the difference in price between the man's order of three burritos and a taco and the woman's order of two burritos and a taco is the price of one burrito.
The man orders the same thing as the woman does, except that he orders one more burrito.
Therefore, the difference in price of their orders is simply the price of one burrito:
$\Rightarrow$ Price of one Burrito = Man's Oder – woman's Order = $2.50 – $1.95 = $0.55
Now, the price of two burritos = $0.55 × 2 = $1.10, and the correct answer is (C).

Example #4:   At a Mexican restaurant, two burritos and five tacos cost the same as four burritos and two tacos. If the restaurant charges $2.50 for a single taco, how much does it charge for two burritos?
(A) $1.25   (B) $2.50   (C) $3.75   (D) $5.00   (E) $7.50

Solution A: **Using Long and Time Consuming Direct Method:**
The cost of a burrito and taco can be translated into two distinct equations using the variable B for burritos and T for tacos. We can then solve the two resulting equations simultaneously.
Since two burritos and five tacos cost the same as four burritos and two tacos:

$\Rightarrow 2B + 5T = 4B + 2T$
Since restaurant charges $2.50 for a single taco:
$\Rightarrow T = 2.50$
Plug-in the value of $T = \$2.50$ in the equation formed above:
$\Rightarrow 2B + 5T = 4B + 2T$
$\Rightarrow 2B + 5(2.50) = 4B + 2(2.50)$
$\Rightarrow 2B + 12.50 = 4B + 5.00$
$\Rightarrow 2B = \$7.50$
Therefore, two burritos cost $7.50, and the correct answer is (E).

Solution B: **Using EZ Short-Cut Method:**
If you read the problem carefully and think smartly, there's an easier and shorter way of solving this problem. You'll realize that two burritos and five tacos cost the same as four burritos and two tacos: $\Rightarrow$ Price of 2 burritos + 5 tacos = Price of 4 burritos + 2 tacos
Let's take away all the items that are the same in the two orders and we're left with three tacos costing the same as two burritos: $\Rightarrow$ Price of 3 tacos = Price of 2 burritos
Now since Price of 1 taco = $2.50
Price of 3 tacos = $2.50 × 3 = $7.50 = Price of 2 burritos.
Therefore, two burritos cost $7.50, and the correct answer is (E).

Example #5:   If $2a + 5b = 20$ and $5a + 2b = 50$, what it is the average of a and b?
(A) 5   (B) 5   (C) 5   (D) 5   (E) 5

Solution A: **Using Long and Time Consuming Direct Method:**
Let's solve the two given equations simultaneously:
$2a + 5b = 20$ [1]
$5a + 2b = 50$ [2]
Multiply equation [1] by (5): $\Rightarrow 10a + 25b = 100$ [3]
Multiply equation [2] by (–2): $\Rightarrow -10a - 4b = -100$ [4]
Now add equation [3] and [4]

$$\begin{array}{rl}
10a \quad + 25b \quad = \quad 100 & [3] \\
\underline{-10a \quad - 4b \quad = -100} & [4] \\
+ 21b \quad = 0 & \\
\Rightarrow b \quad = 0 &
\end{array}$$

Now substitute $b = 0$ in equation [1]:
$2a + 5b = 20$ [1]
$\Rightarrow 2a + 5(0) = 20$
$\Rightarrow 2a = 20$
$\Rightarrow a = 10$

Average of a and $b \Rightarrow \dfrac{a+b}{2} = \dfrac{0+10}{2} = \dfrac{10}{2} = 5$

Therefore, the correct answer is (A).

Solution B: **Using EZ Short-Cut Method:**
If you notice, the question doesn't ask for the value of either "a" or "b" separately, instead it asked for the average of a and b, which is $\dfrac{a+b}{2}$. So don't solve for them separately if you don't have to.

$$\begin{array}{l}
2a + 5b = 20 \qquad \text{[add both equations]} \\
\underline{5a + 2b = 50} \\
7a + 7b = 70
\end{array}$$

$\dfrac{7a + 7b}{7} = \dfrac{70}{7}$ [divide both sides by 7]

$a + b = 10$

$\Rightarrow \dfrac{a+b}{2} = \dfrac{10}{2} = 5$ [again divide both sides by 2]

Therefore, the correct answer is (A).

.PRACTICE EXERCISE WITH DETAILED EXPLANATIONS

Question #1: If $a = 7 \times 9765$ and $b = 7 \times 8765$, what is the value of $a - b$?
  (A) 1,000 (B) 2,000 (C) 3,500 (D) 4,250 (E) 7,000

Solution A: **Using Long and Time Consuming Direct Method:**
  $\Rightarrow a - b = (7 \times 9765) - (7 \times 8765) = 68355 - 61355 = 7{,}000$
  Therefore, the correct answer is (E).

Solution B: **Using EZ Short-Cut Method:**
  $\Rightarrow a - b = (7 \times 9765) - (7 \times 8765) = 7(9765 - 8765) = 7(1000) = 7{,}000$

Question #2: If $x \neq \frac{1}{2}$ and $\dfrac{57}{2x-1} = \dfrac{57}{19}$, then what is the value of x?
  (A) 10 (B) 17 (C) 19 (D) 20 (E) 100

Solution A: **Using Long and Time Consuming Direct Method:**
  $\Rightarrow \dfrac{57}{2x-1} = \dfrac{57}{19}$
  $\Rightarrow 57(2x - 1) = (57)(19)$ [cross-multiply both sides of the equation]
  $\Rightarrow 114x - 57 = 1083$ [apply distributive property]
  $\Rightarrow 114x = 1083 + 57 = 1140$ [add 57 to both sides of the equation]
  $\Rightarrow x = \dfrac{1140}{114} = 10$ [divide both sides of the equation by 114]
  Therefore, the correct answer is (A).

Solution B: **Using EZ Short-Cut Method:**
  If you notice, the numerators in both the fractions are the same. When two fractions are equal, and if the tops (numerators) of the fractions are equal, then the bottoms (denominators) must also be equal.
  $\Rightarrow 2x - 1 = 19$
  $\Rightarrow 2x = 19 + 1 = 20$ [add 2 to both sides of the equation]
  $\Rightarrow x = \dfrac{20}{2} = 10$ [divide both sides of the equation by 2]

Question #3: If $2x - 5 = 96$, what is the value of $2x + 5$?
  (A) 50.5 (B) 100 (C) 101 (D) 106 (E) 111

Solution A: **Using Long and Time Consuming Direct Method:**
  First, solve for x from the given equation:
  $\Rightarrow 2x - 5 = 96$
  $\Rightarrow 2x = 96 + 5 = 101$ [add 5 to both sides of the equation]
  $\Rightarrow x = 101 \div 2 = 50.5$ [divide both sides of the equation by 2]
  Now, plug in the value of x in the given expression to find its value:
  $\Rightarrow 2x + 5 = 2(50.5) + 5 = 101 + 5 = 106$
  Therefore, the correct answer is (D).

Solution B: **Using EZ Short-Cut Method:**
  The best approach is to observe that $2x + 5$ is exactly 10 more than $2x - 5$, so the answer must be 10 more than 96, which is $96 + 10 = 106$.
  If you are not able to observe the above, the next best approach would be to do only one step in solving the equation by adding 5 to both sides: $2x = 96 + 5 = 101$.
  Now again add 5 to both sides: $2x + 5 = 101 + 5 = 106$.

Question #4:   If $x + 2y = 8$ and $x + y = 10$, what is the value of $2x + 2y$?

(A) 10   (B) 20   (C) 30   (D) 40   (E) 50

Solution A: **Using Long and Time Consuming Direct Method:**

We can solve the two equations simultaneously to find the value of x and y.

$\Rightarrow x + 2y = 8$ [1]

$\Rightarrow x + y = 10$ [2]

Now let's solve the two equations simultaneously (subtract Equation [2] from Equation [1]):

$\Rightarrow \quad x \quad + 2y \quad = \quad 8$ [1]

$\Rightarrow \underline{-x \quad - y \quad\quad = -10}$ [2]

$\quad\quad\quad 1y \quad\quad = -2$

Plug the value of y in Equation #2 to find the value of x:

$\Rightarrow x + y = 10$ [2]

$\Rightarrow x - 2 = 10$

$\Rightarrow x = 12$

Finally substitute the value of x and y to evaluate $2x + 2y \Rightarrow 2x + 2y = 2(12) + 2(-2) = 24 - 4 = 20$

Therefore, the correct answer is (B).

Solution B: **Using EZ Short-Cut Method:**

The best approach is to observe that we are asked to find the value of $2x + 2y$ which is double of $x + y$:

$\Rightarrow x + y = 10$

$\Rightarrow 2x + 2y = 20$ [multiple the whole equation by 2]

Question #5:   If $a^2 \neq b^2$, then what is the value of $\dfrac{a^2 - b^2}{b^2 - a^2} \times \dfrac{a - b}{b - a}$

(A) -1 (B) 0   (C) 1   (D) 2   (E) 10

Solution A: **Using Long and Time Consuming Direct Method:**

$\Rightarrow \dfrac{a^2 - b^2}{b^2 - a^2} \times \dfrac{a - b}{b - a}$

$\Rightarrow \dfrac{(a + b)(a - b)}{(b + a)(b - a)} \times \dfrac{(a - b)}{(b - a)}$ [factor: $a^2 - b^2 = (a + b)(a - b)$ and $b^2 - a^2 = (b + a)(b - a)$]

$\Rightarrow \dfrac{(a - b)}{(b - a)} \times \dfrac{(a - b)}{(b - a)}$ [cancel common factors]

$\Rightarrow \dfrac{(a - b)}{-(a - b)} \times \dfrac{(a - b)}{-(a - b)}$ [take ($-$) sign out of the parenthesis in the denominator & again cancel]

$\Rightarrow -1 \times -1 = 1$

Therefore, the correct answer is (C).

Solution B: **Using EZ Short-Cut Method:**

This problem is a lot easier than it appears. The smart thing to notice is that, in any fraction, if the numerator is the negative of the denominator, then that fraction equals -1.

For instance: $\dfrac{5 - 7}{7 - 5} = -\dfrac{2}{2} = -1$.

$\Rightarrow \dfrac{a^2 - b^2}{b^2 - a^2} \times \dfrac{a - b}{b - a} = (-1) \times (-1) = 1$

Similarly, if you were asked to find the sum of the two fractions, you can apply the same EZ Shortcut:

$\Rightarrow \dfrac{a^2 - b^2}{b^2 - a^2} + \dfrac{a - b}{b - a} = (-1) + (-1) = -2$

CHAPTER 4.0: EZ TIPS FOR TRAPS & TRICKS

4.1 ABOUT MATH TRAPS AND TRICKS

One of the most important things that make the standardized math test problems trickier than most regular test problems are the *vicious* traps that are very *deviously* inserted in the problems. In this section, you will also learn how to use test-taking strategies, and be able to recognize and avoid common traps so that you become more successful in solving the math problems.

Fortunately, there are only a few traps that occur repeatedly, but in slightly different forms in different questions. If you learn how these traps work and how you can avoid them – dealing with even the trickiest traps will become easier; and you'll do much better, even on the more difficult math questions. If your answer is wrong and if you didn't make any errors in your calculations, chances are that your incorrect answer is an indication that you got *mired* into a trap.

LEARN HOW THE TEST-MAKERS THINK:
The best way to understand the whole test-makers psyche is to learn to think the way they think. For a moment, place yourself in the test-maker's position. The first thing the test-maker does is to write a question-stem and throw in the correct answer as one of the five answer choices. However, hold on, he isn't done yet. He still has four empty spots to fill. Therefore, he needs to come up with four incorrect answers, which is not a very easy task. For the test-makers to come up with answers that will appeal to people, they have to know how a normal test-taker thinks.

If people who don't know how to solve a problem are going to guess – our test-makers want to make sure they guess wrong. The test-makers spend an awful amount of time and effort into creating incorrect answer choices. The test-makers have had extensive experience with math tests, and they exactly know all the potential ways that the students may mess up a question. Hence, they first try to figure out all the mistakes a careless test-taker might make, and then *flawlessly* include those answers among the choices.

THE TRAPPY DISTRACTERS:
One way of coming up with the four incorrect answer choices or the *"trappy distracters"* is simply to pick random answers or answers that are closely clustered around the correct answer. Now this is a relatively easier task for the test-makers. However, there is one problem – the test-takers who don't know how to solve a problem wouldn't see the obvious answer, and might guess at random. The test-makers do not want the test-takers to guess randomly, because if they did, they might actually pick the right answer. Therefore, the test-makers want to come up with the wrong answer choices that are the most obvious but incorrect answer choices that tempt the test-takers to pick them. These tricky answer choices are traps that seem right but are actually wrong. A trap can be anything but right.

Math traps look right because they're the answers you're most likely to get if you fall into the traps and make one of the simple mistakes that the test-makers have already thought of. Then, when students make one of those already anticipated mistakes and see their wrong answer listed as one of the answer choices, they get tempted to pick that answer instead of checking their work and looking for the right one.

The test-makers already know that you are going to be a little nervous and panicky when you take the test. They take this as an opportunity and don't forget to take full advantage of it. Now if you are a little shaken and confused, desperate to answer something or anything, it won't be very difficult for you to convince yourself that any of the answers that seem to be correct is indeed correct, especially in that panicked state of mind.

This is how nervous people take standardized math tests:

First: They start solving a question with their heart pounding and breath puffing.
Second: They peek down at the answer choices to see if they are on the right track.
Third: They look at the answer choices after each step, just to see if their answer is listed there.
Fourth: As soon as they find their answer listed – BINGO! They fall prey to one of the pre-fabricated traps that allure them into picking an answer that seems right but is actually incomplete or otherwise wrong.

FACTS OF MATH TRAPS & TRICKS:

- The first thing to recognize is the fact that traps are out there, and are probably hiding among many answer choices, trying to trick you.
- The second thing is to understand that unless you approach the question with a plan, you are much more likely to fall prey to one of the vicious traps.

Now we will explain the different types of traps, but first read the following example for your reference:

Example #1:   A couple goes to a Mexican restaurant, the man orders three burritos and one taco, and was charged $2.50. The woman orders two burritos and one taco, and was charged $1.95. What is the price of two burritos?
(A) $0.55   (B) $1.05   (C) $1.10   (D) $1.25   (E) $1.70

MISREADING/MISUNDERSTANDING THE QUESTION:

Read Through the Question – Entirely, Properly, & Thoroughly: The moment you see a question, obviously, the first thing that you would do is read the question. Now this may seem a little too obvious. Of course, you have to read the question in order to answer it. How else can you solve the problem? Yes, it is obvious to read the question; however, in reality, this is not quite as obvious as it seems. Apparently, there are different ways to read the question. The point we are trying to make here is that you need to carefully read the question – entirely, properly, and thoroughly, before you even begin to attempt to solve the problem. Read carefully enough to determine what is being asked, so that you know what you're trying to find before you even start looking for it, and what you have to work with to help you find it.

For majority of test-takers, a significant number of their wrong answers in the math section are a result of nothing more than simple reading errors. One may know very well how to do the math involved, but that is going to be useless if they answer the wrong question. Nothing can be more frustrating than to choose the wrong answer when you know how to do the math. If you can somehow avoid reading mistakes, which is not that difficult, these questions can become relatively easy. Such types of careless mistakes can be devastating on your test score. You can very easily reduce the number of reading mistakes you make in the math section by reading the questions carefully. Always, re-read the question, especially the question-stem, and be on the lookout for misleading phrases, before selecting your final answer.

While reading the problem and before answering the question, think carefully about the following:
- Determine what's asked in the question – develop the ability to decode question-stems quickly & accurately. With practice, just by taking a glimpse at the problem, you'll quickly recognize exactly what is being asked.
- Rephrase the question to make sure you understand it correctly.

You are much more likely to get caught-up in a trap, misunderstand it, or make a careless mistake, if you don't read the question properly. A small clue or buzzword, easily unnoticed, can mean the difference between a right and a wrong answer, which may cost you a point. It's crucial that you pay close attention to precisely what's asked in the question. In fact, many problem-solving questions invite you to misread them. Hence, read carefully and avoid the potential traps. Moreover, if you try to start solving the problem before reading the question all the way through, you may end up doing some unnecessary work, which may not be required to answer the question. Always remember that you don't necessarily have to use all the information given in order to answer the question.

For Instance: In the example given above, you may realize how important it is to read the question properly. It contains some classic traps that are very easy to fall into if you don't read the questions carefully. It looks pretty straightforward; however, if you read through it carefully, you will see a slight twist. You'll notice that you are asked to find the price of two burritos. Many students will get this example wrong by finding the price of one burrito and then forgetting to double it to find the price of two burritos, which is precisely what is being asked in the question. Make sure to do all the required steps. Of course, you can be sure that the test-maker will include the partial answer among the four wrong answer choices to tempt you to pick it.

AVOID REPEATED NUMBERS:

Avoid answers that repeat numbers from the problem, that is, numbers that you have already seen in the problem, even if they have a minor manipulation. It's quite silly, but test-makers think you may simply pick an answer because you remember it from the problem itself.

For Instance: In the example given above, avoid picking answer-choice (A) because it's the difference between the two numbers given in the problem: $2.50 and $1.95. Also, avoid picking answer-choice (D) because it is half of $2.50, which is already given in the problem.

DON'T USE YOUR PERSONAL OPINION OR APPLY ANY OUTSIDE OR EXTRANEOUS KNOWLEDGE:

While solving any problem in math, try not to use any personal opinion or any outside or extraneous knowledge. What we mean by this is, don't try to rationalize the problem to an extent that you cross the scope or the context of the problem. Many students tend to involve their personal opinion while solving a problem, and sometimes without even realizing it. Don't let that happen to you. Use only the information given in the problem, and nothing outside of it. Therefore, always keep in mind that your answer should be based solely and exclusively on the information provided in the question – don't allow your own experiences or assumptions to interfere with your ability to find the correct answer to the question.

For Instance: In the example given above, if you get an answer for the price of a burrito as $0.25 or $7.50, don't think that the market rate for a burrito is significantly lower or higher. If in your opinion, a burrito should normally cost in the range of $2 – $4, and you get $0.55 or $7.50 as your answer, just go ahead and pick what you get, don't let your personal opinion about the price of a burrito, consciously or subconsciously, get in your way. Many times, you may get the price of a burrito to be substantially lower or higher than what you personally think, and you may doubt your own answer, which may actually be correct. For the purpose of your problem, a burrito can cost $0.10 or even $10, or any other amount for that matter.

UNDER-DONE PARTIAL TRAP ANSWERS:

Think of a "partial under-done answer" as an "under-done" cookie – it's done but not completely done, it needs some more work done, and hence it's no good. On math problems, if a question requires you to do more than one step, it's very easy to go wrong by thinking that you are finished before you actually are. You may do one step, and think that you have successfully found the correct answer. What you don't realize is there is another step that needs to be performed in order to solve the problem correctly and completely. What you found was a partial answer, and to find the correct answer you have to do another step. This is a perfect opportunity for the test-makers to throw in a partial answer as a trap. Since the test-makers already know that some people may find a partial answer, hence they like to include, among the answer choices, answers that are partial completions of the problems as potential traps. Therefore, just in case if you get halfway through a problem and decide that you're done, the answer you have arrived at will probably be there, waiting for you to pick it.

For Instance: If a question gives an equation, such as $5x + 2 = 52$, and asks for the value of $2.5x$, one may correctly find the value of x as 10, but then may forget to get the value of $2.5x$ by multiplying 10 by 2.5 and getting 25. The test-makers will want to include 10 among the answer choices. Now if this incorrect answer-choice weren't there, test-takers who didn't do this last step, might realize that they made a mistake, and eventually figure out the correct answer by redoing it. However, the test-makers would prefer that they just get it wrong by picking the trap answer.

OVER-DONE TRAP ANSWERS:

Think of an "over-done answer" as an "over-done" cookie – it's done but excessively done, it got more work done than needed, and hence it's no good. Although there is no logical explanation why any test-taker would want to do more work than needed, however, some test-takers who actually get the correct answer may do an extra step and mess-up their answer. That extra step could be something totally foolish, like adding the two numbers in the problem together, or subtracting them. Therefore, avoid doing any extra unwanted steps.

For Instance: If a question asks you to find 12% of 80, one may correctly find 9.6, but then they would either add it to 80 and get 89.6 or subtract it from 80 and come up with 70.4. The test-makers will want to include 89.6 or 70.4 among the answer choices. Now if these two incorrect answer choices weren't there, test-takers who had done this extra completely unwanted step, might realize they had made a mistake, and eventually figure out the correct answer by redoing it. However, the test-makers would prefer that they just get it wrong by picking the trap answer.

MOST OBVIOUSLY WRONG ANSWERS ARE ALMOST ALWAYS THERE:

If you make a careless mistake when you read the question – you can be sure that the test-maker will include that answer among the four wrong answer choices to tempt you to pick it. In fact, the test-makers have spent hours coming up with all the possible and potential ways for you to mess-up the problem. In fact, some questions are often deliberately designed to be confusing and contain obvious traps. In most of the math questions, the answer choices normally contain the obvious mistakes that a test-taker is expected to make. If you make one of these mistakes, your final answer will be among the answer choices, and you'll pick it, and get the question wrong. Although it's a careless and a very easy mistake to make, it can cost you a point on your test. It's rather easy to make such careless mistakes while you are working through the problems quickly. In fact, most difficult problems contain one or more potential loopholes, and the test makers will include trap answers to snag people who make those mistakes. So beware of such misleading answer choices that try to trick you in picking the wrong answer while making your final choice. That's why we recommend that you read the question properly and make sure you know what's being asked in the question.

POTENTIAL TRAPS ARE ALWAYS THERE:
Even if there's a small chance that a test-taker might fall prey to a potential trap, the test-makers want it to be there. Hence, the test-makers will probably include those answers among the answer choices. Again, there's no good mathematical reason why a test-taker would want to do these things, but the test-makers realize the fact that you don't always need a good reason to go wrong. If the test-makers just picked the incorrect answers at random, a test-taker would be much less likely to fall into their traps.

BEWARE OF THE WRONG BUT TEMPTING ANSWER-CHOICES:
Beware, some of the choices are given in such a manner that they are the obvious mistakes one might make. If you solve a given problem and get an answer, and even if your answer is listed as one of the given choices, this may not necessarily guarantee that your answer is correct. The answer choices contain some of the most obviously wrong answers. Therefore, as soon as you finish solving a problem, always take a moment to reread the problem before you pick an answer to make sure you've actually answered the question you have been asked. Make sure you answer the question that's being asked and not what you think is being asked. Read through all of the possible answers before selecting one. Then reread the question to make sure the answer you have selected really answers the question. At least a few, if not all of the choices given, correspond to answers you would obtain by making simple and common errors, such as adding instead of subtracting, multiplying instead of dividing, or confusing area and perimeter. So read the question carefully and beware of these wrong but tempting answer choices, they are there to trick you so you would pick them.

4.2   HOW TO AVOID PICKING TRAP ANSWERS

The best way to prevent you from picking a trap answer is by doing the following:

Firstly: If you are solving a math problem directly, the best way to avoid falling prey to one of the traps that the test-makers have laid for you is by completely ignoring the answer choices until you have determined that you have reached your final answer. Trap answers are often the values you would get at the mid-point of the process of working out a problem or by making some of the obvious mistakes. If you take a peek at the answers before getting to your final answer, you may get tricked into thinking either that you've solved the question correctly or that you have reached the correct answer before you actually have. Therefore, first try to solve the question without looking at the answer choices. Once you have found your final answer – only then see if your final answer is listed among the given answer choices. By waiting to look at the answer choices until after you've solved the problem, you'll be able to block or by-pass some of these vicious traps.

Secondly: Before you start solving the problem, always take a moment to figure out the level of difficulty of the problem you are working on to decide whether you've done enough work to get to the correct answer, and for the test-makers to think you "deserve" to get the problem right.
- If you are on an easy math question $\Rightarrow$ you should be able to get to the correct answer in usually one step.
- If you are on a medium math question $\Rightarrow$ you should be able to get to the correct answer in usually two steps.
- If you are on a difficult math question, $\Rightarrow$ you should be able to get to the correct answer in usually three or more steps.

Thirdly: It is sometimes a good idea to check your answer by plugging it back into the question-stem before picking your final answer. This will ensure that you didn't make any errors or get trapped.

Fourthly: Finally, solve the question carefully and cautiously. Execute each calculation accurately and correctly. Also, make sure you solve what you have been asked to solve, and not anything extra that is not required.

No Non-Sense Test: You can prevent yourself from falling into a trap by applying the "No Non-Sense Test". That is, use common sense on the problem and figure out if there are any answer choices that simply don't make sense – if there are any such choices, eliminate them immediately.

For Example: What is the solution set to the inequality: $7x > 5x + 16$?
(A) $x > -8$ (B) $x < 8$ (C) $x > 8$ (D) $x < -8$ (E) $x > 16/7$

Solution: Let's first try to solve the problem:
$\Rightarrow 7x > 5x + 16$
$\Rightarrow 2x > 16$
$\Rightarrow x > 8$
Next, let's check if we actually got the correct answer by evaluating cases and see if it **makes sense**:
Since $x > 8$, let's plug-in a case where x is greater than 8, let's say 9 and see if it works, if it does work than we have the correct answer.
$\Rightarrow 7x > 5x + 16$
$\Rightarrow 7(9) > 5(9) + 16$
$\Rightarrow 63 > 45 + 16$
$\Rightarrow 63 > 61$ TRUE, so our answer is correct!
Since $x > 8$, let's plug-in a case where x is less than 8, let's say 7 and see if it doesn't works, if it doesn't work than we have the correct answer.
$\Rightarrow 7x > 5x + 16$
$\Rightarrow 7(7) > 5(7) + 16$
$\Rightarrow 49 > 35 + 16$
$\Rightarrow 49 > 51$ FALSE, so our answer is correct!

4.3 HIDE OR SEEK THE ANSWER-CHOICES

Whether to seek or look at the answer choices before you begin to solve a question, or hide them, is a controversial topic. Different books suggest different things. We have studied this issue in detail, and come up with a detailed analysis of some clear advantages and disadvantages of both approaches.

Advantages of Scanning Through Answer-Choices Before Solving: There are some advantages of scanning through all the answer choices before even attempting to work out a question. Scanning the answer choices can prevent you from doing some extra work, and help you save time.

(A) First scanning the answers will provide valuable information about the format in which the answer choices are given so that you can straight away solve the problem to get the answer in the desired format. This will prevent you from putting your answers in a form that is not given. For instance, you might be able to determine, whether your answer should be left in a radical form or converted to a fractional or a decimal approximation; whether your polynomial answer should be left in factored-form or distributed-out; whether you need to express the probability in a percent, a fractional, or a decimal form; or whether you need to reduce a ratio or a fraction to its lowest terms. Knowing all this in advance will save you time and effort. For example, if all the answer choices were given in the fractional form such as 7/8, it would be a waste of time to solve your answer in the decimal form, such as 0.875.

(B) First scanning the answer choices may warn you early in your solution process if you are on the wrong track. For instance, if all the answer choices are round numbers, such as, 10, 25, 50, etc, and if you feel, your answer is going to be in decimals, then you'll know that something is wrong, and you can check your solution before moving on with the solution process.

(C) First scanning the answer choices will also tell you how spread out or closely clustered the answer choices are and you can accordingly use the degree of approximation. For instance, if all the answer choices are spread-out, such as 5, 25, 50, etc., you can easily approximate your numbers.

(D) First scanning the answer choices will also help you make a quick "make-sense" check before you start working on a problem, and may help you eliminate some of the "absurd" or "out of range" answer choices right away.

Advantages of Not Scanning Through Answer-Choices Before Solving: There are some advantages of not scanning through all the answer choices before even attempting to work out a question. Not scanning the answer choices can prevent you from falling prey to some of the traps explained earlier in this section.

What to do? The decision is yours to make whether or not to look at the answer choices before solving a problem. Whenever you have to make a decision in life, when you have to choose one of the two options, and when there are some very lucrative advantages and harmful disadvantages in both options, you should attempt to squeeze out the best of both approaches and try to quarantine the bad oranges. In other words, what you should do is scan the answer choices before you begin to solve the problem in a manner that gives you the advantages of first scanning the answer choices but at the same time try not to memorize or retain them to the extent that you fall for a trap. You have to do this very carefully.

4.4   APPROACHES FOR EASY & DIFFICULT QUESTIONS

DIFFERENT APPROACHES FOR EASY & DIFFICULT QUESTIONS:
There should be different approaches to solve different problems of different levels of difficulty. We can divide the problems according to their levels of difficulty into three groups: easy or basic, moderate, and difficult or advanced. Keeping this in mind, as you work through a problem, first determine if the question is easy, moderate, or difficult.

If a Math section has been arranged in order of difficulty, with the easiest problems coming first and the hardest problems coming last, the first few questions are basic, the middle few are moderately difficult, and the last few are very difficult. However, not all math sections are arranged in order of difficulty. In this case, your only option is to use your best judgment and determine the level of difficulty of the problem you are tackling. Moreover, level of difficulty is a relative term – a question that is easy for one may be difficult for the other, and vice versa. Note that this only has to be a rough estimate. Always make sure that you treat an easy question differently from a more difficult question.

On the more basic or easy questions, you may find that you know the answer right away and are able to work through them rather quickly without much difficulty. Whereas, when working through some of the more difficult or complex questions, it's very important to spend some extra time thinking about your approach, and looking for traps and hidden information, so that you aren't tricked or misled. However, you'll be surprised; some of the easy questions may also contain traps, and some of the difficult questions may not contain any traps. Remember to be suspicious and avoid some of the obvious errors. Never lose your focus and make sure you always know what's being asked in the question.

EASY QUESTIONS:
Easy questions are usually straightforward, all the information you need to solve the problem may be provided in the question-stem or in the figure. While answering any question, you must always be cautious and careful; however, easy questions usually don't contain traps and hidden information, and are not typically tricky and misleading.
Traps: Easy questions usually don't contain traps, even if there is a trap, it would be just one simple trap – so don't worry too much about traps.
Hidden Information: Easy questions usually don't contain hidden information that may help you solve the problem – so don't worry too much about decoding any hidden information.
Tricky: Easy questions are not usually there specifically to trick you – so don't worry too much about being tricked.
Misleading: Easy questions are not usually written to be misleading and deceptive – so don't worry too much about being misled.

AVOID THE FOLLOWING TRAPS ON EASY QUESTIONS:
* **Easy Questions have Easy Answers:** On easy questions, avoid difficult or complex answers; usually easy questions have easy answers, and any difficult answers are usually wrong. Therefore, if some of the answer choices are too complex, be suspicious, and try to avoid them.
* **It's Easy to Answer Easy Questions:** On easy questions, avoid answers that you get with a lot of time and effort; usually it's easy to answer easy questions. Therefore, if you get an answer with a lot of time and effort, be suspicious, and check your solution – you may have missed something or made some sort of an error.

EZ CAUTION: There are exceptions, an easy question may have a difficult answer, and for some of you, it may be difficult to solve some of the easy questions. However, this is not very likely to happen.

DIFFICULT QUESTIONS:
Difficult questions are not usually straightforward, not all the information you need to solve the problem may not be provided in the question-stem or in the figure. While answering any question, you must always be extra cautious and

careful; especially, difficult questions usually contain traps and hidden information, and are typically tricky and misleading.

Traps: Difficult questions usually contain traps, some of which may be complex, and there may be multiple traps – so watch out and beware of the traps.

Hidden Information: Difficult questions usually contain hidden information that may help you solve the problem – so you often need to decode hidden information so that it becomes more visible to you.

Tricky: Difficult questions are usually there specifically to trick you – so make sure you don't get tricked.

Misleading: Difficult questions are usually written to be misleading and deceptive – so don't let them mislead you or sidetrack you, just focus on what you need to find out.

AVOID THE FOLLOWING TRAPS ON DIFFICULT QUESTIONS:

- **Difficult Questions have Difficult Answers:** On difficult questions, avoid easy or simple answers; usually difficult questions have difficult answers, and any easy answers are usually wrong. Therefore, if some of the answer choices are too simple, be suspicious, and try to avoid them.

- **It's Difficult to Answer Difficult Questions:** On difficult questions, avoid answers that you get too quickly within a short time, and too easily without much effort; usually it's difficult to answer difficult questions. Therefore, if you get an answer too quickly within a short time and too easily without much effort, be suspicious and check your solution – you may have missed something or made some sort of an error.

EZ CAUTION: There are exceptions, a difficult question may have an easy answer, and for some of you, it may be easy to solve some of the difficult questions. However, this is not very likely to happen.

Now let's look at a few solved examples and evaluate some of the most common traps and errors in detail.

Example #1:   A couple goes to a Mexican restaurant, the man orders three burritos and one taco, and was charged $2.50. The woman orders two burritos and one taco, and was charged $1.95. What is the price of two burritos?
  (A) $0.55   (B) $1.05   (C) $1.10   (D) $1.25   (E) $1.70

Solution: The cost of a burrito and taco can be translated into two distinct equations using the variable B for burritos and T for tacos. You could then solve the two equations simultaneously.
  Since three burritos and one taco cost $2.50: $\Rightarrow 3B + 1T = \$2.50$ $\Rightarrow$ Equation #1
  Since two burritos and one taco cost $1.95: $\Rightarrow 2B + 1T = \$1.95$ $\Rightarrow$ Equation #2
  Now let's solve these two equations simultaneously (subtract Equation #2 from Equation #1):
  $\Rightarrow \ 3B \ \ + 1T \ \ = \ \$2.50$ $\Rightarrow$ Equation #1
  $\Rightarrow \underline{-2B \ \ - 1T \ \ = -\$1.95}$ $\Rightarrow$ Equation #2
  $\quad \ \ 1B \qquad \qquad = \$0.55$
  $\quad \ \ 2B \qquad \qquad = \$0.55 \times 2 = \$1.10$
  Therefore, two burritos cost $1.10, and the correct answer is (C)

  Trap #1: The first mistake one can make is to pick answer-choice (A) because it's the difference between the two numbers given in the problem: $2.50 – $1.95 = $0.55. This is clearly wrong!

  Trap #2: The second mistake one can make is to pick answer-choice (D) because it is half of $2.50, which is already given in the problem: ½ × $2.50 = $1.25. This is clearly wrong!

  Trap #3: The third mistake one can make is to find the price of 1 burrito $0.55 and pick answer-choice (A). The question asks for the price of 2 burritos not one. This is a partial answer, you need to do one more step and double the price of one burrito. This is clearly wrong!!

  Trap #4: The fourth mistake one can make is to find the price of 2 tacos by plugging-in $B = 0.55$ in Equation #1 and getting $1.70 and picking answer-choice (E). In this case, you have done more than you were required to do, the question asks for the price of 2 burritos and not 2 tacos. This is clearly wrong!
  $\Rightarrow 3B + 1T = \$2.50$
  $\Rightarrow 3(0.55) + 1T = \$2.50$
  $\Rightarrow T = 2.50 - 1.65 = \$0.85$
  $\Rightarrow 2T = \$0.85 \times 2 = \$1.70$

As you can see above, almost all of the four wrong answer choices contain a value that one can easily obtain if they make one small mistake.

Example #2: At a Mexican restaurant, two burritos and five tacos cost the same as four burritos and two tacos. If the restaurant charges $2.50 for a single taco, how much does it charge for two burritos?
(A) $1.25   (B) $2.50   (C) $3.75   (D) $5.00   (E) $7.50

Solution: The cost of a burrito and taco can be translated into two distinct equations using the variable B for burritos and T for tacos. You could then solve the two equations simultaneously.
Since two burritos and five tacos cost the same as four burritos and two tacos:
$\Rightarrow 2B + 5T = 4B + 2T$
Since restaurant charges $2.50 for a single taco:
$\Rightarrow T = 2.50$
Plug-in the value of $T = \$2.50$ in the equation formed above:
$\Rightarrow 2B + 5T = 4B + 2T$
$\Rightarrow 2B + 5(2.50) = 4B + 2(2.50)$
$\Rightarrow 2B + 12.50 = 4B + 5.00$
$\Rightarrow 2B = \$7.50$
Therefore, two burritos cost $7.50, and the correct answer is (E),

Trap #1: The first mistake to make is to pick answer-choice (B) because it's the same as $2.50, which is already given in the problem. This is clearly wrong!

Trap #2: The second mistake to make is to pick answer-choice (A) because it's half of $2.50, which is already given in the problem: ½ × $2.50 = $1.25. This is clearly wrong!

Trap #3: The third mistake to make is to find the price of 1 burrito by halving $7.50, which is price of 2 burritos and getting $3.75 and pick answer-choice (C). The question asks for the price of 2 burritos not one. In this case, you have done more than you were required to do, the question asks for the price of 2 burritos and not I burrito. This is clearly wrong!!

Trap #4: The fourth mistake to make is to find the price of 2 tacos by doubling $T = 2.50$ and getting $5.00 and picking answer-choice (D). In this case, you have found something totally different than what you were required to do, the question asks for the price of 2 burritos and not 2 tacos. This is a difficult problem and it can't be so easy to solve it in just one step. This is clearly wrong!

Examples #3: At a certain restaurant, the price of a burrito is 20 percent more than the price of a taco, and the price of a taco is half as much as the price of a quesadilla. If a quesadilla costs $12.50, how much less than a quesadilla does a burrito cost?
(A) $5.00   (B) $6.25   (C) $7.50   (D) $8.75   (E) $9.90

Solution: The price of a Quesadilla $\Rightarrow \$12.50$
The price of a Taco is half as much as the price of a Quesadilla $\Rightarrow$ ½ × $12.50 = $6.25
The price of a Burrito is 20 percent more than the price of a Taco $\Rightarrow \$6.25 \times 1.2 = \$7.50$

Since a burrito costs $7.50, and you may immediately pick answer-choice (C), which is the wrong answer.

However, wait a minute, in this case, the question doesn't ask for the price of a burrito, instead, it asks for how much less than a quesadilla, does a burrito cost. The buzzword in this question is "less".

To find out how much less is the price of a burrito than the price of a quesadilla, subtract the price of a burrito from the price of a quesadilla.
$\Rightarrow \$12.50 - \$7.50 = \$5$

Therefore, the correct answer is (A).

Examples #4: At a certain restaurant, the price of a burrito is 20 percent less than the price of a taco, and the price of a taco is twice as much as the price of a quesadilla. If a quesadilla costs $12.50, how much more than a quesadilla does a burrito cost?
(A) $5.00   (B) $6.25   (C) $7.50   (D) $8.75   (E) $20.00

Solution: The price of a Quesadilla $\Rightarrow$ $12.50
The price of a Taco is twice as much as the price of a Quesadilla $\Rightarrow$ 2 × $12.50 = $25
The price of a Burrito is 20 percent less than the price of a Taco $\Rightarrow$ $25 × 0.8 = $20

Since a burrito costs $20, and you may immediately pick answer-choice (E), which is the wrong answer.

However, wait a minute, in this case, the question doesn't ask for the price of a burrito, instead, it asks for how much more than a quesadilla, does a burrito cost. The buzzword in this question is "more".

To find out how much more is the price of a burrito than the price of a quesadilla, subtract the price of a quesadilla from the price of a burrito.
$\Rightarrow$ $20 – $12.50 = $7.50

Therefore, the correct answer is (C).

.PRACTICE EXERCISE WITH DETAILED EXPLANATIONS

Question #1: If $x + y = 2$ and $x = 10$, then what is the value of $x + 2y$?

(A) −8   (B) 6   (C) −6   (D) −26   (E) 26

Solution:
$\Rightarrow x + y = 2$
$\Rightarrow 10 + y = 2$ [plug-in $x = 10$]
$\Rightarrow y = -8$ [solve for y]

Trap #1: At this point, some people would think that the correct answer to the problem is −8, as it also appears as one of the given answer-choice (A). However, this is not the correct answer to the question. The question asks for the value of $x + 2y$, and not just for the value of y. Therefore, you need to perform one more step, that is, plug-in the value of x and y in $x + 2y$.

$\Rightarrow x + 2y = 10 + 2(-8) = 10 - 16 = -6$
Now this is the correct answer to the question, which is choice (C).

Trap #2: If for some reason, you forgot to put the minus sign, you would get the following answer, coincidentally, which also happens to be one of the answer-choice (E)
$\Rightarrow x + 2y = 10 + 2(8) = 10 + 16 = 26$

Trap #3: If for some reason, you put the minus sign for x also, you would get the following answer, coincidentally, which also happens to be one of the answer-choice (D)
$\Rightarrow x + 2y = -10 + 2(-8) = -10 - 16 = -26$

Trap #4: If for some reason, you put the minus sign for x instead of y, you would get the following answer, coincidentally, which also happens to be one of the answer-choice (B)
$\Rightarrow x + 2y = -10 + 2(8) = -10 + 16 = 6$

Question #2: How much will it cost to fence in a field that is 12 feet long and 72 feet wide with fence that costs $10 a yard?

(A) $8,640   (B) $1,680   (C) $560   (D) $420   (E) $168

Solution: We are given the dimensions of a rectangular field and the cost per yard of fencing it.

Trap #1: The first mistake to make is to find the area of the field in square feet, which is 12 × 72 = 864, and then multiplying by 10 to find the cost, which is, 864 × 10 = $8,640. Notice, this is given as one of the answer choices (A).

To find the amount of fencing required, we need to find the perimeter of the field not the area.
$\Rightarrow$ Perimeter of Field = 2(12 + 72) = 2(84) = 168 feet

Trap #2: The second mistake to make is to pick 168 as the answer. Notice, this is given as one of the answer choices (E).

Remember, we still need to find the cost of the fencing required.

Trap #3: The third mistake to make is to find the cost of the fence by multiplying the 168 feet by $10 and get 1,680. Notice, this is given as one of the answer choices (B).

Since the rate of fencing is given in per yard, we first need to convert the feet into yard.
$\Rightarrow$ Since there are 3 feet in 1 yard: 168 feet = 168 ÷ 3 = 56 yards
$\Rightarrow$ Cost of Fencing = 56 × 10 = $560
Now this is the correct answer to the question, which is choice (C).

Trap #4: The fourth mistake to make is to somehow mess up the calculations by thinking that there are 4 feet in 1 yard: 168 ÷ 4 = 42. Cost = 42 × 10 = $420. Notice, this is given as one of the answer choices (D).

CHAPTER 5.0: EZ SMART GUESSING

HIGHLIGHTS:
5.1 Types of Guessing
5.2 About EZ Smart Guessing

EZ OPTIONS: To answer every math question on the test, you'll often have the following two options:
Either: by solving it mathematically using EZ Direct or Alternate approaches
Or: by Guessing

SOLVE OR GUESS? MAKE THE DECISION: Reading the question carefully and properly before beginning to answer it is all the more important because then you'll be in a better position to decide whether you want to solve it or guess it. You only have a few seconds to make this decision. You must become an expert in this practice – deciding which problems to solve and which ones to guess. This strategy also has real life applications and implications, something you'll use both professionally and personally.

Budget the Amount of Time & Effort to Put into Each Question: Depending on where you are on the test and how much time is remaining, budget the amount of time and effort to put into each question. Sometimes, it may not be worth your time, and you may be better off guessing than solving, and saving time for other questions.
- Determine the question's level of difficulty relative to your skills, and if you'll be able to solve the question quickly without much difficulty – try to recognize if you usually find this type of problem to be easy or difficult.
- Determine if you know how to solve the question, and if you are usually good at answering this type of question, or if you normally do well on this type of question. Only you know what type of questions give you particular trouble. For instance, if you're terrible at percents and hit a percent question, you should move through it rather quickly to allow time to answer other questions more accurately and completely.

(A) When to Solve Mathematically: In general, if you are comfortable with the problem and the math being tested, or if you know how to solve the problem easily – don't waste time in guessing – the fastest, and the most effective way is to solve the problem mathematically using our EZ Direct or Alternative Methods instead of trying to guess it.

Solve mathematically if you think:
- the problem is easy enough for you to solve, or
- the problem will not take too long to solve, or
- it's a problem that you usually do well on, or
- you have confidence solving this particular type of problem

(B) When to Guess: In general, if you are not very comfortable with the problem, or if you are clueless and have no idea how to solve the problem by using our EZ Direct or Alternative Method, or you tried solving the problem and are still stuck – don't waste time in solving – the only choice that you have is to take your best guess, bank your time, and move on to the next question, instead of trying to solve it.

Solve by guessing if you think:
- the problem is too difficult for you to solve, or
- the problem will take too long to solve and there isn't enough time, or
- it's a problem that you don't usually do well on, or
- you don't have enough confidence solving this particular type of problem

EZ TIP: Remember, just because you don't know how to solve a question mathematically doesn't mean that the question is impossible to answer or you won't be able to figure out the correct answer.

5.1   TYPES OF GUESSING

Guessing can be of the following two different types:
(i)   **Random Guessing** – blind guessing
(ii) **EZ Smart Guessing** – educated and intelligent guessing using POE

(i) Random Guessing: Random Guessing is the worst form of guessing. If you don't have any idea of the correct answer and can't eliminate even a single choice, and if you have to guess, then you have to make a random guess. However, this is not likely to happen very often; in most cases, you should be able to do some sort of elimination.

If you're running out of time and several questions remain unanswered, make sure to answer each question by guessing something or anything. In the rare but possible case, when you are not able to eliminate even a single choice, don't waste your time – just close your eyes and pick any one answer-choice, and hope that you get lucky!

(ii) EZ Smart Guessing: EZ Smart Guessing is the more sophisticated form of guessing by making educated and intelligent guesses using Process of Elimination. The key to EZ Smart Guessing is using the Process of Elimination to its maximum by eliminating as many wrong answer choices as possible, and then by making an intelligent guess from the remaining choices.

EZ Smart Guessing gives you a better shot at getting to the correct answer even when you don't know how to solve a problem. As a rule of thumb, if you are able to eliminate at least one answer-choice using logic or common sense, then perhaps that's the time you should make a smart guess from one of the remaining choices and move on. Take a closer look at the answer choices and think about what the problem is asking. If you are still unable to narrow down the answer choices, reread the question, and try again. In general, try not to guess unless you eliminate some answer choices, except if you have no other option.

The rest of this section is dedicated to EZ Smart Guessing – the educated and intelligent way of guessing using POE. The strategies that we explain in this section will make you better at guessing and eliminating answers to any math question on your test.

5.2   ABOUT EZ SMART GUESSING

EZ SMART GUESSING USING POE: ELIMINATE "OUT OF RANGE" AND MAKE AN INTELLIGENT GUESS:
If you want to play the guessing game, make an EZ Smart Guess, that is, first eliminate all the "out of range" and obviously wrong answer choices to narrow down your options, and then guess intelligently from among the remaining answer choices. Your main objective should be to figure out one statement and hence eliminate as many answer choices as you can while doing as little work as possible. While using the guessing strategy, it is imperative to learn how to eliminate wrong answers quickly and most effectively.

EZ STEP-BY-STEP METHOD: While using EZ Smart Guessing Strategy, apply the following steps:

STEP 1: Use POE: Eliminate Answer-Choices: The first step in making an intelligent guess is to use the Process of Elimination to the maximum and eliminate as many answer choices as possible.
While guessing and using POE, think about the given problem, and do the following:
   (A) Eliminate Out-of-Range answer choices that don't make sense – choices that seem crazy, strange, weird, odd, absurd, bizarre, unreasonable, or irrational.
   (B) Eliminate obviously wrong answer choices that are clearly wrong – choices that seem fundamentally or noticeably wrong.

STEP 2: Guess From the Remaining Answer-Choices: After you have eliminated all possible answer choices, make a guess from the remaining ones.

EZ NOTE: Before you indulge yourself in the guessing game, make sure you master our EZ Smart Guessing Strategies for making intelligent guesses.

EZ TIPS FOR SMART GUESSING:

TIP #1: On easy questions – your first response is usually correct, that is, doing the first thing that comes into your mind will often fetch you the right answer.

TIP #2: On difficult questions – your first response is usually wrong, that is, doing the first thing that comes into your mind will often fetch you the wrong answer.

TIP #3: On medium problems – your first response is usually correct half of the time, and wrong the other half of the time.

Guessing + Other Strategies: An important point to know while guessing is that it doesn't work well in isolation; instead, it works best when used in alliance with the other strategies discussed in this module. So guess, but don't guess in isolation. There are a lot of problem solving techniques that can help you become a better guesser. Look at each choice offered, as some may be obviously incorrect. Make use of anything you can – common sense, logic, estimation, picking numbers, back-solving – to eliminate some answer choices before you guess, and improve your odds of picking the correct answer.

GUESSING + PROCESS OF ELIMINATION + USING OTHER STRATEGIES = EZ SMART GUESSING

Higher the Elimination, Higher the Chances of Getting the Correct Answer: The more answer choices you are able to eliminate, the better your chances are of guessing the correct answer from what's left over. Often times, many questions will have answer choices that are obviously wrong or don't make sense – in such cases, you may automatically arrive at the correct answer. Usually, two or three of the answer choices in most questions are absurd – eliminate them and make a guess. Occasionally, four of the five answer choices will be absurd; when this happens, your answer is no longer a guess.

Keep Moving Forward: Try to answer every question to the best of your ability, and always quickly move forward through the test. It sure feels good to be able to solve every problem mathematically on a given math test, but if you end up guessing sometimes, don't feel bad. It's okay to guess on a few questions; even the most expert test-takers make few intelligent guesses on their test. Spending too much time on tricky questions earlier in the test can prevent you from taking a good crack at questions you can handle later on in the test or even finishing the test on time. By spending more time on the questions you know how to answer, you're more likely to get a better score, even if you have to guess blindly on a few questions. Therefore, it is better to spend more time on the problems you know how to solve, and quickly move on by guessing on the problems that you don't know how to solve.

GUESSING AND STANDARDIZED TESTS:

Some people perceive guessing on a question to be a terrible way of answering it. They think guessing is more or less like accepting defeat and giving up on the question. However, guessing is an integral part of standardized tests, in which you may have to make a guess at some point.

Our EZ Smart Guessing Strategies are especially useful on Standardized Tests. You may run into some questions that you don't know how to solve. At that point, you either have to skip those questions or make a guess. Sometimes, the wise thing to do is to make your best guess. Moreover, very few students are going to know how to solve each and every question, and almost everyone has to make a guess at some point or the other. So guessing is somewhat inevitable on standardized tests, it's something you may have to indulge in.

Since you may have to guess, it's better to have a plan of attack for guessing efficiently and effectively than to waste time and then finally end up making a random and wild guess. Therefore, your only option to answer the questions that are at or beyond your skill level is by applying our EZ Smart Guessing Strategies. As you'll see, our EZ Smart Guessing Strategies will make most of these difficult questions easier and solvable.

Guessing is Not the Best Strategy, but it's Better than Nothing: Although guessing is usually not the greatest approach to achieve a higher score, but if you have no idea how to solve a problem, or if you do not see your answer among the answer choices, or if the problem is complicated or too difficult for you – your only option is to either make a guess or skip it. In fact, making an intelligent guess is a good strategy for answering some typical types of questions.

Multiple-Choice Format and Guessing: Since your test is entirely a multiple-choice test, it is particularly vulnerable to using good guessing strategies. On every question, the correct answer is always right there in front of you. The only difference is that it's just hidden among a cluster of wrong answers. All you have to do is find the correct answer – if not by solving it, then by guessing your way to the correct answer by using EZ Smart Guessing with the process of elimination.

Don't Random Guess Without Trying to Smart Guess: During the course of your test, you will probably find at least a few multiple-choice questions that you have no idea how to solve. Do not straight away random guess these questions. You should only infrequently make a random guess, especially if you have at least spent some time to work on it. Even if you don't know how to solve a problem correctly, you may still realize and deduce a lot of information, and sometime that information can help you a great deal in eliminating some of the answer choices. At the very minimum, you can at least get started on a problem, eliminate a few answer choices, and then make an intelligent guess.

HOW TO AVOID PICKING CRAZY ANSWERS:

The test-makers know it very well that people taking the test sometimes do crazy things under pressure. The test-makers are so bogged down in trying to provide answer choices that anticipate all the mistakes a test-taker is likely to make on a problem that in the process, they often forget to make certain that all of these answer choices make sense. Therefore, the test-makers like to include, among the answer choices, numbers that a test-taker may arrive at – even though they don't make much sense.

For a moment, forget about the math, and just look at the answer choices with a clear mind. Even if you are rusty with the math involved, there is no way that all of the answer choices given would seem to be right to you. Hence, in an effort to anticipate your potential wrong answers, the test-makers give you some answer choices that are simply "absurd" and "crazy".

HOW TO SPOT "OUT OF RANGE" CRAZY ANSWER-CHOICES:

Crazy answer choices are choices that are strange, weird, odd, absurd, or bizarre. Crazy answer choices can be spotted by taking a step back, and looking at the problem, and its answer choices with a clear mind, and at their face value.

Following are some of the examples of crazy answers:

(A) If you are at least able to determine that the correct answer must be positive, but some of the answer choices are negative ⇒ you can easily eliminate those answer choices that have negative values, and then make an EZ Smart Guess.

(B) If you are at least able to determine that the correct answer must be even, but some of the answer choices are odd ⇒ you can easily eliminate those answer choices that have odd values, and then make an EZ Smart Guess.

(C) If you are at least able to determine that the correct answer must be in a specific unit, but some of the answers choices are in other units ⇒ you can easily eliminate those answer choices that are in incorrect units, and then make an EZ Smart Guess.

(D) If you are at least able to determine that the correct answer must be a whole number, but some of the answer choices are in terms of fractions or decimals ⇒ you can easily eliminate those answer choices that are in terms of fractions or decimals, and then make an EZ Smart Guess.

(E) If you are at least able to determine that the correct answer must be between a certain range of numbers, but some of the answer choices are outside that range ⇒ you can easily eliminate those answer choices that are outside the range, and then make an EZ Smart Guess.

(F) If you are at least able to determine that the correct answer choice must be less than a certain number, but some of the answer choices are greater than that number ⇒ you can easily eliminate those answer choices that are greater than that number, and then make an EZ Smart Guess.

(G) If you are at least able to determine that the correct answer must be less than 100%, but some of the answer choices are greater than 100% ⇒ you can easily eliminate those answer choices that are greater than or equal to 100%, and then make an EZ Smart Guess.

(H) If you are at least able to determine that the correct answer must be a ratio that is less than 1, but some of the answer choices have ratios that are greater than 1 ⇒ you can easily eliminate those answer choices that have ratios greater than or equal to 1, and then make an EZ Smart Guess.
For instance, if you are told that a profit of $75,000 is to be divided in some ratio among three partners, and asked for the largest share. If the profits were divided equally, each share would be worth $25,000. If it is divided unequally, the largest share has to be at least greater than $25,000. Hence, you can immediately eliminate answer choices that have $25,000 or less.

IMPORTANCE OF TEST BOOKLET AS SCRATCH PAPER ON POE:

Use of your test booklet as scratch paper is essential to organize your thinking in the math section, especially while using POE. You need to record your progress of elimination of answer choices. While using POE, as soon as you discover a specific answer-choice to be wrong, make sure that you eliminate it and cross it off on your test booklet. This will prevent you from picking them later through carelessness or desperation. Moreover, you may not realize the importance of doing this, but it's psychologically very inspiring to see your possible answers narrowed down to fewer and fewer choices. This will also boost your confidence and make you feel that you are getting closer to the correct answer. You can quietly whisper in your own ears, "Yeah, one down, four more to go!"

Now, let's look at some of the solved examples. In each example, the solution provided will help you determine which crazy answer choices you should eliminate. At that point, you simply have to make a guess. Remember, not to struggle too much when you have to guess, simply make an EZ Smart Guess, and move on.

Example #1:   If the average of 10, 15, 20, and n is 25, what is the value of n?
(A) 0   (B) 20   (C) 25   (D) 50   (E) 55

Solution: If the average of four numbers is 25, and three of them are less than 25, the other one must be greater than 20.

$\Rightarrow$ Eliminate (A) and (B) and take a guess on (C), (D), or (E).

Consequently, if you are further able to realize that since 10 and 15 are a lot less than 25, n will probably be a lot more than 25

$\Rightarrow$ Now you can even eliminate (C) as well, and guess either (D) or (E). This leaves you with a 50-50 shot at guessing the correct answer.

Note: We have explained how to solve such problems in the module on averages.

By the way, the actual correct answer is (E).

Example #2:   John receives a sales commission of 75 cents for every $50.00 worth of merchandise he sells. What percent is his commission?
(A) 1.5%   (B) 2%   (C) 5%   (D) 25%   (E) 125%

Solution: Obviously, you can notice that a commission of 75 cents on $50 is pretty small.

$\Rightarrow$ Eliminate (D) and (E), and take a guess on (A), (B), or (C).

Consequently, if you are further able to realize that 1% of $50 is 50 cents, then you know the commission is a little more than 1%.

$\Rightarrow$ Now you can even eliminate (C) as well, and guess either (A) or (B). This leaves you with a 50-50 shot at guessing the correct answer.

Note: We have explained how to solve such problems in the module on percents.

By the way, the actual correct answer is (A).

Finding the Correct Answer While Guessing: The following examples illustrates an important point: even if you know how to solve a problem, and you are immediately able to see that four of the five choices are absurd – just pick the remaining choice, and move on.

Example #3:   The average of 10 numbers is –10. If the sum of six of them is 100, what is the average of the other four?

                    (A) –50   (B) 0   (C) 25   (D) 50   (E) 75

Solution: The main point to realize in this problem is that, if the average of all 10 numbers is negative, so should be the sum.

Since, the sum of the first six numbers is positive, so the sum (and the average) of the others has to be negative.
$\Rightarrow$ Eliminate (B), (C), (D), and (E) since all them are positive.

This leaves nothing to take a guess on; the only remaining answer-choice is (A)

By the way, the actual correct answer is (A).

Example #4:   The ratio of apples to oranges in a fruit basket is 9:7. If there are 256 fruits in the basket, how many apples are there in the basket?

                    (A) 52   (B) 72   (C) 144   (D) 292   (E) 512

Solution: Since there are a total of 256 fruits in the basket, there must be fewer than 256 apples:

$\Rightarrow$ Eliminate (D) and (E) since both of them are more than 256.

Moreover, since the ratio of apples to oranges is 9:7, there must be more apples than oranges, and it should be close to half-and-half, half of 256 is 128.

$\Rightarrow$ Eliminate (A) and (B) since 52 & 72 are way less than half of 128

This leaves nothing to take a guess on; the only remaining answer-choice is (C)

By the way, the actual correct answer is (C).

▪PRACTICE EXERCISE WITH DETAILED EXPLANATIONS

Question #1: If the average of 100, 150, 200, and *n* is 250, what is the value of *n*?
  (A) 0   (B) 200   (C) 250   (D) 500   (E) 550

Solution: If the average of four numbers is 250, and three of them are less than 250, the other one must be greater than 200.

⇒ Eliminate (A) and (B) and take a guess on (C), (D), or (E).

Consequently, if you are further able to realize that since 100 and 150 are a lot less than 250, *n* will probably be a lot more than 250

⇒ Now you can even eliminate (C) as well, and guess either (D) or (E).

By the way, the actual correct answer is (E).

Question #2: John receives a sales commission of 25 cents for every $50.00 worth of merchandise he sells. What percent is his commission?
  (A) 0.5%   (B) 0.75%   (C) 5%   (D) 25%   (E) 125%

Solution: Obviously, you can notice that a commission of 25 cents on $50 is pretty small.

⇒ Eliminate (D) and (E), and take a guess on (A), (B), or (C).

Consequently, if you are further able to realize that 1% of $50 is 50 cents, then you know the commission is a little less than 1%.

⇒ Now you can even eliminate (C) as well, and guess either (A) or (B).

By the way, the actual correct answer is (A).

Finding the Correct Answer While Guessing:

Question #3: The average of 10 numbers is –20. If the sum of six of them is 100, what is the average of the other four?
  (A) –75   (B) 0   (C) 25   (D) 50   (E) 75

Solution: The main point to realize in this problem is that, if the average of all 10 numbers is negative, so should be the sum.

Since, the sum of the first six numbers is positive, so the sum (and the average) of the others has to be negative.

⇒ Eliminate (B), (C), (D), and (E) since all them are positive.

This leaves nothing to take a guess on; the only remaining answer-choice is (A)

By the way, the actual correct answer is (A).

Question #4: The ratio of apples to oranges in a fruit basket is 9:7. If there are 512 fruits in the basket, how many apples are there in the basket?
  (A) 112   (B) 124   (C) 288   (D) 584   (E) 1024

Solution: Since there are a total of 512 fruits in the basket, there must be fewer than 512 apples:

⇒ Eliminate (D) and (E)

Moreover, since the ratio of apples to oranges is 9:7, there must be more apples than oranges, and it should be close to half and half, half of 512 is 256.

⇒ Eliminate (A) and (B) since 112 & 124 are way less than half of 256.

This leaves nothing to take a guess on; the only remaining answer-choice is (C)

By the way, the actual correct answer is (C).

CHAPTER 6.0: EZ ALTERNATE STRATEGIES

On the first page of each math section, you will see somewhat similar directions. They ask you to solve each problem in the section using your scratch paper. Then they ask you to pick the best answer-choice out of the given ones, and select the corresponding option.

These directions are very simple and straightforward. They basically suggest that you ignore the fact that these are multiple-choice questions. They recommend that you just solve each problem, and then look at the five choices to select the best/correct one. Nevertheless, as you will learn in this section, this is not always the best strategy to answer multiple-choice questions, at least not for some of the typical types of problems.

TWO WAYS TO ANSWER QUESTIONS: Math questions can be solved using one of the following two approaches:
- Solve by using **EZ Straightforward Traditional Methods** (explained in Content-Knowledge Review-Modules)
- Solve by using **EZ Alternative Methods** (explained in this section)

As the name suggests, alternative strategies are strategies that give you an *"alternate"* or *"optional"* way to solve problems, which are not traditional textbook style methods. This is why we call them non-traditional methods, and are categorized as *"EZ Alternative Strategies"* to solve math problems.

In this section, you'll learn some of the most powerful and effective techniques that may help you avoid or evade algebra, and will enable you to solve some problems without using traditional algebra. These techniques may be useful when you don't know how to solve a problem the straightforward way using algebra, and is a great way to make confusing problems more clear.

At first, some people may be skeptical about using these strategies, as they may appear to be vague and not the real way to answer the questions. Don't worry – you'll get more than enough exposure to these strategies in this section. So take your time and try to get familiar and comfortable working with these strategies, and be flexible in your approach to solving new problems by recognizing the opportunities to employ them.

It may take a little time and practice to get the hang of EZ Alternate Strategies, but they are invaluable and indispensable for answering some math questions. In fact, mastering these strategies is essential for anyone developing good math test-taking skills.

Our EZ Alternate strategies will help you transform algebra questions into arithmetic questions and make things a lot easier for you, especially when you want to **bypass** the algebra. It is an exceptional method for solving questions particularly when you have no clue as to where to start. In the normal course, you would have to miss -out on such questions; however, with the help of our EZ Alternative Strategies, you can still answer them correctly as long as you understand the basic logic given in the question.

EZ ALTERNATIVE STRATEGIES ARE EASIER:
Of course, you're free to work through a problem in a straightforward way; however, you are by no means required to do so. In fact, it frequently works to your advantage to use an alternative approach. There are some special types of questions, which can be solved much easily by using one of our alternative strategies. Now, maybe you just love to solve complicated algebraic expressions or translate word problems into algebraic equations. Fine, do it that way! However, keep in mind, oftentimes, using our EZ Alternative Methods can be much easier and less likely to produce errors on most of the questions. After going through this section, you'll realize that using EZ Alternative Strategies can come in handy on your Math test, so try to make the most of these alternate strategies.

EZ ALTERNATIVE STRATEGIES CAN BE TIME-CONSUMING:
Generally, applying alternative strategies may be more time-consuming than applying other conventional methods, and hence should only be used sparingly. Even though EZ Alternative Strategies may require a little more time than traditional methods, the results are worth the extra effort. Make sure to check the remaining time, and the number of questions left in the section before you use this approach. However, unlike other books, we have streamlined our alternative strategies in a manner that will help you apply them most efficiently by minimizing your time and maximizing

your results. In fact, sometimes, EZ Alternative Strategies can be faster than setting up equations or using complicated formulas. It can save a great deal of time if used correctly and wisely.

EZ ALTERNATIVE STRATEGIES ALWAYS WORK:
Some strategies allow you to eliminate a few choices so you can make a smart guess; however, when EZ Alternative Strategies are applied, they'll always lead you to the right answer. The important point to note is if you are uncomfortable with the direct approach of solving a problem algebraically, you don't have to omit these questions. You can use these alternative strategies and always get the right answer. Sometimes, even if you can do the algebra, you should still use this approach if you think you can solve the problem quickly or will be less likely to make a mistake. With the proper use of these tactics, you can correctly solve many questions that you may not know how to do otherwise. The good thing about our EZ Alternative Strategies is that if they are applied correctly, they are guaranteed to nail the correct answer every time they are used. The only reason not to use it on a particular problem is if you can quickly solve the problem directly.

EZ ALTERNATIVE STRATEGIES ON COMPLEX QUESTIONS:
EZ Alternative Strategies are often the quickest and easiest way to solve some of the most complicated problems. You may have already used these strategies inadvertently several times when you come across multiple-choice questions that you had a hard time dealing with. Now we want you to learn to use EZ Alternative Strategies systematically and methodically.

EZ ALTERNATIVE STRATEGIES WORKS ONLY IN MULTIPLE CHOICE QUESTIONS:
Without the answer choices, it's not possible to apply alternative strategies. The only way to solve such problems is by using traditional methods. However, if you are given multiple answer choices and one of them has to be correct, it is possible to find the correct answer by applying our EZ Alternative Strategies.

EZ ALTERNATIVE STRATEGIES ARE IMPORTANT BACK-UP STRATEGIES:
Sometimes while reading a question, it happens that you completely blank out and for some reason you are not able to solve the problem directly by using techniques that are more traditional. In such cases, EZ Alternative Strategies prove to be a useful back-up tool. EZ Alternative Strategies work well in a wide range of questions, which makes it a lucrative option when you're uncertain how to approach a particular question in the traditional way. It's always a good idea to know different ways to solve the same problem. Just in case, if one method of solving the problem doesn't work, you have the option to try another one. Moreover, in some special types of problems, the only way to answer a question is by applying one of our EZ Alternative Strategies.

EZ ALTERNATIVE METHODS AND STANDARDIZED TESTS:
Our EZ Alternate Strategies are especially useful on Standardized Tests. You may run into some questions that you don't know how to solve. Your only option to answer the questions that are at or beyond your skill level is by applying our EZ Alternate Strategies. As you'll see, our EZ Alternate Strategies will make most of these difficult questions easier and solvable. Our EZ Alternate Strategies is a great way to slash down the level of difficulty of a question by at least a couple of notches.

THREE TYPES OF QUESTIONS: We can categorize all math questions into the following three main categories:
- Problems that can only be answered using EZ Straightforward Traditional Methods (very few questions)
- Problems that can only be answered using EZ Alternative Methods (very few questions)
- Problems that can be answered using either method (most questions)

WHEN TO USE AND WHEN NOT TO USE EZ ALTERNATIVE STRATEGY:
In this section, you'll see that often there's more than one way to solve a math problem. All the methods are equally correct and legitimate, as long as they get you to the right answer. Your concern should be to pick an approach that will solve the problem faster for you. It's essential that you figure out which technique works best for different types of problems. This will vary from question to question. EZ Alternative Strategies will help you answer most multiple-choice questions; however, as invaluable as these techniques are, use them only when needed. As a thumb rule, if you know how to solve a question directly and you are confident that you can do it easily, accurately, and reasonably quickly – don't think twice, just go ahead and do it! Use the back-solving strategy only on a problem that you can't solve directly or if they are more time consuming.

(A) When to Use EZ Straightforward Traditional Methods: For questions on which you have a natural aptitude, it makes sense for you to work out your solutions using a more straightforward approach. In most cases, the best approach is to use the traditional approach, by translating the question-stem into mathematical expressions. Therefore, if a question looks like the one you can readily handle by using a straightforward traditional approach, work through it immediately using one of our EZ straightforward methods covered in our content knowledge review modules.

Consider using EZ Straightforward Methods to solve a problem if:
- the question is a simple straightforward problem, or
- it seems that the question can be easily and quickly solved algebraically, or
- you are easily able to connect with the problem, or
- translating the question-stem into algebra is fairly simple, or
- the answer choices include variables or ugly complicated quantities, such as, radicals and variables – plugging them in takes too much time and effort, or
- the problem can be made easier by juggling with the algebra that is involved rather than by testing possibilities, or
- you are able to easily understand the problem and have already solved such problems algebraically

(B) When to Use EZ Alternative Methods: For questions on which you don't have a natural aptitude, it makes sense for you to work out your solutions using an alternate approach. You may be surprised, by using our EZ Alternate Strategies, you'll be well on your way to finding the correct answer, and that too on questions which you could never solve before or with which you have had trouble. It's a great tool to solve problems that are almost impossible to solve algebraically. It may also help avoid many careless mistakes that one would make while doing algebra. Moreover, there are a few selected types of questions, which can only be solved using one of our EZ Alternative Strategies. In fact, in such cases, the use of alternate strategies is not only essential but also inevitable; without it, these problems are difficult and nearly impossible to answer correctly.

Consider using EZ Alternative Methods to solve a problem if:
- the question is a complex problem, or
- it seems that the question will take too long and is too tedious to solve algebraically, or
- you are not able to connect with the problem and nothing clicks, or
- translating the question-stem into algebra is fairly complex, or
- the answer choices are all rather simple numbers, or
- the problem can be made easier by testing possibilities rather than by juggling with the algebra that is involved, or
- you simply don't understand the problem and have never solved such problems algebraically

Look for your Ideal Method: Since there are multiple ways to solve any given math problem, you shouldn't be looking for an ideal method that works for everybody, but the fastest and easiest method that works for you. As you already know, time is of the essence on standardized tests, so you should compare the value of your time with the alternative methods. The right method is the method that is quickest and simplest for you. This can also be a personal preference, which may vary from person to person. In addition, this will also differ from question to question.

Apply Traditional or Alternative Methods: Some problems are easier to solve using our EZ Straightforward Methods, while other problems can be very easily solved using our EZ Alternative Methods. With time, you may find that you get more comfortable using EZ straightforward methods for certain types of questions, and our EZ alternative methods for others. As you work through your test preparation, pay attention to the types of questions you are most comfortable with, and the questions that give you the greatest difficulty. Once you get enough experience, you'll learn when to apply which approach in solving specific types of problems. With practice, you'll need to build-up a sense of situations when EZ Alternate Methods can be most beneficial. At that point, you'll be in a better position to decide which approach to use to solve a specific type of problem. The key is to be **open** to apply different approaches to solve different problems. Look for the approach that works best for you for any given question – and apply it!

Whether you are using EZ Straightforward Methods or EZ Alternative Methods, always remember, the only thing that matters is that you need to find as many correct answers as you can, and as quickly as possible. Your math test is all about results, and the only result that matters is the correct answer-choice!

TYPES OF EZ ALTERNATIVE STRATEGIES:

The following are the two most important and useful EZ Alternative Strategies:
- EZ Back-Solving/Back-Door Strategy
- EZ Plug-In Numbers Strategy

CHAPTER 7.0: EZ BACK-SOLVING STRATEGY

HIGHLIGHTS:
7.1 Applying the EZ "C" Rule
7.2 Exceptions to the EZ "C" Rule
7.3 EZ Back-Solving For "Largest" or "Smallest" Answers
7.4 When EZ Back-Solving is Essential
7.5 EZ Back-Solving for Simple Questions
▪ Practice Exercise with Detailed Explanations

There are usually two ways to approach and solve a problem:
- **Forward Solving** (by directly solving from the question-stem using the straightforward approach)
- **Backward Solving** (by indirectly solving from the answer choices using the backward approach)

Throughout your academic life until now, and even in our content-knowledge review-modules, you have been taught how to solve problems using the straightforward approach. However, sometimes it's easier to work **backwards** from the answer choices to the question-stem than working straight **forward** from the question-stem to the answer. In such cases, working **"backwards"** or **"back-solving"** may be the best approach, which is also known as the **"back-door"** strategy.

Sometimes if you are not able to solve a problem directly or can't figure out how to approach it, using the answer choices may give you an alternate way to solve a problem by substituting the answer choices to back-solve a problem. In such cases, the answer choices give you some very valuable hints and they become your tools to help you work backwards to find the right answer. We call this **EZ Back-Solving Strategy**, which essentially means plugging the answer choices back into the question-stem until you find the one that fits the guidelines or conditions given in the question.

On every multiple-choice question, the correct answer is right in front of you. It's just hidden among the five answer choices – one is correct and the remaining four are wrong. All you have to do is find the correct one. This means you can sometimes **short-circuit** the problem by substituting each answer-choice into the question-stem in order to see which one works. In fact, in certain cases, working backwards could actually be a more efficient method than solving the problem directly.

EZ Back-Solving Strategy can often be applied on many word problems, especially if running answer choices through the question-stem turns out to be easier and quicker than going through the whole translation process of the word problems into setting up equations and then solving.

Back-Solving is normally used to solve for an unknown. For Instance, look at the following example:

For Example: If $x^2 - 11x + 18 = 0$, then $x = ?$
(A) (1, 2)   (B) (1, 5)   (C) (5, 9)   (D) (0, 10)   (E) (2, 9)

In the above example, you're asked to solve a quadratic equation to find the value of a variable. For some reason, you may not be able to factor the quadratic expression, and you can't remember the quadratic formula. In such a situation, you can still solve the question and be able to get the correct answer by substituting the answer choices into the equation until you find the one that works.

You'll see how to solve this question, later in this section.

IDEA BEHIND EZ BACK-SOLVING STRATEGY: The idea behind EZ Back-Solving Strategy is simple – testing the given answer choices and figuring out which one is correct. In other words, EZ Back-Solving is a strategy that allows you to use the answer choices to work backwards through the question-stem, that is, substituting answer choices into the question-stem to see which one works. The answer-choice that satisfies or agrees with the condition(s) and/or relationship(s) laid out in the question-stem is the correct answer.

First, pick an answer choice and temporarily presume it's the correct answer to the given question. Then plug that answer choice into the question-stem to determine if it is in fact correct, that is, if it works. If it does work, then that's the correct answer, you pick it and go on to the next question. If it doesn't work, you eliminate it and try another one, until you find the one that works. If this sounds too confusing, don't worry, we have streamlined the whole process of back-solving in a well organized and systematic step-by-step method.

EZ NOTE: There is only one number in the whole world that will make these problems work, and fortunately it has to be one of the five answer choices. So, never try to plug-in any other numbers in such types of problems. These problems ask for specific numeric answers.

USING TEST BOOKLET AS SCRATCH PAPER ON EZ BACK-SOLVING STRATEGY: It's important to keep track and make notes while using EZ Back-Solving Strategy. Always make sure to mark down the answer-choice you are substituting, and circle it. Then try each of the answer choices, crossing them off as you eliminate them. This way you'll know which answer choices you have already tested. Never try to do this process in your mind, as it's almost impossible to do so.

WHEN TO USE AND WHEN NOT TO USE EZ BACK-SOLVING STRATEGY:

(A) When To Use EZ Back-Solving Strategy: You should use EZ Back-Solving Strategy only when you are asked to solve for an unknown and you don't know how to solve the problem directly, but understand the question and the relationship between the variables and know what needs to be done to answer the question; however, you want to avoid doing the algebra involved. In most cases, back-solving is more time consuming than solving it directly. Generally, it is safe to use the back-solving technique when the answer choices have specific numbers. Therefore, when the arithmetic is simple and you understand what's being asked in the question, it's okay to find the answer by checking each choice and eliminating wrong choices. However, in problems that are more complicated, this can take more time than finding a solution through mathematical reasoning.

(B) When Not To Use EZ Back-Solving Strategy: You should not use EZ Back-Solving Strategy if you know how to easily solve the question directly. In most cases, direct-solving is much easier and faster than back-solving. You must remember that every problem that can be solved using EZ Back-Solving Strategy can also be solved directly and perhaps in less time. Therefore, if you are confident you can directly solve a problem quickly and accurately, you should just go ahead and solve it directly, and save EZ Back-Solving Strategy for other problems that you can't easily solve directly, since it can be more time-consuming.

Note: Just because a question contains numbers in the answer choices, it doesn't mean that you can always back-solve. There can be instances where back-solving doesn't make any sense.
It needs to be noted that Back-Solving works only when the question asks for a single value, such as x or y.
It can't be used when the question asks for the value of multiple numbers or expressions, such as $(x + y)$ or $(x - y)$
The reason for this is that it won't be possible to know how much of the answer is x and how much is y.

PARTS OF EZ BACK-SOLVING STRATEGY: Our EZ Back-Solving Strategy can be divided into the following five parts:
- Applying the EZ "C" Rule
- Exceptions to the EZ "C" Rule
- EZ Back-Solving For Largest/Smallest Answers
- When EZ Back-Solving is Essential
- EZ Back-Solving for Easy Questions

7.1   APPLYING THE EZ "C" RULE

APPLYING THE EZ "C" RULE: WHEN ANSWER-CHOICES ARE ARRANGED IN ORDER:
In most math questions, the answer choices (A), (B), (C), (D), and (E), to all numerical multiple-choice questions are almost always listed in either increasing order (arranged from smallest to largest) or decreasing order (arranged from largest to smallest). Although in most cases, answer choices are arranged in order, there are a few cases when the answer choices are not arranged in order. While using the EZ Back-Solving Strategy, it's beneficial to start back-solving with the middle answer-choice, which is "C". Note that there are exceptions to this rule, where you may have to plug-in each one of the answer choices starting with the answer-choice (A) in order to determine the correct answer. Nevertheless as a rule, it's often helpful to start with choice "C". While applying the EZ "C" Rule, just by plugging in one answer-choice, you should be able to eliminate at least two to three of the answer choices in most cases.

EZ STEP-BY-STEP METHOD: While using our EZ Back-Solving Strategy, apply the following steps,:
(Note: assuming, the answer choices (A), (B), (C), (D), and (E) are listed in increasing order)

STEP 1: First, identify the specific value the question asks, that is, the value that the answer choices represent. Then, start with plugging-in answer-choice "C" into the question-stem, and work through the problem.

STEP 2: **(i)** If "C" works, you've found the correct answer; you don't need to go any further. STOP. You're done.
(ii) If "C" doesn't work, eliminate it, and you'll usually be able to determine whether the correct answer is larger or smaller than the middle choice, which means that you should be able to determine whether "C" is too small or too big, and whether you need to test a larger or a smaller answer-choice. This information will also enable you to eliminate two more answer choices.

STEP 3: Choice "C" will be either too small or too big, leaving you with only two answers that could possibly be correct. Next, you simply have to plug-in one more answer-choice to get to the correct answer.

(i) If you think "C" is too small, you'll know immediately that you'll need a larger number, so you can eliminate (A) and (B), which are even smaller, and choose the next larger number.
Now, the answer must be either (D) or (E), and trying just one of these will give you the answer.

(ii) If you think "C" is too large, you'll know right away that you'll need a smaller number, so you can eliminate (D) and (E), which are even larger, and choose the next smaller number.
Now, the answer must be either (A) or (B), and trying just one of these will give you the answer.

At this point, in all, you'll be able to eliminate three choices, which mean you'll have narrowed down the choices to two.

STEP 4: Next, try plugging-in answer-choice (B) if you need a smaller number or (D) if you need a bigger number. If (B) or (D) works, it is the correct answer; you don't need to go any further. STOP. You're done.
(i) If (D) is still too small, eliminate it, and by default, the answer must be (E).
(ii) If (B) is still too large, eliminate it, and by default, the answer must be (A).

STEP 5: Now your answer must be the other one, your obvious answer is (A) if you still need a smaller number or (E) if you still need a bigger number, provided you didn't make any errors or any silly mistakes in the earlier steps. However, just to be sure, try plugging-in answer-choice (A) or (E), and it will work.
Note: If you're worried about making an error and if you have the time, go ahead and check the third choice, just to be sure.

Our EZ "C" Rule is primarily useful on problems with numerical answer choices and problems where you're able to determine whether the choice you tried was too high or too low.

EZ TIP: The answer may not always be the first choice you pick. However, usually, when you start with (C) and if it doesn't work, you may be able to tell whether it is too large or too small – and that will tell you which direction to go and which of the remaining choices to try next.

EZ HINT: This approach may appear time-consuming, but you can make it more efficient by first trying choice "C". It takes a while to get used to EZ Back-Solving Strategy, but with practice, it can be nearly as fast as solving a problem the traditional way. Therefore, while using EZ Back-Solving Strategy you only have to check at the most two answer choices in order to get to the correct answer.

EZ EXCEPTION: Don't start with "C" if some other choice is much easier to work with. If you start with "B" and it is too small/big, you'll either be able to eliminate four of the choices (B, C, D, and E) or eliminate only two choices (A and B), instead of three, but you will save time if plugging-in choice "C" would be messier.

The following examples will not only help you better understand the concept given above, but they will also illustrate how to implement it in a real test-question:

Example #1:   If $6(n - 2) = n + 13$, then $n = $?
        (A) 1   (B) 2   (C) 3   (D) 4   (E) 5

Solution A: **Using EZ Back-Solving Method:**
        The correct answer should yield in a true equation.
        Let's back-solve, starting with answer-choice (C)

        Plug-in answer-choice (C): $n = 3$
        $\Rightarrow 6(3 - 2) = 3 + 13$
        $\Rightarrow 6 \neq 16$

        Since the LHS is a lot smaller than the RHS, we need a bigger value for n.
        This means, we can not only eliminate (C), but we can also eliminate answer choices (B) and (A). The correct answer has to be either (D) or (E).

        Plug-in answer-choice (D): $n = 4$
        $\Rightarrow 6(4 - 2) = 4 + 13$.
        $\Rightarrow 12 \neq 17$

        Again, since the LHS is still smaller than the RHS, we need even bigger value for n.
        This means, we can also eliminate (D).
        Now, at this point, by default, our obvious correct answer has to be answer-choice (E).
        Nevertheless, let's evaluate it anyways, just for our satisfaction:

        Plug-in answer-choice (E): $n = 5$
        $\Rightarrow 6(5 - 2) = 5 + 13$
        $\Rightarrow 18 = 18$

        Since we looking for a true equations, this is exactly what we have now.

        Therefore, the correct answer-choice is (E)

Solution B: **Using EZ Direct Method:**
        $\Rightarrow 6(n - 2) = n + 13$
        $\Rightarrow 6n - 12 = n + 13$ [apply distributive property]
        $\Rightarrow 6n - n = 13 + 12$ [group like-terms: subtract n from both sides and add 12 to both sides]
        $\Rightarrow 5n = 25$ [combine like-terms]
        $\Rightarrow n = 5$ [divide both sides of the equation by 5]

Example #2:   If the average (arithmetic mean) of 10, 12, 20, 22, and n is 15, what is the value of n?
        (A) 11   (B) 16   (C) 21   (D) 26   (E) 31

Solution A: **Using EZ Back-Solving Method:**
        The correct answer should yield 15 as the average.
        Let's back-solve, starting with answer-choice (C)

Plug-in answer-choice (C): $n = 21$
Next, let's see if the average of 10, 12, 20, 22, and 21 is equal to 15.
$\Rightarrow (10 + 12 + 20 + 22 + 21) \div 5 = 85 \div 5 = 17$

Since 17 is too big, we need a smaller value of average.
This means, we can not only eliminate (C), but we can also eliminate answer choices (D) and (E). The correct answer has to be either (B) or (A).

Plug-in answer-choice (B): $n = 16$
Next, see if the average of 10, 12, 20, 22, and 16 is equal to 15.
$\Rightarrow (10 + 12 + 20 + 22 + 16) \div 5 = 80 \div 5 = 16$

Since 16 is too big, we need a smaller value of average.
This means, we can eliminate (B),
Now, at this point, by default, our obvious correct answer has to be answer-choice (A).
Nevertheless, let's evaluate it anyways, just for our satisfaction:

Plug-in answer-choice (A): $n = 11$
Next, see if the average of 10, 12, 20, 22, and 11 is equal to 15.
$\Rightarrow (10 + 12 + 20 + 22 + 11) \div 5 = 75 \div 5 = 15$

Since we know the average is 15, this is exactly what we have now.

Therefore, the correct answer-choice is (A).

Solution B: **Using EZ Direct Method:**
$\Rightarrow (10 + 12 + 20 + 22 + n) \div 5 = 15$
$\Rightarrow (64 + n) \div 5 = 15$ [combine like terms]
$\Rightarrow 64 + n = 15 \times 5$ [multiply both sides of the equation by 5]
$\Rightarrow n = 75 - 64 = 11$ [subtract 64 from both sides of the equation]

Example #3:   A company's profits have doubled for each of the 4 years it has been in existence. If the total profits for the last 4 years were $15 million, what were the profits in the first year of operation?
(A) $1 million   (B) $2 million   (C) $3 million   (D) $4 million   (E) $5 million

Solution A: **Using EZ Back-Solving Method:**
The correct answer should yield a profit of $15 million for all 4 years.
Let's back-solve, starting with answer-choice (C)

Plug-in answer-choice (C): $3 million
If the 1st year's profit were $\Rightarrow$ $3 million
Then, the 2nd year's profit would be $\Rightarrow$ $6 million
And, the 3rd year's profit would be $\Rightarrow$ $12 million
And, the 4th year's profit would be $\Rightarrow$ $24 million
Total Profit for all 4 years $\Rightarrow\Rightarrow\Rightarrow\Rightarrow$ $\Rightarrow$ $45 million

Since the profit for all 4 years is only $15 million, this is much bigger than what we are looking for, and we need a smaller number.
This means, we can not only eliminate (C), but we can also eliminate answer choices (D) and (E).
The correct answer has to be either (B) or (A)

Plug-in answer-choice (B): $2 million
If the 1st year's profit were $\Rightarrow$ $2 million
Then, the 2nd year's profit would be $\Rightarrow$ $4 million
And, the 3rd year's profit would be $\Rightarrow$ $8 million
And, the 4th year's profit would be $\Rightarrow$ $16 million
Total Profit for all 4 years $\Rightarrow\Rightarrow\Rightarrow\Rightarrow$ $\Rightarrow$ $30 million

Since the profit for all 4 years is only $15 million, this is still much bigger than what we are looking for, and we need a smaller number.
This means, we can also eliminate (B).

Now, at this point, our obvious correct answer has to be answer-choice (A). Nevertheless, let's evaluate it anyways, just for our satisfaction:

Plug-in answer-choice (A): $1 million
If the 1st year's profit were $\Rightarrow$ $1 million
Then, the 2nd year's profit would be $\Rightarrow$ $2 million
And, the 3rd year's profit would be $\Rightarrow$ $4 million
And, the 4th year's profit would be $\Rightarrow$ <u>$8 million</u>
Total Profit for all 4 years $\Rightarrow\Rightarrow\Rightarrow\Rightarrow$ $\Rightarrow$ $15 million

Now, the profit for all 4 years = $15 million
Since we know profit for all 4 years = $15 million, this is exactly what we have now.

Therefore, the correct answer-choice is (A).

Solution B: **Using EZ Direct Method:**
Let the profit for 1st year   = n
Then the profit for 2nd year   = $2n$
And the profit for 3rd year   = $4n$
And the profit for 4th year   = <u>$8n$</u>
Total profit for all 4 years $\Rightarrow$ =$15n$
Equate $15n$ with the total profit for all 4 years, which is $15 million
$\Rightarrow 15n = 15$
$\Rightarrow n = 1$ [divide both sides of the equation by 15]

Example #4:   An insurance company provides coverage according to the following rules: the policy pays 80 percent of the first $1,250 of the cost and 50 percent of the cost above $1,250. If a patient had to pay $525 of the cost of a certain procedure himself, how much did the procedure cost?
(A) $1,000   (B) $1,200   (C) $1,400   (D) $1,600   (E) $1,800

Solution A: **Using EZ Back-Solving Method:**
Since each answer-choice represents a possible amount of the procedure's cost, we can pick an answer-choice, assuming it is the cost of the procedure, and apply the insurance company's policy rules on that choice. The answer-choice that results in the patient paying $525 is the correct answer.

We are given that the policy pays 80% of the first $1,250, so the patient pays 20% of the first $1,250 of the cost. We are also given that the policy pays 50% of any cost above $1,250, so that means the patient must pay 50% of the cost above $1,250.

Let's back-solve, starting with answer-choice (C):

Plug-in answer-choice (C): $1,400
If it's correct, then the procedure costs $1,400.
The patient pays 20% of the first $1,250 $\Rightarrow$ 0.20 × $1250 = $250
The part of the cost above $1,250 is $1,400 − $1250 $\Rightarrow$ $150
Since the patient pays 50% of that, the patient's share is ½ of $150 $\Rightarrow$ 0.5 × 150 = $75
Total expense for the patient $\Rightarrow$ $250 + $75 = $325

Since the patient's actual expense is $525, this is much smaller than what we are looking for.
This means, we can not only eliminate (C), but we can also eliminate answer choices (B) and (A).
The correct answer has to be either (D) or (E)

Plug-in answer-choice (D): $1,600
If it's correct, then the procedure costs $1,600.

The patient pays 20% of the first $1,600 $\Rightarrow$ 0.20 × $1,250 = $250
The part of the cost above $1250 is $1,600 – $1,250 $\Rightarrow$ $350
Since the patient pays 50% of that, the patient's share is ½ of $350 $\Rightarrow$ 0.5 × 350 = $175
Total expense for the patient $\Rightarrow$ $250 + $175 = $425

Since the patient's actual expense is $525, this is still smaller than what we are looking for.
This means, we can also eliminate (D).
Now, at this point, by default, our obvious correct answer has to be answer-choice (E).
Nevertheless, let's evaluate it anyways, just for our satisfaction:

Plug-in answer-choice (E): $1,800
If it's correct, then the procedure cost $1,800.
The patient pays 20% of the first $1,250 $\Rightarrow$ 0.20 × $1,250 = $250
The part of the cost above $1,250 is $1,800 – $1,250 $\Rightarrow$ $550

Since the patient pays 50% of that, the patient's share is ½ of $550 $\Rightarrow$ 0.5 × 550 = $275
Total expense for the patient $\Rightarrow$ $250 + $275 = $525

Since we know the patient pays $525, this is exactly what we have now.

Therefore, the correct answer-choice is (E).

Solution B: **Using EZ Direct Method:**
Let, the cost of procedure = n
$\Rightarrow$ 20% of $1,250 + 50% of ($n$ – 1,250) = $525

$$\Rightarrow \frac{20}{100} \times 1,250 + \frac{50}{100} \times (n - 1,250) = 525$$

$$\Rightarrow 250 + \frac{(n - 1,250)}{2} = 525$$

$$\Rightarrow 2\left[250 + \frac{(n - 1,250)}{2}\right] = 2\left[525\right] \qquad \text{[multiply both sides of the equation by 2]}$$

$\Rightarrow$ 500 + (n – 1,250) = 1,050   [apply distributive property]
$\Rightarrow$ n – 750 = 1,050   [combine like-terms]
$\Rightarrow$ n = 1,050 + 750 = 1,800   [add 750 to both sides of the equations]

7.1.1: SPECIAL CASES – SKIPPING (B) OR (D):
While applying the "C" Rule in some problems, you may be able to make an intelligent guess and skip an answer-choice. For instance, look at the following example:

Example #5:   A man's wealth of $275,000 is to be divided among three children in the ratio of 2:3:6. What is the value of the largest share?
(A) $25,000   (B) $75,000   (C) $90,000   (D) $125,000   (E) $150,000

Solution A: **Using EZ Back-Solving Method:**
Let's back-solve, starting with answer-choice (C)

First, plug-in answer-choice (C): $90,000
If the largest share = $90,000
Then, the second largest share = $45,000 (one-half of $90,000)
And, the smallest share = $30,000 (one-third of $90,000)
Total Wealth = $90,000 + $45,000 + $30,000 = $165,000

Since this is way too smaller than the actual wealth, we need a bigger number.
This means, we can not only eliminate (C), but we can also eliminate answer choices (B) and (A).
The correct answer has to be either (D) or (E)

Now since $165,000 is way too small, let's skip (D) for now, and try answer-choice (E):

Next, plug-in answer-choice (E): $150,000
If the largest share = $150,000
Then, the second largest share = $75,000 (one-half of $150,000)
And, the smallest share = $50,000 (one-third of $150,000)
Total Wealth = $150,000 + $75,000 + $50,000 = $275,000

Since we know the actual total wealth is $275,000, this is exactly what we have now.

Therefore, the correct answer-choice is (E).

Solution B: **Using EZ Direct Method:**
Ratio of share $\Rightarrow$ 2:3:6
$\Rightarrow 2x + 3x + 6x = \$275,000$ [add all parts of the ratio and equate it with the sum of the parts]
$\Rightarrow 11x = \$275,000$ [combine like-terms]
$\Rightarrow x = \$25,000$ [divide both sides of the equation by 11]
Largest Share $\Rightarrow 6x = \$25,000 \times 6 = \$150,000$

7.2   EXCEPTIONS TO THE EZ "C" RULE

There are certain exceptions to our EZ "C" Rule. While working backwards on some of the problems, you'll always be able to eliminate answer-choice (C); however, occasionally, you may not be sure whether you need a larger number or a smaller number. In such cases, instead of wasting time trying to decide, simply try all the answer choices until you get to the right one. For such types of problems, it may be a good idea to just start from answer-choice (A) and work through the answer choices in alphabetical order. Keep trying until you find the answer that fits the information in the question. You may get lucky in the first couple of attempts. However, even in the worst-case scenario, you'll never have to try more than four of the five answer choices. Since if none of the first four choices you tried worked out, then by default, the correct answer has to be the fifth one, assuming you didn't make any errors.

Following are a few examples where you may have to test each and every answer-choice:

Example #1:   If $x^2 - 11x + 18 = 0$, then $x = ?$
(A) (1, 2)   (B) (1, 5)   (C) (5, 9)   (D) (0, 10)   (E) (2, 9)

Solution A: **Using EZ Back-Solving Method:**
Since we have to find the value of x, we have to test each one of the choices until we find the answer that gives us 0 for both values.

(A) (1, 2)   If $x = 1$ $\Rightarrow 1^2 - 11(1) + 18 = 0$ $\Rightarrow 1 - 11 + 18 = 0$ $\Rightarrow 8 \neq 0$ ✗
               If $x = 2$ $\Rightarrow 2^2 - 11(2) + 18 = 0$ $\Rightarrow 4 - 22 + 18 = 0$ $\Rightarrow 0 = 0$

(B) (1, 5)   If $x = 1$ $\Rightarrow 1^2 - 11(1) + 18 = 0$ $\Rightarrow 1 - 11 + 18 = 0$ $\Rightarrow 8 \neq 0$ ✗
               If $x = 5$ $\Rightarrow 5^2 - 11(5) + 18 = 0$ $\Rightarrow 25 - 55 + 18 = 0$ $\Rightarrow -12 \neq 0$

(C) (5, 9)   If $x = 5$ $\Rightarrow 5^2 - 11(5) + 18 = 0$ $\Rightarrow 25 - 55 + 18 = 0$ $\Rightarrow -12 \neq 0$ ✗
               If $x = 9$ $\Rightarrow 9^2 - 11(9) + 18 = 0$ $\Rightarrow 81 - 99 + 18 = 0$ $\Rightarrow 0 = 0$

(D) (0, 10)   If $x = 0$ $\Rightarrow 0^2 - 11(0) + 18 = 0$ $\Rightarrow 0 - 0 + 18 = 0$ $\Rightarrow 18 \neq 0$ ✗
               If $x = 10$ $\Rightarrow 10^2 - 11(10) + 18 = 0$ $\Rightarrow 100 - 110 + 18 = 0$ $\Rightarrow 8 \neq 0$

(E) (2, 9)   If $x = 2$ $\Rightarrow 2^2 - 11(2) + 18 = 0$ $\Rightarrow 4 - 22 + 18 = 0$ $\Rightarrow 0 = 0$ ✓
               If $x = 9$ $\Rightarrow 9^2 - 11(9) + 18 = 0$ $\Rightarrow 81 - 99 + 18 = 0$ $\Rightarrow 0 = 0$

Solution B: **Using EZ Direct Method:**
$x^2 - 11x + 18 = 0$
$\Rightarrow (x - 2)(x - 9) = 0$ [factor the quadratic equation into two binomials]
Either: Or:
$x - 2 = 0$ $x - 9 = 0$
$\Rightarrow x = 2$ $\Rightarrow x = 9$
Therefore, the Solution Set is: {2, 9}

Example #2:   What is the value of x if $\dfrac{x+1}{x-3} - \dfrac{x+2}{x-4} = 0$?

           (A) 5   (B) 4   (C) 3   (D) 2   (E) 1

Solution A: **Using EZ Back-Solving Method:**
Since we have to find the value of x, we have to test each one of the choices until we find the answer that gives us 0.

(A) 5 $\Rightarrow \dfrac{5+1}{5-3} - \dfrac{5+2}{5-4} = 0$ $\Rightarrow \dfrac{6}{2} - \dfrac{7}{1} = 0$ $\Rightarrow 3 - 7 = 0$ $\Rightarrow -4 \neq 0$ ✘

(B) 4 $\Rightarrow \dfrac{4+1}{4-3} - \dfrac{4+2}{4-4} = 0$ $\Rightarrow \dfrac{5}{1} - \dfrac{6}{0} = 0$ $\Rightarrow$ undefined   ✘

(C) 3 $\Rightarrow \dfrac{3+1}{3-3} - \dfrac{3+2}{3-4} = 0$ $\Rightarrow \dfrac{4}{0} - \dfrac{5}{-1} = 0$ $\Rightarrow$ undefined   ✘

(D) 2 $\Rightarrow \dfrac{2+1}{2-3} - \dfrac{2+2}{2-4} = 0$ $\Rightarrow \dfrac{3}{-1} - \dfrac{4}{-2} = 0$ $\Rightarrow -3 - (-2) = 0$ $\Rightarrow -1 \neq 0$ ✘

(E) 1 $\Rightarrow \dfrac{1+1}{1-3} - \dfrac{1+2}{1-4} = 0$ $\Rightarrow \dfrac{2}{-2} - \dfrac{3}{-3} = 0$ $\Rightarrow -1 - (-1) = 0$ $\Rightarrow 0 = 0$ ✔

Solution B: **Using EZ Direct Method:**
This problem is fairly difficult to solve it directly, however, if you are a pro in algebra, go ahead and solve it the direct way:

$\Rightarrow \dfrac{x+1}{x-3} - \dfrac{x+2}{x-4} = 0$

$\Rightarrow \dfrac{(x+1))(x-4) - (x+2)(x-3)}{(x-3)(x-4)} = 0$ [subtract the fractions by taking the common denominator]

$\Rightarrow \dfrac{x^2 - 4x + x - 4 - (x^2 - 3x + 2x - 6)}{(x-3)(x-4)} = 0$ [use FOIL in the numerator to multiply the factors]

$\Rightarrow \dfrac{x^2 - 3x - 4 - (x^2 - x - 6)}{(x-3)(x-4)} = 0$ [combine like-terms]

$\Rightarrow \dfrac{x^2 - 3x - 4 - x^2 + x + 6}{(x-3)(x-4)} = 0$ [get rid of the parenthesis in the numerator]

$\Rightarrow \dfrac{-2x + 2}{(x-3)(x-4)} = 0$ [again combine like-terms]

$\Rightarrow -2x + 2 = 0$ [cross-multiply]
$\Rightarrow -2x = -2$ [subtract 2 from both sides of the equation]
$\Rightarrow x = 1$ [divide both sides of the equation by −2]

7.3   EZ Back-Solving For Largest/Smallest Answers

For Questions Asking for "Largest" or "Smallest" Answer-Choice:

7.3.1: For Largest Quantity – Start with the Largest Answer-Choice:

On problems that ask for the largest number satisfying a certain property or condition – you should start with the largest answer-choice, working your way through the answer choices in descending order. Since you are asked to find the largest number satisfying a certain property or a condition, even if some of the smaller numbers offered as answer choices also satisfy the condition, your job is to find the largest one. Therefore, it doesn't matter whether any of the smaller choices work, what you need is the largest number. Of course, the same rule applies for problems that ask for the smallest number.

EZ Tip: In questions that ask for the greatest, maximum, or largest value, the answer-choice offering the largest number is rarely correct. Hence, if you ever need to guess on questions asking about the largest value, the one answer-choice you should avoid picking is the largest answer-choice. Of course, the same advice applies for questions that ask for the least, minimum, or smallest values.

Example #1:   What is the largest possible value of integer, n, such that $\dfrac{120}{2^n}$ is an integer?

    (A) 1   (B) 2   (C) 3   (D) 4   (E) 5

Solution A: **Using EZ Back-Solving Method:**

Since we have to find the largest possible value of integer n, such that $\dfrac{120}{2^n}$ is an integer, let's start testing answer choices starting from the largest number, which is, choice (E)

Plug-in answer-choice (E) 5 $\Rightarrow \dfrac{120}{2^n} = \dfrac{120}{2^5} = \dfrac{120}{32} = 3.75$ ✘

Plug-in answer-choice (D) 4 $\Rightarrow \dfrac{120}{2^n} = \dfrac{120}{2^4} = \dfrac{120}{16} = 7.5$ ✘

Plug-in answer-choice (C) 3 $\Rightarrow \dfrac{120}{2^n} = \dfrac{120}{2^3} = \dfrac{120}{8} = 15$ ✓

Since we are looking for the largest number, we don't have to go any further, the correct answer-choice is (C).

7.3.2: For Smallest Quantity – Start with the Smallest Answer-Choice:

On problems that ask for the smallest number satisfying a certain property or condition – you should start with the smallest answer-choice, working your way through the answer choices in ascending order. Since you are asked to find the smallest number satisfying a certain property or a condition, even if some of the larger numbers offered as answer choices also satisfy the condition, your job is to find the smallest one. Therefore, it doesn't matter whether any of the larger choices work, what you need is the smallest number. Of course, the same rule applies for problems that ask for the largest number.

EZ Tip: In the questions that ask for the least, minimum, or smallest value, the answer-choice offering the smallest number is rarely correct. Hence, if you ever need to guess on questions asking about the smallest value, the one answer-choice you should avoid picking is the smallest answer-choice. Of course, the same advice applies for questions that ask for the greatest, maximum, or largest values.

Example #2: What is the smallest possible value of integer, n, such that $\dfrac{112}{2^n}$ is not an integer?

(A) 1   (B) 2   (C) 3   (D) 4   (E) 5

Solution A: **Using EZ Back-Solving Method:**

Since we have to find the smallest possible value of integer n, such that $\dfrac{112}{2^n}$ is not an integer, let's start testing answer choices starting from the smallest answer-choice:

(A) 1 $\Rightarrow \dfrac{112}{2^n} = \dfrac{112}{2^1} = \dfrac{112}{2} = 56$ $\Rightarrow$ It's an integer   ✘

(B) 2 $\Rightarrow \dfrac{112}{2^n} = \dfrac{112}{2^2} = \dfrac{112}{4} = 28$ $\Rightarrow$ It's an integer   ✘

(C) 3 $\Rightarrow \dfrac{112}{2^n} = \dfrac{112}{2^3} = \dfrac{112}{8} = 14$ $\Rightarrow$ It's an integer   ✘

(D) 4 $\Rightarrow \dfrac{112}{2^n} = \dfrac{112}{2^4} = \dfrac{112}{16} = 7$ $\Rightarrow$ It's an integer   ✘

(E) 5 $\Rightarrow \dfrac{112}{2^n} = \dfrac{112}{2^5} = \dfrac{112}{32} = 3.5$ $\Rightarrow$ It's not an integer   ✓

Therefore, the correct answer-choice is (E).

7.4   WHEN EZ BACK-SOLVING IS ESSENTIAL

WHEN THE ONLY WAY TO ANSWER THE QUESTION IS BY BACK-SOLVING THE ANSWER-CHOICES:

There are some multiple-choice questions, which cannot be answered directly; instead, you have to test almost all of the answer choices in order to find the correct answer. These questions ask which of the five answer choices satisfy a certain condition. On these types of problems, you are not really back-solving, actually there is nothing to solve. You are essentially testing which of the answer choices satisfy the condition given in the problem. Usually, in such situations, these types of questions cannot be answered directly in a straightforward manner, and you have to look at the answer choices and test each one of them until you find one that works. At that point, you can stop – since none of the other choices could be correct.

EZ HINT: Since there is no particular order to follow in which to test the answer choices, it makes sense to first test the easier answer choices. For instance, it is usually easier to test whole numbers than fractions, and positive numbers than negative numbers.

EZ TIP: In such types of questions, it is always better to start with answer-choice (E), the right answer is rarely one of the first few choices. However, this may not always be true.

These types of questions usually start with a phrase, such as, "which of the following...?"

Example #1: Which of the following is not equivalent to $\dfrac{4}{5}$?

(A) $\dfrac{20}{25}$ (B) 0.80   (C) 80%   (D) $\dfrac{4}{7} \times \dfrac{7}{5}$ (E) $\dfrac{4}{7} \div \dfrac{7}{5}$

Solution: In this problem, we have to test each of the five answer choices until we find the one that satisfies the condition that it is not equal to 2/5. Since there is no predefined order to follow, you can just test each of the answer-choice in the order that seems most convenient to you:

(A) $\dfrac{20}{25}$ $\Rightarrow \dfrac{20}{25} \div \dfrac{5}{5}$ $\Rightarrow \dfrac{4}{5}$ ✘

(B) 0.80 $\Rightarrow 0.80 \times \dfrac{100}{100} = \dfrac{80}{100} = \dfrac{8}{10} \div \dfrac{2}{2}$ $\Rightarrow \dfrac{4}{5}$ ✗

(C) 80% $\Rightarrow \dfrac{80}{100} = \dfrac{8}{10} \div \dfrac{2}{2}$ $\Rightarrow \dfrac{4}{5}$ ✗

(D) $\dfrac{4}{7} \times \dfrac{7}{5}$ $\Rightarrow \dfrac{4}{\cancel{7}} \times \dfrac{\cancel{7}}{5}$ $\Rightarrow \dfrac{4}{5}$ ✗

(E) $\dfrac{4}{7} \div \dfrac{7}{5}$ $\Rightarrow \dfrac{4}{7} \times \dfrac{5}{7}$ $\Rightarrow \dfrac{20}{49}$ ✓

Therefore, the correct answer-choice is (E)

7.5 EZ BACK-SOLVING FOR SIMPLE QUESTIONS

EZ BACK-SOLVING FOR EASY COMPUTATIONAL TYPES OF QUESTIONS:

EZ Back-Solving can also be applied to solve some of the most basic computational questions. In fact, for some basic questions, it may be easier and quicker to work backwards by checking the answers than solving the problem. Therefore, it is sometimes a good idea to first look at the answer choices before starting to work on the problem.

Example #1:   Which of the following numbers is the closest to the square root of 0.0026?
              (A) 0.02   (B) 0.5   (C) 0.05   (D) 0.005   (E) 0.09

Solution: One way to answer this question it to actually calculate the exact square root of 0.0026 and then determine which of the answer choices is closest to your answer.
$\Rightarrow \sqrt{0.0026} = 0.0509$ $\Rightarrow$ this is closest to 0.05 which is choice (C).

The other easier way is to square each of the answer choices and see which one is closest to 0.0026.

(A) 0.02 $\Rightarrow 0.02^2$ $= 0.0004$ ✗

(B) 0.5 $\Rightarrow 0.5^2$ $= 0.25$ ✗

(C) 0.05 $\Rightarrow 0.05^2$ $= 0.0025$ ✓

(D) 0.005 $\Rightarrow 0.005^2$ $= 0.000025$ ✗

(E) 0.09 $\Rightarrow 0.09^2$ $= 0.0081$ ✗

Therefore, the correct answer choice is (C).
Note: In general, it is often easier to calculate the square than a square root.

▪ PRACTICE EXERCISE WITH DETAILED EXPLANATIONS

Applying the EZ "C" Rule:

Question #1:   If the sum of five consecutive even integers is 600, what is the smallest of these integers?
(A) 108   (B) 110   (C) 112   (D) 114   (E) 116

Solution A: **Using EZ Back-Solving Method:**
The correct answer should yield in 600 as the sum of the five consecutive integers.
Let's back-solve, starting with answer choice (C)

Plug-in answer choice (C): 112
If 112 is the smallest integer, the integers are: 112, 114, 116, 118, 120; and their sum is 580.
Since 580 is too small, this means, we can not only eliminate (C), but we can also eliminate answer choices (B) and (A). The correct answer has to be either (D) or (E)

Plug-in answer choice (D): 114
If 114 is the smallest integer, the integers are 114, 116, 118, 120, 122; and their sum is 590.
Since 590 is still too small, this means, we can also eliminate (B).
Now, at this point, by default, our obvious correct answer has to be answer choice (A). Nevertheless, let's evaluate it anyways, just for our satisfaction:

Plug-in answer choice (E): 116
If 116 is the smallest integer, the integers are 116, 118, 120, 122, 124; and their sum is 600
Since the sum of five consecutive integers is 600, this is exactly what we have got.
Therefore, the correct answer choice is (E).

Solution B: **Using EZ Direct Method:**
$n + (n + 2) + (n + 4) + (n + 6) + (n + 8) = 600$
$\Rightarrow 5n + 20 = 600$ [combine like-terms]
$\Rightarrow 5n = 600 - 20 = 580$ [subtract 20 from both sides of the equation]
$\Rightarrow n = 580 \div 5 = 116$ [divide both sides of the equation by 5]

Question #2:   A man has a book collection in which half of the books are literature books, 5 books are history books, and the rest of the $\frac{2}{5}$ of the books are science books. How many books are in the collection?

(A) 50   (B) 60   (C) 70   (D) 80   (E) 90

Solution A: **Using EZ Back-Solving Method:**
Let's back-solve, starting with answer choice (C)

Plug- in answer choice (C): 70
If the collection had 70 books, half of the books, which is 35 books were literature, 5 were history books, so literature + history books were 35 + 5 = 40, the remaining are 70– 40 = 30 science books.
Is 30 exactly $\frac{2}{5}$ of 70? $\Rightarrow$ NO, $\frac{2}{5}$ of 70 = 28
Eliminate answer choice (C)
Since 30 is too big, eliminate (D) and (E). The correct answer has to be either (B) or (A)

Plug-in answer choice (B): 60
If the collection had 60 books, half of the books, which is 30 books were literature, 5 were history books, so literature + history books were 30 + 5 = 35, the remaining are 60 – 35 = 25 science books.
Is 25 exactly $\frac{2}{5}$ of 60? $\Rightarrow$ NO, $\frac{2}{5}$ of 60 = 24

Since 25 is still too big, eliminate answer choice (B).
Now, at this point, by default, our obvious correct answer has to be answer choice (A). Nevertheless, let's evaluate it anyways, just for our satisfaction:

Plug-in answer choice (A): $n = 50$
If the collection has 50 books, half of the books, which is 25 books are literature, 5 are history books. Therefore, literature + history books are 25 + 5 = 30 books, the remaining are 50 − 30 = 20 books.

Is 20 exactly $\dfrac{2}{5}$ of 50? ⇒ YES, $\dfrac{2}{5}$ of 50 = 20

Therefore, the correct answer choice is (A).

Solution B: **Using EZ Direct Method:**
Let the total number of books in the collection = n

$\Rightarrow n = \dfrac{2}{5}n + \dfrac{1}{2}n + 5$

$\Rightarrow n - \dfrac{2}{5}n - \dfrac{1}{2}n = 5$ [group like-terms on one side of the equation]

$\Rightarrow \dfrac{1}{10}n = 5$ [combine like-terms]

$\Rightarrow n = 5 \times 10 = 50$ [multiply both sides of the equation by 10]

Question #3:   In a certain school, the ratio of boys to girls is 2:5. If there are 75 more girls than boys, how many boys are there?
(A) 10   (B) 20   (C) 25   (D) 40   (E) 50

Solution A: **Using EZ Back-Solving Method:**
The correct answer should yield a ratio of 2:5.
Let's back-solve, starting with answer choice (C)

Plug-in answer choice (C): 25
If there are 25 boys, then there are 25 + 75 = 100 girls.
Now, the ratio of boys to girls = 25:100 = 1:4
Since we know the ratio of boys to girls is 2:5 or 0.4, the ratio of 1:4 or 0.25 is too small, which means we need a bigger number for boys.
This means, we can not only eliminate (C), but we can also eliminate answer choices (B) and (A).

Plug-in answer-choice (D): 40
If there are 40 boys, then there are 40 + 75 = 115 girls.
Now, the ratio of boys to girls = 40:115 = 8:23
Since we know that the ratio of boys to girls is 2:5 or 0.4, the ratio of 8:23 or 0.34 is still too small, which means we still need a bigger number for boys.
This means, we can also eliminate answer choices (D).

Now, at this point, our obvious correct answer has to be answer choice (E). Nevertheless, let's evaluate it anyways, just for our satisfaction:
Plug-in answer choice (E): 50
If there are 50 boys, then there are 50 + 75 = 125 girls.
Now, the ratio of boys to girls = 50:125 = 2:5
Since we know the ratio of boys to girls is 2:5, this is exactly what we have got.
Therefore, the correct answer choice is (E).

Solution B: **Using EZ Direct Method:**
Ratio of Boys to Girls ⇒ 2:5
Let's say the number of Boys = n
And, the number of Girls = $n + 75$
Now, we can form the following equation or proportion:

$$\Rightarrow \frac{2}{5} = \frac{n}{n+75}$$

$\Rightarrow 5n = 2(n + 75)$ [cross multiply both sides of the equation]

$\Rightarrow 5n = 2n + 150$ [apply distributive property]

$\Rightarrow 3n = 150$ [subtract $2n$ from both sides of the equation]

$\Rightarrow n = 150 \div 3 = 50$ [divide both sides of the equation by 3]

Question #4: A bushel of apples contains one red apple for every 10 apples in the basket. If 2 out of every 5 red apples are considered to be of cherry red shade, and there are 24 cherry red apples in the basket, how many apples are there in the bushel?

(A) 600   (B) 650   (C) 700   (D) 750   (E) 800

Solution A: **Using EZ Back-Solving Method:**

The correct answer should yield 24 cherry red apples.

Let's back-solve, starting with answer choice (C)

Plug-in answer choice (C): 700

If there are 700 apples, and 1 in 10 are red apples, then the number of red apples: $\Rightarrow 700 \div 10 = 70$

If there are 70 red apples, and 2 in 5 are cherry red apples, then the number of cherry red apples:

$$\Rightarrow \frac{2}{5} \times 70 = 28$$

Since there are 24 cherry red apples, 28 is too big. So we need a smaller number for cherry red apples, which means we need a smaller number for total apples.

This means, we can not only eliminate (C), but we can also eliminate answer choices (D) and (E). The correct answer has to be either (B) or (A)

Plug-in answer-choice (B): 650

If there are 650 apples, and 1 in 10 are red apples, then the number of red apples: $\Rightarrow 650 \div 10 = 65$

If there are 65 red apples, and 2 in 5 are cherry red apples, then the number of cherry red apples:

$$\Rightarrow \frac{2}{5} \times 65 = 26$$

Since there are 24 cherry red apples, 26 is still too big. So we need even a smaller number for cherry red apples, which means we need even a smaller number for total apples.

This means, we can also eliminate (B).

Now, at this point, by default, our obvious correct answer has to be answer choice (A). Nevertheless, let's evaluate it anyways, just for our satisfaction:

Answer Choice (A): 600

Plug-in answer-choice (A): 600

If there are 600 apples, and 1 in 10 are red apples, then the number of red apples: $\Rightarrow 600 \div 10 = 60$

If there are 60 red apples, and 2 in 5 are cherry red apples, then the number of cherry red apples:

$$\Rightarrow \frac{2}{5} \times 60 = 24$$

Since the number of cherry red apples is 24, this is exactly what we have got.

Therefore, the correct answer choice is (A).

Solution B: **Using EZ Direct Method:**

Ratio of Total Apples to Red Apples = 10:1

Ratio of Red Apples to Cherry Red Apples = 5:2

Total	:	Red	Red:	Cherry	
10	:	1	5	:	2	[write both ratios in order so that the common part is the middle]
50	:	5	5	:	2	[make the common part equal]

Ratio of Total Apples to Red Apples to Cherry Red Apples = 50:5:2

Since we know there are 24 cherry red apples, the scaling factor is 12

So, the number of Cherry Red Apples = 50 × 12 = 600

Exceptions to the EZ "C" Rule:

Question #5: What is the possible value of integer, n, such that $\dfrac{64}{2n}$ is a prime number?

(A) 1   (B) 2   (C) 4   (D) 8   (E) 16

Solution A: **Using EZ Back-Solving Method:**
Since we have to find an answer that is a prime number, we have to test each one of the choices until we find the answer that is a prime number.

Plug-in answer choice (A) 1 $\Rightarrow \dfrac{64}{2n} = \dfrac{64}{2 \times 1} = \dfrac{64}{2} = 32$ ✗

Plug-in answer choice (B) 2 $\Rightarrow \dfrac{64}{2n} = \dfrac{64}{2 \times 2} = \dfrac{64}{4} = 16$ ✗

Plug-in answer choice (C) 4 $\Rightarrow \dfrac{64}{2n} = \dfrac{64}{2 \times 4} = \dfrac{64}{8} = 8$ ✗

Plug-in answer choice (D) 8 $\Rightarrow \dfrac{64}{2n} = \dfrac{64}{2 \times 8} = \dfrac{64}{16} = 4$ ✗

Plug-in answer choice (E) 16 $\Rightarrow \dfrac{64}{2n} = \dfrac{64}{2 \times 16} = \dfrac{64}{32} = 2$ ✓

Since 2 is a prime number, the correct answer choice is (E).

Solution B: **Using EZ Direct Method:**
Factor Pairs of 64:   1, 2, 4, 8, 16, 32, and 64

For $\dfrac{64}{2n}$ to be a prime number, n has to be 16

CHAPTER 8.0: EZ PLUG-IN NUMBERS STRATEGY

HIGHLIGHTS:
8.1 EZ Plug-in For Numeric Answers
8.2 EZ Plug-in For Variable Answers
8.3 EZ Plug-in For Problems with Multiple Variable Equations
8.4 EZ Plug-in For Special Format Answers
▪ Practice Exercise with Detailed Explanations

EZ Plug-In Numbers Strategy is just another version of the back-solving strategy, as it also transforms algebra problems into arithmetic problems. EZ Plug-In Numbers Strategy is perhaps one of our most useful math techniques, by using which you'll be able to solve complicated problems more easily and quickly than you can ever imagine. Therefore, practice this method so that you can use it effectively on tough problems.

EZ Plug-In Numbers Strategy means solving a problem by plugging-in EZ Smart Numbers in place of the variables; that is, testing the various answer choices and finding out which one is correct. If you understand the question, the relationship between the variables, and know what to do – simply evaluate each of the answer choices with the numbers you picked, and determine which answer-choice is equal to the answer you had previously obtained. The answer that satisfies the conditions and/or relationships laid out in the problem is the correct answer. This is how our EZ Plug-In Numbers Strategy works.

Look at the following two examples:

Example A: If 2 apples cost $4 dollars, then how many dollars would 5 apples cost?
(A) $2.50   (B) $1.60   (C) $10.00   (D) $0.625   (E) $0.40

Example B: If n apples cost p dollars, then how many dollars would m apples cost?

(A) $\dfrac{mn}{p}$ (B) $\dfrac{np}{m}$ (C) $\dfrac{mp}{n}$ (D) $\dfrac{m}{np}$ (E) $\dfrac{p}{mn}$

You'll see how to solve this question, later in this section.

Obviously, the first example looks much easier to solve than the second example. However, the question is, why does the first one seem so much easier than the second one, or why does the second one seem so much harder than the first one?

If you look at both questions more closely, they are identical, except for the fact that the first one uses simple numbers (2, 4, and 5) and the second one contains ugly variables (n, p, and m). Therefore, the use of variables (i.e., algebra) instead of numbers (i.e., arithmetic) make things appear more complex. In fact, for most people, algebra is always going to be harder than arithmetic. Moreover, no matter how good one is at algebra, one is always definitely going to be better at arithmetic.

For most of us, numbers are easier to work with than variables, and hence, you are much more vulnerable to making mistakes when manipulating variables than real numbers. In general, your brain, processes "2 + 5" more easily than it does "$x + y$". Therefore, instead of struggling with the algebra, just assume that a certain undefined value has a specific numerical value.

FROM ABSTRACT TO CONCRETE: Sometimes you may find yourself stuck on a math question, or it may seem more difficult than it actually is, just because the question is too general or abstract. These types of problems are especially confusing because the problem contains exasperating unknown values, instead of any actual numbers. Normally, problems that involve numbers are easier to understand. In such cases, you'll realize that although the problem involves the values of certain numbers; however, those values will never be given. As a result, the problem is quite abstract. A good solution to this problem is to make the problem more concrete and solvable by picking real numbers to stand in for those values, when they aren't provided to you.

Such math problems aren't meant to have just one specific number as the correct answer. You are expected to write a function, an equation, or a formula that will answer the question regardless of the value of the numbers. This number can have any value, and that function would still give you the correct answer. You can use algebra to solve these questions, but there is usually a better way. The correct answer will work for any number, and not just one value. Plugging-in a number is normally used to solve for an unknown. After going through this section, you'll realize that our EZ Plug-In Numbers Strategy makes even some of the most difficult problems fairly easy to answer. This strategy is not very easy to master, but with practice, you should be able to get better at applying it. If this sounds too confusing, don't worry, we have streamlined the whole process of back-solving in a well organized and systematic step-by-step method.

INVISIBLE OR VISIBLE VARIABLES: The variables that we have been talking about so far may be invisible or visible. Sometimes the variables in the question aren't very visible or obvious, in which case they are invisible variables. For instance, a question may not mention any actual variable, such as, *x* or *y*; however, it may contain remainders, percents, fractions, or ratios of some unknown amount – all of which are more like invisible variables. While at other times the variables in the question are very visible or evident, in which case they are visible variables. For instance, a question may mention actual variables, such as, *x* or *y*; which are more like visible variables.

WHEN TO USE AND WHEN NOT TO USE EZ PLUG-IN NUMBERS STRATEGY:

(A) When to Use EZ Plug-In Numbers Strategy: You should use our EZ Plug-In Numbers Strategy only when you don't know how to solve the problem directly, but understand what needs to be done to answer the question. In such cases, picking numbers may especially prove to be useful and helpful. Use this strategy when the question involves remainders or when the answer choices are in terms of fractions, ratios, percents, or variables.

(B) When Not to Use EZ Plug-In Numbers Strategy: You should not use the plug-in number strategy if you know how to solve the question directly. In most cases, direct solving is much quicker and easier than plugging-in numbers. In most cases, plugging-in numbers is more time consuming than solving it directly. However, in a few cases, plugging-in numbers becomes essential in answering the problem.

USING TEST BOOKLET AS SCRATCH PAPER ON EZ PLUG-IN NUMBERS STRATEGY:
It's important to keep track and make notes while using EZ Plug-In Numbers Strategy. Always make sure to write down the number you are plugging-in. Once you find the answer to the problem in terms of that number, circle it. Then try each of the answer choices, crossing them off as you eliminate them. This way you'll know what numbers you picked and which answer choices you have already plugged into those numbers. Never try to do this process in your head, it's almost impossible to do so.

TYPES OF EZ PLUG-IN NUMBERS STRATEGY:
The following are the two types of problems where you should consider using EZ Plug-In Numbers Strategy, when the answer choices contain variables – invisible or visible:
- EZ Plug-in For Numeric Answers (Invisible Variables)
- EZ Plug-in For Variable Answers (Visible Variables)
- EZ Plug-in For Problems with Multiple Variable Equations
- EZ Plug-in For Special Format Answers

8.1 EZ PLUG-IN FOR NUMERIC ANSWERS

Invisible or Hidden Variables: Sometimes the variables in the question aren't very visible or obvious, in which case they are invisible variables. For instance, a question may not mention any actual variable, such as, *x* or *y*; however, it may contain remainders, percents, fractions, or ratios of some unknown amount – all of which are more like invisible variables.

8.1.1: FOR PROBLEMS WITH REMAINDERS AS ANSWER-CHOICES:

For remainder problems that don't specify any actual values, that is, when they include remainder of some unspecified numerical quantity and contain remainders in the answer choices, consider using EZ Plug-In Numbers Strategy.

EZ NOTE: Remainder problems may seem quite complex but they are not that difficult. In fact, they are much easier than they appear. Many students have a notion that the key to solving remainder problems is to find the value of the variables involved – this not only takes up a lot of time but also causes a lot of confusion, and that type of complicated problem solving is usually neither necessary nor recommended. Remainder problems can usually be solved very easily by simply using EZ Plug-In Numbers Strategy. Actually, it is usually the fastest way to solve problems related to remainders, and often, this may be the only way to solve these types of problems.

EZ SMART NUMBERS: If a problem involves remainders, make the computation easier by picking EZ Smart Numbers. When picking a number on a problem involving remainders, the easiest and best number to pick is the number that you arrive at after adding the remainder to the number you're dividing by.

EZ SPOT: It's easy to spot remainder problems. These problems contain one of the following buzz words/phrases: remainder, residue, leftover, what's left, etc.

Example #1:   When "*n*" is divided by 5, the remainder is 1. What is the remainder when 2*n* is divided by 5?
(A) 2   (B) 3   (C) 4   (D) 5   (E) 6

Solution: Since the question asks for the remainder, so that's the invisible variable in the answer choices. Now let's first pick an EZ smart number for remainder.
We have to find a number that leaves a remainder of 1 when divided by 5. Since the remainder when *n* is divided by 5 is 1, pick any multiple of 5 and add 1. The easiest multiple to work with is 5 itself.
Hence, a good selection would be (5 + 1) = 6, since when 6 is divided by 5, the remainder is 1.
Now plug-in 6 for *n* and see what happens to the remainder when:
$\Rightarrow$ 2*n* is divided by 5
$\Rightarrow$ 2(6) is dived by 5
$\Rightarrow$ 12 is divided by 5
$\Rightarrow$ 12 ÷ 5 = 2 with remainder = 2
Therefore, if *n* = 6, then 2*n* = 12, which, when divided by 5, leaves a remainder of 2.
Note: this problem doesn't depend on knowing the value of *n*. In fact, *n* has an infinite number of possible values. The reminder will remain to be 2 regardless of the value of *n*.
Therefore, the correct answer is (A).

8.1.2: FOR PROBLEMS WITH PERCENTS AS ANSWER-CHOICES:

For percent problems that don't specify any actual values, that is, when they include percents of some unspecified numerical quantity and contain percents in the answer choices, consider using EZ Plug-In Numbers Strategy.

EZ SMART NUMBERS: If a problem involves percents, make the computation easier by picking EZ Smart Numbers. When picking a number on a problem involving percents, the easiest and best number to pick is 100 for the unspecified amount because it is easy to calculate percents of 100. Since percent is always out of 100, the answer you work out will automatically be in percent, and you won't have to perform the extra step of converting your answer into percent. Moreover calculating percents of 100 is extremely easy; picking any other number may make the problem more complicated.

Example #2: At a certain state college, each student takes exactly one foreign language. One-fifth of the students take French, one-eighth of the remaining students take Italian, and the rest take Spanish. What percent of the students take Spanish?

    (A) 10%   (B) 20%   (C) 25%   (D) 50%   (E) 70%

Solution: Since the question asks for the percent of students who take Spanish, so that's the invisible variable in the answer choices. Now let's first pick an EZ smart number for total number of students.

Since this problem involves percents, lets assume that the total number of students = 100

Number of students taking French = $\dfrac{1}{5} \times 100 = 20$

Remaining students = $100 - 20 = 80$

Number of students taking Italian = $\dfrac{1}{8} \times 80 = 10$

Remaining students = $80 - 10 = 70$

Number of students taking Spanish = 70

Since our total number of students is 100, we don't have to convert our answer into percents; therefore, 70% of the student takes Spanish.

Therefore, the correct answer is (E).

8.1.3: FOR PROBLEMS WITH FRACTIONS AS ANSWER-CHOICES:

For fraction problems that don't specify any actual values, that is, when they include fractional parts of some unspecified numerical quantity and contain fractions in the answer choices, consider using EZ Plug-In Numbers Strategy.

EZ NOTE: These types of problems give out a lot of information to work with, but they almost never give the whole of the parts. You are expected to find the fractional part without knowing the specific whole. These problems are supposed to work regardless of the whole, that is, they work under any situation.

EZ SMART NUMBERS: If the problem involves fractions, make the computation easier by picking EZ Smart Numbers. When picking a number on a problem involving fractions, the easiest and best number to pick is a number that is divisible by or is the common multiple of all the denominators of the fraction given in the problem. This number is likely to be the least common denominator of all the fractions involved.

Example #3: Mary spends one-half of her salary on rent. She spends one-third of her remaining salary on utilities. She spends one-fourth of her salary on paying miscellaneous bills. If Mary has no other expense and saves the rest of her salary in a savings account, what fraction of her salary does she save in her savings account?

    (A) $\dfrac{1}{3}$ (B) $\dfrac{1}{4}$ (C) $\dfrac{1}{6}$ (D) $\dfrac{1}{8}$ (E) $\dfrac{1}{12}$

Solution: Since the question asks for the fraction of Mary's salary, so that's the invisible variable in the answer choices. Now let's first pick an EZ smart number for total salary.

The problem involves three fractions: 1/2, 1/3, and 1/4, let's assume that the total salary was $12.
(12 is the least common denominator and is divisible by all three denominators 2, 3, and 4)

Amount of Salary spent on Rent = $\dfrac{1}{2} \times 12 = \$6$

Remaining Salary after paying Rent = $\$12 - \$6 = \$6$

Amount of Salary spent on Utilities = $\dfrac{1}{3} \times 6 = \$2$

Remaining Salary after paying Rent & Utilities = $\$6 - \$2 = \$4$

Amount of Salary spent on Misc. Bills = $\dfrac{1}{4} \times 12 = \$3$

Remaining Salary after paying Rent & Utilities & Misc. Bills = $\$4 - \$3 = \$1$

Fraction of salary saved in savings account = 1 out of 12 = $\dfrac{1}{12}$

Therefore, the correct answer is (E).

8.1.4: FOR PROBLEMS WITH RATIOS AS ANSWER-CHOICES:

For ratio problems that don't specify any actual values, that is, when they include ratios of some unspecified quantity and contain ratios in the answer choices, consider using EZ Plug-In Numbers Strategy.

EZ SMART NUMBERS: If a problem involves ratios, make the computation easier by picking EZ Smart Numbers. When picking a number on a problem involving ratios, the easiest and best number to pick is a number that is divisible by all the parts of the ratio. This number is likely to be the least common multiple of all the ratios involved.

Example #4: A building has two-ninth of its floors below ground. What is the ratio of the number of floors above ground to the number of floors below ground?
(A) 7:2   (B) 5:2   (C) 2:7   (D) 2:5   (E) 7:5

Solution: Since the question asks for the ratio of floors above ground, so that's the invisible variable in the answer choices. Now let's first pick an EZ smart number for total number of floors.
Since the problem involves fractions and ratios, let's assume that the total number of floors is 18.
(18 is divisible by both the numerator and denominator of 2/9)

Number of floors below ground = $\dfrac{2}{9} \times 18 = 4$

Number of floors above ground = $18 - 4 = 14$
Ratio of the number of floors above ground to the number of floors below ground = 14:4 = 7:2
Therefore, the correct answer is (A).

8.1.5: EXCEPTIONS: WHEN NOT TO USE PLUG-IN NUMBERS STRATEGY:

In some problems, a quantity might be unknown to you; however, it may actually be specified in the problem in some other way. Even though the whole may not be given in the problem, the whole may not be completely unspecified or indeterminable. For instance, you may be given a part of the total, and you can use that information to determine the whole. You can usually solve such problems by figuring out how big the known part is, and then use that information to find the size of the whole. In such cases, you cannot use EZ Plug-In Numbers Strategy and use EZ Smart Numbers to assign real numbers to the unknowns.

EZ TIP: As a rule of thumb, if there is even one specified amount in a problem, you generally cannot use EZ Plug-In Numbers Strategy and use EZ Smart Numbers to solve it.

Example #5: In a home library, there are one-half history books and two-ninth science books. The remainder of the collection consists of political books. If there are 55 political books, how many books are there in the entire home library?
(A) 99   (B) 101   (C) 110   (D) 192   (E) 198

Solution: Although we don't know the total number of books in the home library, the total is not completely unspecified. We know a part of the total: 55 political books. We can use this information to find the total. Do not make the mistake of using plugging numbers strategy and use smart numbers here. Instead, solve it by figuring out how big the known part is; and then use that information to find the total number of books in the entire home library.

$\Rightarrow$ History Books + Science Books + Political Books = Total Books

$\Rightarrow \dfrac{1}{2} + \dfrac{2}{9} + P = 1$

$\Rightarrow P = 1 - \dfrac{1}{2} - \dfrac{2}{9} = \dfrac{18}{18} - \dfrac{9}{18} - \dfrac{4}{18} = \dfrac{5}{18}$

$\Rightarrow$ Political Books = $55 = \dfrac{5}{18}$ of total books

$\Rightarrow 55 = \dfrac{5}{18} x$

$\Rightarrow x = 55 \times \dfrac{18}{5} = 198$

Therefore, the correct answer is (E).

Example #6: If a student allocated one-half of his annual budget for rent, one-quarter for tuition, one-sixth for food, and the remaining $900 for other expenses, what was his total annual budget?
(A) 9,000   (B) 10,200   (C) 10,800   (D) 16,200   (E) 21,600

Solution: Rent Fraction + Tuition Fraction + Food Fraction + Other Expenses Fraction = Total Budget

$$\Rightarrow \frac{1}{2} + \frac{1}{4} + \frac{1}{6} + E = 1$$

$$\Rightarrow E = 1 - \frac{1}{2} - \frac{1}{4} - \frac{1}{6} = \frac{24}{24} - \frac{12}{24} - \frac{6}{24} - \frac{4}{24} = \frac{24}{24} - \frac{22}{24} = \frac{2}{24} = \frac{1}{12}$$

Other Expense = $900 = $\frac{1}{12}$ of total budget

$$\Rightarrow 900 = \frac{1}{12}x$$

$$\Rightarrow x = 900 \times 12 = 10,800$$

Therefore, the correct answer is (C).

Example #7: Mary spends two-thirds of her savings on a car, and then spends one-fourth of her remaining savings on furniture. If the furniture cost her $500, how much were Mary's original savings?
(A) $6,000   (B) $4,000   (C) $3,000   (D) $2,000   (E) $1500

Solution: Cost of Car   = Two-Thirds of her Savings
Cost of Furniture = One-Fourth of One-Third of Original Savings = 1/4 of 1/3 = 1/12 of Original Savings
Original Savings = 12 times Cost of Furniture = 12 × $500 = $6,000
Therefore, the correct answer is (A).

8.2   EZ PLUG-IN FOR VARIABLE ANSWERS

Visible Variables: Sometimes the variable in the question are very visible or evident, in which case they are visible variables. For instance, a question may mention actual variables, such as, x or y; which are more like visible variables.

The only thing that's difficult about these questions is that they use variables instead of numbers. EZ Plug-In Numbers Strategy is an extremely important strategy for making sense out of problems that contain variables instead of numbers. Instead of trying to solve these complex problems algebraically, it is much easier to solve them by picking numbers. These questions have answers that use given quantities whose numerical values will not be given. In such problems, assigning a value that is easy to compute with can simplify the problem, and enable you to check your answer choices. For most of us, variables make a question significantly complex. Instead of trying to work with unknown variables, we can pick concrete values for the variables. So, get rid of those variables and make the questions real by picking numbers in place of variables. These questions include a condition that you can express in the form of a formula, even if it's a verbal one. So, pick numerical values to find or check answers that involve formulas. Any answer-choice that does not work for the concrete values cannot be the correct answer.

Therefore, whenever you come across a problem that contains variables in the question and in the answer choices, you should automatically be prompted to consider using our EZ Plug-In Numbers Strategy.

Variable problems that do not specify a value is another instance where EZ Plug-In Numbers Strategy can be a successful strategy. For problems that contain variables in the answer choices, that is, when all the answer choices are in the form of variables, consider using EZ Plug-in Numbers Strategy.

EZ STEP-BY-STEP METHOD: While using our "EZ Plug-In Number" Strategy, apply the following steps:

STEP 1: Pick EZ Smart Numbers: If the question and its answer choices are all expressed in terms of variables (such as x and y) simply pick numeric values for each of those variables or letters with EZ Smart Numbers that fit the conditions given in the problem.
Note: Use a grid to keep track of your work – pick numbers for each variable and put them in a grid.

STEP 2: Solve the Question with Picked Numbers: Do the math involved, and solve the problem by using the numbers that you picked in step 1, which will yield another number as a result – this is going to be your *"virtual"* answer.
Note: Once you arrive at your virtual answer – underline or circle it.

STEP 3: Test Each Answer-Choice: Evaluate each of the five answer choices with the numbers you had originally picked in step 1. That is, take the numbers you picked for the variables and plug them into the variables in each answer-choice, dropping the ones that don't agree with the conditions given in the question-stem. Whichever answer-choice yields your virtual answer that you had obtained above in step 2, assuming only one choice results in the same number as in the problem, is the correct answer to the question.
Order: The order in which you test the answer choices is not important. However, it makes sense to start with the easiest answer-choice to compute and work towards the hardest. Keep in mind, if the answer choices are too complicated, this approach may take longer than the usual time.

STEP 4: One choice may give you the correct answer, but you must make sure to evaluate each and every answer-choice before making your final selection, even if you have already found the one that works.
Note: Don't stop if the answer-choice you try gives you the same answer that you had obtained originally. Different answer choices may give the same result for one assignment of quantities.

STEP 5: Try different values when more than one answer-choice works: If more than one answer-choice works, that is, yields your virtual answer – you need to rework the problem by picking new set of numbers and test only each of the remaining answer choices, which seemed correct the first time around, until only one answer-choice yields your virtual answer. The correct choice must work for all possible real numbers.
Note: Don't worry, this last step doesn't happen very often and is rarely necessary!
In general, in most cases if you follow our guidelines you can prevent this from happening, and you'll be left with only one correct answer. If not, continue plugging in different set of numbers until you're left with only one correct answer. You wouldn't have to pick another set of numbers to plug-in; and even if you do have to pick another set of numbers to plug-in, you will never have to pick a set of numbers to plug-in the third time. In most cases, you should be able to find the answers with the first pick, if not then the second pick, but you almost never have to make a third attempt. Therefore, in almost all cases you'll be able to eliminate all the incorrect choices in the first attempt itself.

EZ CAUTION: Make sure that you plug-in the same numbers that you had originally picked, that is, keep the values you've picked for the variables constant throughout the problem. Hence, if a variable appears more than once in the same problem, it must be replaced by the same number each time it appears.

TIPS AND GUIDELINES FOR PICKING EZ SMART NUMBERS:
While using EZ Plug-In Numbers Strategy, you should pick EZ smart numbers that you plug-in for the variables. As we already mentioned above, these questions use variables (indicated by letters) to represent the values that you are asked to consider. You can make the problem more concrete by making "logical" substitutions of numbers for the variables. Although these types of problems are designed to work with any number, you'll realize that certain numbers work better than other numbers. Hence, our method will work with any numbers; however, things will be a lot easier if you keep in mind the following guidelines and tips when selecting numbers to plug-in.

When picking a number on a variable problem, there is no golden number to pick, you just have to pick numbers that meet the conditions given in the problem. Try your best to pick simple numbers that are easy to work with and will make the calculations simpler. For instance, let's say a problem involves five consecutive numbers. It would be easier to pick 1, 2, 3, 4, and 5. Alternatively, of course, you could also pick some "ugly" numbers, such as, 17,578, 17, 579, 17,580, 17,581, and 17,582. Either way, the math will still work out the same; however, with the second selection, you will make your life miserable by making the calculations much tougher than necessary, and still get the same result.

Sometimes the best way to select a number is to use a little common sense and logic while picking numbers to plug-in or substitute. For instance, if the problem involves hours and days, it might make sense to pick 24. Likewise, if the problem involves minutes and hours, a good number would probably be 60.

Pick numbers and replace the variables with numbers that are easy-to-use, not necessarily the ones that make sense in real life. It's perfectly fine to ignore reality while picking numbers. For instance, a school can have 5 students or 10,000 students; apples can cost $1 or $10 each; cars or trains can go at 5 miles per hour or 1,000 miles per hour – it really doesn't matter!

The success and effectiveness of this strategy depends primarily on your ability to pick easy convenient numbers. Make sure you check the special cases to get the full picture. Therefore, while picking number(s) to plug-in – try to pick numbers that will make the problem easy for you to work on.

Following are some guidelines for deciding which numbers to use while applying this strategy:
- Try to pick easy positive numbers, such as 2, 3, 5, 10, etc., or negative numbers, such as –2, –3, –5, –10, etc.
- Pick numbers between 0 & 1; and 0 & –1 (such as, ¼, ½, 1/5, etc. are often useful)
- The best big numbers to pick are the multiples of 10 (such as, 10, 100, etc., are sometimes useful)
- Try to pick numbers from both sides of the topic tested in the question. For instance, if the question is about positive versus negative, plug in both a positive number and a negative number.

NUMBERS TO AVOID PICKING: Avoid picking numbers with special properties that may make more than one answer choice work. For instance: for a certain question, let's suppose you plug in $x = 5$, and your answer works out to be 25. Now, if $5x$ and x^2 are both among the answer choices, you'll have two choices that match your intermediate answer, and you'll have to re-work these two options again by picking different numbers.
Keep in mind the following in order to avoid cases in which more than one answer-choice works:
(A) Try to avoid picking numbers 0 or 1: Since 0 times any number is 0, and 1 times any number does not change that number, these may result in more than one correct answer-choice.
(B) Try to avoid picking numbers that already appear in the question-stem or the answer choices. If there is a number that already exists in the problem, it may result in more than one correct answer-choice.
(C) Try to avoid picking the same numbers for different variables. While picking numbers on a problem containing more than one variable, make sure to pick a different number for each variable. If you pick the same number for two different variables, it may result in more than one correct answer-choice.
Therefore, avoid using 0, 1, any number that is already in the question-stem/answer choices, or the same number for different variables, because these numbers have special properties. Often, when you plug-in one of these numbers, you may find that more than one answer-choice appears to work, and then you have to try plugging-in another number to decide among the remaining answer choices.

The following examples will not only help you better understand the concept given above, but they will also illustrate how to implement it in a real test-question:

Example #1A: If 2 apples cost $4 dollars, then how many dollars would 5 apples cost?
(A) $2.50   (B) $1.60   (C) $10.00   (D) $0.625   (E) $0.40

Solution: Price of 2 apples = $4
Price of 1 apple = $4 ÷ 2 = $2
Price of 10 apples = $2 × 5 = $10
Therefore, the correct answer is (C).

Example #1B: If n apples cost p dollars, then how many dollars would m apples cost?

(A) $\dfrac{mn}{p}$ (B) $\dfrac{np}{m}$ (C) $\dfrac{mp}{n}$ (D) $\dfrac{m}{np}$ (E) $\dfrac{p}{mn}$

Solution A: **Using EZ Plug-In Numbers Method:**
The question asks: If n apples cost p dollars, then how many dollars would m apples cost?
Pick EZ smart numbers   ⇒ $n = 2$, $p = 4$, $m = 5$
The question now becomes: If 2 apples cost 4 dollars, then how many dollars would 5 apples cost?
This is easy to find, we can get the price of 5 apples by setting up a simple direct proportion:
$$\Rightarrow \frac{2}{5} = \frac{4}{x}$$
⇒ $2x = 20$
⇒ $x = 10$
So when $n = 2$, $p = 4$, and $m = 5$, the correct answer should equal 10.
Now, let's plug-in these numbers in each of the answer choices and find out which one equals 10.

(A) $\dfrac{mn}{p}$ $\Rightarrow \dfrac{5 \times 2}{4}$ $\Rightarrow \dfrac{10}{4}$ $\Rightarrow 2.5$ ✗

(B) $\dfrac{np}{m}$ $\Rightarrow \dfrac{2 \times 4}{5}$ $\Rightarrow \dfrac{8}{5}$ $\Rightarrow 1.6$ ✗

(C) $\dfrac{mp}{n}$ $\Rightarrow \dfrac{5 \times 4}{2}$ $\Rightarrow \dfrac{20}{2}$ $\Rightarrow 10$ ✓

(D) $\dfrac{m}{np}$ $\Rightarrow \dfrac{5}{2 \times 4}$ $\Rightarrow \dfrac{5}{8}$ $\Rightarrow 0.625$ ✗

(E) $\dfrac{p}{mn}$ $\Rightarrow \dfrac{4}{5 \times 2}$ $\Rightarrow \dfrac{4}{10}$ $\Rightarrow 0.4$ ✗

Therefore, the correct answer is (C), since that's the only one that yields 10.

Solution B: **Using EZ Direct Method:**
The question asks: If n apples cost p dollars, then how many dollars would m apples cost?
Since quantity and price are directly proportional, let's set up a direct proportion.
Let the price of m apples be "x"

$\Rightarrow \dfrac{n}{m} = \dfrac{p}{x}$

$\Rightarrow nx = mp$ [cross multiply both sides of the equation]

$\Rightarrow x = \dfrac{mp}{n}$ [divide both sides of the equation by n]

Therefore, if n apples cost p dollars, then m apples would cost $\dfrac{mp}{n}$ dollars.

Example #2:   If a school needs p pencils each month for each student, and is there are s students in the school, for how many months will a stock of q pencils last?

(A) $\dfrac{pq}{s}$ (B) $\dfrac{ps}{q}$ (C) $\dfrac{qs}{p}$ (D) $\dfrac{p}{qs}$ (E) $\dfrac{q}{ps}$

Solution A: **Using EZ Plug-In Numbers Method:**
Let's Pick EZ smart numbers $\Rightarrow$ the school needs 2 pencils each month for each student $\Rightarrow p = 2$
                                     $\Rightarrow$ the school has 5 students $\Rightarrow s = 5$
                                     $\Rightarrow$ the school has a stock of 20 pencils $\Rightarrow q = 20$
The school needs $2 \times 5 = 10$ pencils per month; therefore, the stock of 20 pencils will last 2 months.
Now, lets plug-in $p = 2$, $s = 5$, $q = 20$ in each of the answer choices and find out which one equals 2.

(A) $\dfrac{pq}{s}$ $\Rightarrow \dfrac{2 \times 20}{5}$ $= \dfrac{40}{5}$ $= 8$ ✗

(B) $\dfrac{ps}{q}$ $\Rightarrow \dfrac{2 \times 5}{20}$ $= \dfrac{10}{20}$ $= \frac{1}{2}$ ✗

(C) $\dfrac{qs}{p}$ $\Rightarrow \dfrac{20 \times 5}{2}$ $= \dfrac{100}{2}$ $= 50$ ✗

(D) $\dfrac{p}{qs}$ $\Rightarrow \dfrac{2}{20 \times 5}$ $= \dfrac{2}{100}$ $= \dfrac{1}{50}$ ✗

(E) $\dfrac{q}{ps}$ $\Rightarrow \dfrac{20}{2 \times 5}$ $= \dfrac{20}{10}$ $= 2$ ✓

Therefore, the correct answer is (E), since that's the only one that yields 2.

Solution B: **Using EZ Direct Method:**
Number of pencils needed for each student each month = p
Number of students = s
Total number of pencils needed each month = ps
Stock of pencil = q
$\Rightarrow$ Number of months a stock of q pencil will last = q/ps

8.2.1: EZ PLUG-IN NUMBERS STRATEGY FOR COMPLEX WORD PROBLEMS:

EZ Plug-In Numbers Strategy can often simplify some of the most complex word problems. Since they are some of the most difficult types of problems on the test, you should expect them to be tricky with many traps. Reading them for the first time might make your head spin and you may get totally stumped. Without the knowledge of our EZ Plug-In Numbers Strategy, you might be baffled by such questions. However, they'll become much simpler when you try to solve them using EZ Plug-in Numbers Strategy by substituting numbers in place of the variables. You'll be able to answer them quickly and easily than working out the algebra.

Example #3:   A machine produces s screws every hour at a cost of c cents per screw. If the machine operates for h hours and m minutes, how much money will it spend, in dollars, on the production of screws?

(A) $\dfrac{(60h+m)cs}{600}$ (B) $\dfrac{(h+m)cs}{600}$ (C) $\dfrac{(h+60m)cs}{100}$ (D) $\dfrac{(h+m)cs}{6000}$ (E) $\dfrac{(60h+m)cs}{6000}$

Solution: Let's start by picking EZ smart numbers.
Assume that the machine produces 10 screws per hour at a cost of 5 cents each.
Then, it spends 50 cents per hour on manufacturing screws, and in 2 hours and 30 minutes (2.5 hours), it will spend $1.25.
Now let's plug in $s = 10$, $c = 5$, $h = 2$, $m = 30$ in the answer choices & see which one yields 1.25 or 5/4

(A) $\dfrac{(60h+m)cs}{600}$ $\Rightarrow$ $\dfrac{[60(2)+30](5)(10)}{600}$ $\Rightarrow$ $\dfrac{(150)(50)}{600}$ $\Rightarrow$ $\dfrac{25}{2}$ ✗

(B) $\dfrac{(h+m)cs}{600}$ $\Rightarrow$ $\dfrac{(2+30)(5)(10)}{600}$ $\Rightarrow$ $\dfrac{(32)(50)}{600}$ $\Rightarrow$ $\dfrac{8}{3}$ ✗

(C) $\dfrac{(h+60m)cs}{100}$ $\Rightarrow$ $\dfrac{[2+60(30)](5)(10)}{100}$ $\Rightarrow$ $\dfrac{(182)(50)}{100}$ $\Rightarrow 91$ ✗

(D) $\dfrac{(h+m)cs}{6000}$ $\Rightarrow$ $\dfrac{(2+30)(5)(10)}{6000}$ $\Rightarrow$ $\dfrac{(32)(50)}{6000}$ $\Rightarrow \dfrac{4}{15}$ ✗

(E) $\dfrac{(60h+m)cs}{6000}$ $\Rightarrow$ $\dfrac{[60(2)+30](5)(10)}{6000}$ $\Rightarrow$ $\dfrac{(150)(50)}{6000}$ $\Rightarrow \dfrac{5}{4}$ ✓

Therefore, the correct answer is (E), since that's the only one that yields 5/4.

8.2.2: WHEN EZ PLUG-IN NUMBERS STRATEGY IS ESSENTIAL:

There are certain problems that can only be answered by using our EZ Plug-In Numbers Strategy. These problems are somewhat different from other questions, and are quite unusual. Most students find problems like these astounding and baffling. In these problems, you are asked to reason through word problems involving only variables. In such cases, the use of this strategy is absolutely essential; without it, these problems are impossible to solve.

Example #4:   If m is less than n, which of the following numbers is greater than m and less than n?

(A) mn (B) $n^2 - m^2$ (C) $\dfrac{m+n}{2}$ (D) $n - m$ (E) $\dfrac{mn}{2}$

Solution: Plug-in any two number for m and n, such that $m < n$
Pick EZ smart numbers $\Rightarrow m = 5$ and $n = 7$
Now let's plug these numbers in the answer-choice and see which one results in a value that is greater than m but less than n, i.e., in between 5 and 7:

(A) mn $\Rightarrow (5)(7)$ $= 35$ ✗

(B) $n^2 - m^2$ $\Rightarrow (7)^2 - (5)^2 = 49 - 25$ $= 24$ ✗

(C) $\dfrac{m+n}{2}$ $\Rightarrow \dfrac{5+7}{2} = \dfrac{12}{2}$ $= 6$ ✓

(D) $n - m$ $\Rightarrow 7 - 5$ $= 2$ ✗

(E) $\dfrac{mn}{2}$ $\Rightarrow \dfrac{5 \times 7}{2} = \dfrac{35}{2}$ $= 17.5$ ✗

Therefore, the correct answer is (C), since that's the only one that yields a value between 5 and 7.

Example #5: If the product of three consecutive integers written in increasing order equals the middle integer, what is the LEAST of the three integers?
(A) 2   (B) 1   (C) 0   (D) –2   (E) –1

Solution: Product of Three Consecutive Integers = Middle Integer
$\Rightarrow$ 1st Integer × 2nd Integer × 3rd Integer = 2nd Integer
Now let's try each one of the answer-choice and see which one satisfies this condition:

(A) 2 $\Rightarrow$ If this is the answer then it must be true that $2 \times 3 \times 4 = 3$ ✗

(B) 1 $\Rightarrow$ If this is the answer then it must be true that $1 \times 2 \times 3 = 2$ ✗

(C) 0 $\Rightarrow$ If this is the answer then it must be true that $0 \times 1 \times 2 = 1$ ✗

(D) –2 $\Rightarrow$ If this is the answer then it must be true that $-2 \times -1 \times 0 = -1$ ✗

(E) –1 $\Rightarrow$ If this is the answer then it must be true that $-1 \times 0 \times 1 = 0$ ✓
Therefore, the correct answer is (E), since that's the only one that satisfies the given condition.

8.2.3: EZ Plug-In Numbers Strategy in Odd/Even Problems:
EZ Plug-In Numbers is the best way to tackle odd/even questions. These types of problems are usually not tricky; all you need to do is apply the plug-in numbers strategy. You'll see that picking numbers strategy works especially well with even/odd questions.

Example #6: If m and n are odd integers, which of the following must be an even integer?
(A) $m(n-2)$ (B) $mn + 2$ (C) $(m+2)(n-2)$ (D) $m(n+6)$ (E) $5m + 7n$

Solution: According to the condition given in the question: m and n are both odd integers.
Pick EZ smart numbers $\Rightarrow m = 3$ and $n = 5$
Now let's substitute these numbers in the answer choices and see which one yields an even integer:

(A) $m(n-2)$ $\Rightarrow 3(5-2)$ $= 3(3)$ $= 9$ ✗

(B) $mn + 2$ $\Rightarrow (3)(5) + 2$ $= 15 + 2$ $= 17$ ✗

(C) $(m+2)(n-2)$ $\Rightarrow (3+2)(5-2) = (5)(3)$ $= 15$ ✗

(D) $m(n+6)$ $\Rightarrow 3(5+6)$ $= 3(11)$ $= 33$ ✗

(E) $5m + 7n$ $\Rightarrow 5(3) + 7(5)$ $= 15 + 35$ $= 50$ ✓
Therefore, the correct answer is (E), since that's the only one that yields an even integer.

Example #7: If m is an odd integer and n is an even integer, which of the following must be an odd integer?
(A) $2m + n$ (B) mn (C) $m + 2n$ (D) m^2n (E) mn^2

Solution: According to the condition given in the question: m is an odd integer and n is an even integer.
Pick EZ smart numbers $\Rightarrow m = 3$ and $n = 2$
Now let's substitute these numbers in the answer choices and see which one yields an odd integer:

(A) $2m + n$ $\Rightarrow 2(3) + 2$ $= 6 + 2$ $= 8$ ✗

(B) mn $\Rightarrow (3)(2)$ $= 6$ $= 6$ ✗

(C) $m + 2n$ $\Rightarrow 3 + 2(2)$ $= 3 + 4$ $= 7$ ✓

(D) m^2n $\Rightarrow (3)^2 \times 2$ $= 9 \times 2$ $= 18$ ✗

(E) mn^2 $\Rightarrow 3 \times (2)^2$ $= 3 \times 4$ $= 12$ ✗
Therefore, the correct answer is (C), since that's the only one that yields an odd integer.

EZ Tip: While adding, subtracting, or multiplying even and odd numbers, you can generally assume that whatever happens with one pair of numbers generally happens with similar pairs of numbers.

8.2.4: SPECIAL CASES – WHEN MORE THAN ONE CHOICE WORKS:

While using EZ Plug-In Numbers Strategy, sometimes more than one choice will yield the correct result. When that happens, you must pick another set of numbers to filter out the coincidences. Hence, when you have more than one answer-choice that gives the right answer, you have to pick another set of numbers that works only for one of the remaining answer choices. Look at the following examples:

Example #8:   If $n > 1$, what is the value of $\dfrac{2n + 6}{n^2 + 2n - 3}$

(A) n (B) $\dfrac{n-1}{2}$ (C) $n + 5$ (D) $\dfrac{5n}{2}$ (E) $\dfrac{2}{n-1}$

Solution: According to the condition given in the question: $n > 1$
Pick EZ smart numbers $\Rightarrow n = 2$
Now substitute 2 for n in the question-stem and see which one will yield the following:
$$\Rightarrow \frac{2n + 6}{n^2 + 2n - 3} = \frac{2(2) + 6}{(2)^2 + 2(2) - 3} = \frac{4 + 6}{4 + 4 - 3} = \frac{10}{5} = 2$$
Next, check the answer choices and see which one gives us 2 when $n = 2$

(A) n $\Rightarrow 2$ ✓

(B) $\dfrac{n-1}{2}$ $\Rightarrow \dfrac{2-1}{2} = \frac{1}{2}$ ✗

(C) $n + 5$ $\Rightarrow 2 + 5 = 7$ ✗

(D) $\dfrac{5n}{2}$ $\Rightarrow \dfrac{5(2)}{2} = 5$ ✗

(E) $\dfrac{2}{n-1}$ $\Rightarrow \dfrac{2}{2-1} = 2$ ✓

Unfortunately, as you can see, both answer-choice (A) and (E) results in 2.
This narrows down the possibilities to (A) and (E).
Next, pick another integer for n that is greater than 1: $n = 3$
Now let's substitute 3 for n in the question-stem and see which one will yield the following:
$$\Rightarrow \frac{2n + 6}{n^2 + 2n - 3} = \frac{2(3) + 6}{(3)^2 + 2(3) - 3} = \frac{6 + 6}{9 + 6 - 3} = \frac{12}{12} = 1$$
Next, check the answer choices and see which one gives us 1 when $n = 3$.

(A) n $\Rightarrow 3$ ✗

(E) $\dfrac{2}{n-1}$ $\Rightarrow \dfrac{2}{3-1} = 1$ ✓

Therefore, the correct answer is (E), since that's the only one that still yields 1.

EZ CAUTION: Always remember to try out all the answer choices while using the picking numbers strategy. If you ignored to do this, you might have picked (A) before seeing that (E) also works.

Example #9:   If x and y are consecutive positive integers, which of the following must be an even integer?

(A) xy (B) $xy + 1$ (C) $x + y$ (D) $xy - 1$ (E) $\dfrac{xy}{2}$

Solution: Let's plug-in any two consecutive positive integers for x and y.
Pick EZ smart numbers $\Rightarrow x = 3$ and $y = 4$
Now let's plug these numbers in the answer-choice and see which one results in an even integer:

(A) xy $\Rightarrow 3 \times 4$ = 12   ✓

(B) $xy + 1$ $\Rightarrow (3)(4) + 1$ = 12 + 1   = 13   ✗

(C) $x + y$ $\Rightarrow 3 + 4$ = 7   ✗

(D) $xy - 1$ $\Rightarrow (3)(4) - 1$ = 12 - 1   = 11   ✗

(E) $\dfrac{xy}{2}$ $\Rightarrow \dfrac{(3)(4)}{2}$ $= \dfrac{12}{2}$ $= 6$ ✓

As you can see two of the answer choices yielded even integers.
We first tried odd and even integers, this time let's try even and odd integers.
Let's assume that $\Rightarrow x = 2$ and $y = 3$

(A) xy $\Rightarrow 2 \times 3$ $= 6$ ✓

(E) $\dfrac{xy}{2}$ $\Rightarrow \dfrac{(2)(3)}{2}$ $= \dfrac{6}{2}$ $= 3$ ✗

Therefore, the correct answer is (A), since that's the only one that still yields an even integer.

8.3   EZ PLUG-IN FOR MULTIPLE VARIABLE EQUATIONS

For solving problems with multiple variables, the same EZ Plug-In Numbers Strategy explained earlier can be applied. If a problem consists of several variables that are all related in one equation, apply the following steps:

EZ STEP-BY-STEP METHOD: While using our "EZ Plug-In Number" Strategy, apply the following steps:
STEP 1: Pick numbers for all the variables except one.
STEP 2: Next, solve the equation to find the value of the variable for which you didn't pick a number.
STEP 3: This will give you the values of all the variables in the given equation.
STEP 4: Finally, plug-in these numbers in the answer choice and find the correct matches.

Note: In this case, there are no magic numbers to pick; however, try to pick simple numbers, which yield an integer answer.

Example #1:   If $x = \dfrac{y + 10}{z}$, what is the value of y in terms of x and z?

(A) $\dfrac{xz}{10}$ (B) $x(10 - z)$ (C) $xz - 10$ (D) $10(x - z)$ (E) $10xz$

Solution A: **Using EZ Plug-In Numbers Method:**
Since there is an equation with three variables, we'll have to pick numbers for all but two of the variables. Pick EZ smart numbers $\Rightarrow z = 2$ and $y = 6$

$\Rightarrow x = \dfrac{y + 10}{z} = \dfrac{6 + 10}{2} = \dfrac{16}{2} = 8$

So when $z = 2$ and $y = 6$, $x = 8$
Now, let's plug-in $z = 2$ and $x = 8$ in each of the answer choices and see which one gives $y = 6$

(A) $\dfrac{xz}{10}$ $\Rightarrow \dfrac{8 \times 2}{10}$ $\Rightarrow \dfrac{16}{10}$ $\Rightarrow 1.6$ ✗

(B) $x(10 - z)$ $\Rightarrow 8(10 - 2)$ $\Rightarrow 8(8)$ $\Rightarrow 64$ ✗

(C) $xz - 10$ $\Rightarrow (8)(2) - 10$ $\Rightarrow 16 - 10$ $\Rightarrow 6$ ✓

(D) $10(x - z)$ $\Rightarrow 10(8 - 2)$ $\Rightarrow 10(6)$ $\Rightarrow 60$ ✗

(E) $10xz$ $\Rightarrow 10(8)(2)$ $\Rightarrow 10(16)$ $\Rightarrow 160$ ✗

Therefore, the correct answer is (C), since that's the only one that yields $y = 6$.

Solution B: **Using Direct Method:**

$x = \dfrac{y + 10}{z}$

$\Rightarrow xz = y + 10$ [cross-multiply both sides of the equation]
$\Rightarrow y = xz - 10$ [subtract 10 from both sides of the equation]

8.4   EZ PLUG-IN FOR SPECIAL FORMAT ANSWERS

Occasionally, you may get questions that contain a special phrase in the answer choices. Following are such five types of special phrases:
- "CANNOT BE" – Finding out the EXCEPTION
- "ALWAYS" or "MUST BE" – Find out the option which must always hold true.
- "COULD BE"
- "NOT ENOUGH INFORMATION GIVEN" – Can't be solved
- "ROMAN NUMERAL" Format Answer-Choices

Such types of questions usually test your knowledge of the properties of various kinds of numbers (e.g., odd and even, positive and negative, etc.). There is often no way to proceed answering these question except by applying one of our EZ Alternative Strategies, that is, examining each of the five options. Such types of problems can only be solved with multiple answer choices, and there is no one numeric right answer. Therefore, to answer such problems, you have to analyze the options as part of your solution strategy and look for information in the answer choices. You may also have to consider each answer-choice before picking your correct answer. Moreover, you may need to plug-in more than once, especially on the Roman numeral problems.

8.4.1: EZ STRATEGY FOR "CANNOT BE" TYPE OF QUESTIONS:

There are some problems that ask for the "EXCEPTIONS", and they usually use phrases such as, "which of the following could not be……." or "which of the following cannot be……." etc.

The best way to solve such types of problems is to first determine the conditions given in the question-stem, and then figure out which one of the answer choices does NOT fit that condition under all situations. The following example will help you understand this strategy:

Example #1:   If the ratio of boys to girls at a school picnic is 7:5, which of the following could NOT be the total number of children at the picnic?
(A) 24   (B) 96   (C) 150   (D) 192   (E) 900

Solution: If $7x$ and $5x$ are the number of boys and the number of girls, respectively, at the picnic, then:
The number of children present at the school picnic = $7x + 5x = 12x$.
Therefore, the number of children must be a multiple of 12.
Now, let's see which one of the given answer-choice is not a multiple of 12:

(A) 24 $\Rightarrow 24 \div 12 = 2$ $\Rightarrow$ Evenly divisible by 12   ✓

(B) 96 $\Rightarrow 96 \div 12 = 8$ $\Rightarrow$ Evenly divisible by 12   ✓

(C) 150 $\Rightarrow 150 \div 12 = 12.5$ $\Rightarrow$ NOT evenly divisible by 12 ✗

(D) 192 $\Rightarrow 192 \div 12 = 16$ $\Rightarrow$ Evenly divisible by 12   ✓

(E) 900 $\Rightarrow 900 \div 12 = 75$ $\Rightarrow$ Evenly divisible by 12   ✓

$\Rightarrow$ Since, only answer-choice (C) 150 is not divisible by 12, and therefore it's not possible to have 150 children at the picnic in the given ratio.

EZ EXCEPTION: In the example given above, if instead of the ratio of boys to girls, the ratio given was that of strawberry ice-cream and raspberry ice-cream: Assume that the ratio of the number of pounds of strawberry ice-cream to the number of pounds of raspberry ice-cream consumed at the school picnic was 7:5. Then, it is possible that a total of exactly 150 pounds of these two flavors of ice-creams were consumed: 87.5 pounds of strawberry ice-cream and 62.5 pounds of raspberry ice-cream. In the example given above, however, 150 isn't a possible answer because there has to be a whole number of boys and girls. So be careful, there are some countable quantities that can exclusively be represented in terms of whole numbers, such as, boys and girls, pass and fail, etc.

8.4.2: EZ STRATEGY FOR "ALWAYS" TYPE OF QUESTIONS:

There are some problems that ask for the "ALWAYS" or "MUST BE", and they usually use phrases such as, "which of the following always has to……." or "which of the following must be……." etc.

The best way to solve such types of problems is to first determine the conditions given in the question-stem, and then figure out which one of the answer choices MUST fit that condition under all situations. The following example will help you understand this strategy:

Example #2: If m and n are both odd integers, which of the following must be an even integer?
(A) $2m + n$ (B) mn (C) $mn + 2$ (D) $m + n + 1$ (E) $m + n$

Solution: Let's plug-in any two odd integers for m and n.
Let $m = 5$ and $n = 7$
Now let's plug these numbers in the answer-choice and see which one results in an even integer:

(A) $2m + n$ $\Rightarrow 2(5) + 7 = 10 + 7$ $= 17$ $\Rightarrow$ Odd ✘

(B) mn $\Rightarrow (5)(7)$ $= 35$ $\Rightarrow$ Odd ✘

(C) $mn + 2$ $\Rightarrow (5)(7) + 2 = 35 + 2$ $= 37$ $\Rightarrow$ Odd ✘

(D) $m + n + 1$ $\Rightarrow 5 + 7 + 1$ $= 13$ $\Rightarrow$ Odd ✘

(E) $m + n$ $\Rightarrow 5 + 7$ $= 12$ $\Rightarrow$ Even ✔

Therefore, the correct answer is (E), since that's the only answer-choice, which yields an even integer.

8.4.3: EZ STRATEGY FOR "COULD BE" TYPE OF QUESTIONS:

There are some problems that ask for the "COULD BE" or "CAN BE", and they usually use phrases such as, "which of the following could be……." or "which of the following can be……." etc.

The best way to solve such types of problems is to first determine the conditions given in the question-stem, and then figure out which one of the answer choices COULD fit that condition. The following example will help you understand this strategy:

Example #3: If n is an integer, which of the following could be an even integer?
(A) $\dfrac{19}{n}$ (B) $\dfrac{17}{n}$ (C) $\dfrac{n}{7}$ (D) $\dfrac{13}{n}$ (E) $\dfrac{11}{n}$

Solution: Let's test each one of the answer choices and see which one could result in an even integer:

(A) $\dfrac{19}{n}$ $\Rightarrow$ The only factors of 19 are 1 & 19, and if n is any of these two, it will results in odd integer.

(B) $\dfrac{17}{n}$ $\Rightarrow$ The only factors of 17 are 1 & 17, and if n is any of these two, it will results in odd integer.

(C) $\dfrac{n}{7}$ $\Rightarrow$ The multiples of 7 are many, such as, 14, 21, 28, etc, and if n is 14, it will results in 2, which is an even integer.

(D) $\dfrac{13}{n}$ $\Rightarrow$ The only factors of 13 are 1 & 13, and if n is any of these two, it will results in odd integer.

(E) $\dfrac{11}{n}$ $\Rightarrow$ The only factors of 11 are 1 & 11, and if n is any of these two, it will results in odd integer.

Therefore, the correct answer is (C), since that's the only answer-choice, which yields an even integer.

8.4.4: EZ STRATEGY FOR "NOT ENOUGH INFO GIVEN" TYPE OF QUESTIONS:

There are some problems that ask for the "NOT ENOUGH INFORMATION GIVEN", and they usually use phrases such as, "Not enough information given……." or "Cannot be determined from the given information" etc.

The best way to solve such types of problems is to determine what is needed to solve the problem, and whether there is enough information given in order to solve the problem. If you think that the problem is impossible to solve with the amount of information given, pick this answer-choice; however, be fairly certain before you choose this option. Also, make sure you haven't missed some pertinent information or there isn't an alternate strategy that would allow you to solve the problem from the given information. If you think there is sufficient information given in the problem in order to solve, then you can completely eliminate this answer-choice, and focus on the rest of the answer choices. The following example will help you understand this strategy:

Example #4: The four sides of a parallelogram measure 8 feet, 2 feet, 8 feet, and 2 feet. What is the area of the parallelogram in square feet?
(A) 10 　　　(B) 16 　　　(C) 20 　　　(D) 24 　　　(E) Not enough information is given

Solution: The formula for the area of parallelogram is base times height; however, since in this case we don't know the height, it's impossible to find its area, and hence, there is not enough information given. Therefore, the correct answer is (E).

8.4.5: EZ STRATEGY FOR "ROMAN NUMERAL" FORMAT:

Another type of multiple-choice questions that could appear on your test is the Roman numeral-type questions. These questions consist of three different statements labeled I, II, and III. The five answer choices give various combinations of the given three labeled statements.
- the case could be that only one of the statements is true, or
- the case could be that only two of the statements are true, or
- the case could be that all three statements are true

Chances are that you are not familiar with this type of question format. Don't worry; they are actually a lot easier than they may appear, and the math that's being tested can become significantly easier if you follow our method.

EZ STEP-BY-STEP METHOD: While solving Roman Numeral Format questions, apply the following steps:
STEP 1: First, evaluate each Roman numeral statement as a separate true/false question.
STEP 2: Next, figure out the validity of each of the three statements, determining whether it must be true or not, and mark with a "T" for True or an "F" for False.
STEP 3: Finally, you have to pick the answer choice that lists only the statements that hold true, that is, look for the answer that matches your "T's" and "F's".

EZ Elimination Technique for Roman-Numeral Format Questions: Determining the validity of one statement may let you eliminate more than one answer choice. For instance,
- if you can determine that Statement I is correct ⇒ then you can immediately eliminate every choice that doesn't list Statement I
- if you can determine that Statement I isn't correct ⇒ then you immediately eliminate every choice that does list Statement I

EZ HINT: While picking numbers for variables in Roman numeral problems, consider positive number, negative numbers, and fractions/decimals. You must remember that not all numbers are positive integers. Don't overlook the fact that there are negative numbers and fractions/decimals as well. This is particularly important because negative numbers and fractions between 0 and 1 perform very differently from positive integers.

Example #5: If $n \neq 0$, then which of the following must be true?
I. $n^2 > n$
II. $2n > n$
III. $n + 1 > n$
(A) I only 　　(B) II only 　　(C) III only 　　(D) I and III 　　(E) I, II, and III

Solution: Let's use the picking-numbers technique to evaluate the truth of this statement. So let's evaluate one statement at a time and see which ones have to be true for any kind of number:

Statement I: $n^2 > n$

Input a positive integer: $\Rightarrow n = 5$
$\Rightarrow n^2 = 5^2 = 25$
$\Rightarrow 25 > 5$
$\Rightarrow n^2 > n$ TRUE

Input a negative integer: $\Rightarrow n = -5$
$\Rightarrow n^2 = (-5)^2 = 25$
$\Rightarrow 25 > -5$
$\Rightarrow n^2 > n$ TRUE

Input a fraction: $\Rightarrow n = \frac{1}{2}$
$\Rightarrow n^2 = \frac{1}{4}$
$\Rightarrow \frac{1}{4} > \frac{1}{2}$
$\Rightarrow n^2 > n$ FALSE

Statement II: $2n > n$

Input a positive integer: $\Rightarrow n = 5$
$\Rightarrow 2n = 10$
$\Rightarrow 10 > 5$
$\Rightarrow 2n > n$ TRUE

Input a negative integer: $\Rightarrow n = -5$
$\Rightarrow 2n = -10$
$\Rightarrow -10 > -5$
$\Rightarrow 2n > n$ FALSE

Input a fraction: $\Rightarrow n = \frac{1}{4}$
$\Rightarrow 2n = \frac{1}{2}$
$\Rightarrow \frac{1}{2} > \frac{1}{4}$
$\Rightarrow 2n > n$ TRUE

Statement III: $n + 1 > n$

Input a positive integer: $\Rightarrow n = 5$
$\Rightarrow n + 1 = 6$
$\Rightarrow 6 > 5$
$\Rightarrow n + 1 > n$ TRUE

Input a negative integer: $\Rightarrow n = -2$
$\Rightarrow n + 1 = -1$
$\Rightarrow -1 > -2$
$\Rightarrow n + 1 > n$ TRUE

Input a fraction: $\Rightarrow n = \frac{1}{2}$
$\Rightarrow n + 1 = \frac{1}{2} + 1 = 1.5$
$\Rightarrow 1.5 > 0.5$
$\Rightarrow n + 1 > n$ TRUE

Therefore, the correct answer is (C), since only statement III must be true.

Note: In the example above, if you considered only positive integers greater than 1 for the value of n, you would have assumed that all three statements are true. However, as you can see, that is not the case. If you didn't consider fractions or negative numbers, you would have fallen into the trap and answered the question incorrectly. Only statement III must be true, so choice (C) is the correct answer.

▪PRACTICE EXERCISE WITH DETAILED EXPLANATIONS

EZ Plug-in For Numeric Answers:

For Remainder Problems:

Question #1: When "*n*" is divided by 2, the remainder is 1. What is the remainder when 10*n* is divided by 5?
(A) 0   (B) 1   (C) 2   (D) 4   (E) 5

Solution: Since the question asks for the remainder, so that's the invisible variable in the answer choices. Now let's first pick an EZ smart number for remainder.
We have to find a number that leaves a remainder of 1 when divided by 2.
Since the remainder when *n* is divided by 2 is 1, pick any multiple of 2 and add 1.
The easiest multiple to work with is 2 itself.
Hence, a good selection would be (2 + 1) = 3, since when 3 is divided by 2, the remainder is 1.
Now plug-in 3 for *n* and see what happens to the remainder when:
$\Rightarrow$ 10*n* is divided by 5
$\Rightarrow$ 10(3) is dived by 5
$\Rightarrow$ 30 is divided by 5
$\Rightarrow$ 30 ÷ 5 = 6 with remainder 0
Therefore, if *n* = 3, then 10*n* = 30, which, when divided by 5, leaves a remainder of 0.
Note: this problem doesn't depend on knowing the value of *n*. In fact, *n* has an infinite number of possible values. The reminder will remain to be 0 regardless of the value of *n*.
Therefore, the correct answer is (A).

For Problems with Percents as Answer Choices:

Question #2: The price of an article increased by 20 percent in 1997 and it decreased by 25 percent in 1998. What was the percent change in the price in the whole two-year period?
A) 1%   (B) 5%   (C) 10%   (D) 50%   (E) 100%

Solution: Since the question asks for the percent change in price, so that's the invisible variable in the answer choices. Now let's first pick am EZ smart number for original price.
Since this problem involves percents, lets assume that the original price = 100.
Original Price = $100
Price in 1997 = $100 + (20% of $100) = $100 + $20 = $120
Price in 1998 = $120 – (25% of $120) = $120 – $30 = $90

Total Price Decrease = Original Price – Final Price = $100 – $90 = $10

Since the price fell by $10, the percent decrease = $\dfrac{10}{100}$ × 100% = 10%

Therefore, the correct answer is (C).

For Problems with Fractions as Answer Choices:

Question #3: John spends one-fourth of his salary on rent and two-third less than he spent on rent for the utilities. What fraction of his earnings did he spend on the rent and utilities?
(A) $\dfrac{7}{12}$ (B) $\dfrac{1}{2}$ (C) $\dfrac{5}{12}$ (D) $\dfrac{3}{4}$ (E) $\dfrac{1}{12}$

Solution: Since the question asks for the fraction of John's salary, so that's the invisible variable in the answer choices. Now let's first pick an EZ smart number for total earnings.
The problem involves two fractions: 1/4 and 2/3, let's assume that the total earnings was $12.
(12 is the least common denominator and is divisible by both the denominators 4 and 3)

Amount spent on Rent = $\dfrac{1}{4} \times 12 = 3$

Amount spent on Utilities = $3 - \dfrac{1}{3} \times 3 = 3 - 1 = 2$

Amount spent on Rent + Utilities = $3 + 2 = 5$

Fraction of earning spent of Rent & Utilities = 5 out of 12 = $\dfrac{5}{12}$

Therefore, the correct answer is (C).

For Problems with Ratios as Answer Choices:

Question #4: For a particular trip, a person travels one-twelfth of the total trip by car, one-sixth of the total trip by train, and the rest of the trip by airplane. What is the ratio of the distance covered by car to the distance covered by airplane?

(A) 1:18   (B) 1:12   (C) 1:6   (D) 1:7   (E) 1:9

Solution: Since the question asks for the ratio of the distance covered by car to the distance covered by airplane, so that's the invisible variable in the answer choices. Now let's first pick an EZ smart number for total distance.

The problem involves ratios and fractions, let's assume that the total distance of the whole trip was 12 (the least common denominator of the two fractions 1/12 and 1/6)

Distance covered by car = $\dfrac{1}{12} \times 12 = 1$

Distance covered by train = $\dfrac{1}{6} \times 12 = 2$

Distance covered by airplane = $12 - 1 - 2 = 9$

Ratio $\Rightarrow$ Distance covered by car : Distance covered by airplane = 1:9

Therefore, the correct answer is (E).

EZ Plug-in For Variable Answers:

Question #5: If $a < b$, and c is the sum of a and b, which of the following is the positive difference between b and a?

(A) $2a - c$ (B) $c - a + b$ (C) $2c - a$ (D) $c - a - b$ (E) $2b - c$

Solution A: **Using EZ Plug-In Numbers Method:**

The question asks: If $a < b$, and c is the sum of a and b, which of the following is the positive difference between a and b?

Pick EZ smart numbers $\Rightarrow a = 1$, $b = 2$, $c = 1 + 2 = 3$

Since the positive difference between b and a is 1, the correct answer should equal 1.

Now, let's plug-in these numbers in each of the answer choices, and find out which one equals 1.

(A) $2a - c$ $\Rightarrow 2(1) - 3 = 2 - 3$ $= -1$ ✘

(B) $c - a + b$ $\Rightarrow 3 - 1 + 2$ $= 4$ ✘

(C) $2c - a$ $\Rightarrow 2(3) - 1 = 6 - 1$ $= 5$ ✘

(D) $c - a - b$ $\Rightarrow 3 - 1 - 2$ $= 0$ ✘

(E) $2b - c$ $\Rightarrow 2(2) - 3 = 4 - 3$ $= 1$ ✔

Therefore, the correct answer is (E), since that's the only one that yields 1.

Solution B: **Using EZ Direct Method:**

$\Rightarrow a + b = c$

$\Rightarrow a + b - 2b = c - 2b$ [subtract $2b$ from both sides of the equation]

$\Rightarrow a - b = c - 2b$ [combine like-terms]

$\Rightarrow -(a - b) = -(c - 2b)$ [multiply both sides by -1]

$\Rightarrow b - a = 2b - c$ [apply distributive property]

Question #6: If the sum of five consecutive odd integers is "s", then, in terms of "s", which one of the following is the largest of those integers?

(A) $\dfrac{s-20}{5}$ (B) $\dfrac{s-15}{5}$ (C) $\dfrac{s+10}{5}$ (D) $\dfrac{s+15}{5}$ (E) $\dfrac{s+20}{5}$

Solution A: **Using EZ Plug-In Numbers Method:**
According to the question: "sum of five consecutive odd integers" is "s"
Pick EZ smart numbers: five consecutive odd integers $\Rightarrow$ 1, 3, 5, 7, and 9 (their sum is 25)
Now, plug-in $s = 25$ in all the answer choices and find out which one gives the largest integer, 9.

(A) $\dfrac{s-20}{5}$ $\Rightarrow \dfrac{25-20}{5} = \dfrac{5}{5}$ $= 1$ ✗

(B) $\dfrac{s-15}{5}$ $\Rightarrow \dfrac{25-15}{5} = \dfrac{10}{5}$ $= 2$ ✗

(C) $\dfrac{s+10}{5}$ $\Rightarrow \dfrac{25+10}{5} = \dfrac{35}{5}$ $= 7$ ✗

(D) $\dfrac{s+15}{5}$ $\Rightarrow \dfrac{25+15}{5} = \dfrac{40}{5}$ $= 8$ ✗

(E) $\dfrac{s+20}{5}$ $\Rightarrow \dfrac{25+20}{5} = \dfrac{45}{5}$ $= 9$ ✓

Therefore, the correct answer is (E), since that's the only one that yields 9.

Solution B: **Using EZ Direct Method:**
$\Rightarrow s = n + (n + 2) + (n + 4) + (n + 6) + (n + 8)$
$\Rightarrow s = 5n + 20$ [combine like-terms]
$\Rightarrow 5n = s - 20$ [subtract 20 from both sides of the equation]
$\Rightarrow n = \dfrac{s-20}{5}$ [divide both sides of the equation by 5]

$\Rightarrow n + 8 = \dfrac{s-20}{5} + 8$ [add 8 to both sides of the equation]

$\Rightarrow n + 8 = \dfrac{s-20}{5} + \dfrac{40}{5}$ [rewrite 8 as a fraction with 5 as the denominator]

$\Rightarrow n + 8 = \dfrac{(s-20)+40}{5}$ [combine fractions on right side of the equation]

$\Rightarrow n + 8 = \dfrac{s+20}{5}$ [solve for $n + 8$]

Question #7: If a team played g games and won w of them, what fraction of the games played did the team loose?

(A) $\dfrac{w-g}{w}$ (B) $\dfrac{w-g}{g}$ (C) $\dfrac{g}{g-w}$ (D) $\dfrac{g-w}{w}$ (E) $\dfrac{g-w}{g}$

Solution A: **Using EZ Plug-In Numbers Method:**
Pick EZ smart numbers $\Rightarrow$ Games Played $= g = 3$
                           $\Rightarrow$ Games Won $= w = 2$
                           $\Rightarrow$ Games Lost $= g - w = 3 - 2 = 1$
Fraction of Games Lost $= \dfrac{3-2}{3} = \dfrac{1}{3}$

Now, plug-in these numbers in all the answer choices and find out which one equals 1/3.

(A) $\dfrac{w-g}{w}$ $\Rightarrow \dfrac{2-3}{2} = \dfrac{-1}{2}$ ✗

(B) $\dfrac{w-g}{g}$ $\Rightarrow \dfrac{2-3}{3} = \dfrac{-1}{3}$ ✗

(C) $\dfrac{g}{g-w}$ $\Rightarrow \dfrac{3}{3-2} = \dfrac{3}{1}$ ✘

(D) $\dfrac{g-w}{w}$ $\Rightarrow \dfrac{3-2}{2} = \dfrac{1}{2}$ ✘

(E) $\dfrac{g-w}{g}$ $\Rightarrow \dfrac{3-2}{3} = \dfrac{1}{3}$ ✓

Therefore, the correct answer is (E), since that's the only one that yields 1/3.

Solution B: **Using EZ Direct Method:**
Games Played = g
Games Won = w
Games Lost = $g - w$

Fraction of Games Lost = $\dfrac{g-w}{g}$

Question #8:   A car rental company charges for mileage as follows: n dollars per mile for the first m miles and $n + 1$ dollars per mile for each mile over m miles. How much will the mileage charge be, in dollars, for a trip of t miles, where $t > m$?
     (A) $(t - n)(t + m)$ (B) $nm + t$ (C) $nm + t(n + 1)$ (D) $n(m + t) + 2t$ (E) $t(n + 1) - m$

Solution A: **Using EZ Plug-In Numbers Method:**
According to the condition given in the question: $t > m$
Pick EZ smart numbers for n, m and $t \Rightarrow n = 5$, $m = 2$, $t = 10$
Now let's substitute these numbers in the question-stem, which will yield the following:
$\Rightarrow$ 5 dollars per mile for the first 2 miles, and 6 dollars per mile for each additional mile over 2 miles
Now let's calculate mileage charge for a trip of 5 miles:
$\Rightarrow$ Cost for the first 2 miles: 2×5 = \$10
$\Rightarrow$ Cost for the remaining 8 miles: 8×6 = \$48
$\Rightarrow$ Total cost for 10 miles: = \$58
Now let's plug-in these numbers in all the answer choices and find out which one gives us \$58 when n = 5, m = 2, t = 10.

     (A) $(t - n)(t + m)$ $\Rightarrow (10 - 5)(10 + 2)$ $= 5 \times 12$ $= 60$ ✘

     (B) $nm + t$ $\Rightarrow (5)(2) + 10$ $= 10 + 10$ $= 20$ ✘

     (C) $nm + t(n + 1)$ $\Rightarrow (5)(2) + 10(5 + 1)$ $= 10 + 60$ $= 70$ ✘

     (D) $n(m + t) + 2t$ $\Rightarrow 5(2 + 10) + 2(10)$ $= 60 + 20$ $= 80$ ✘

     (E) $t(n + 1) - m$ $\Rightarrow 10(5 + 1) - 2$ $= 60 - 2$ $= 58$ ✓

Therefore, the correct answer is (E), since that's the only one that yields \$58.

Solution B: **Using EZ Direct Method:**
Total mileage = t miles
Charges per mile for first m miles $\Rightarrow n$ dollars per mile
Charges for first m miles $\Rightarrow \$mn$
Number of miles after n miles = $(t - m)$ miles
Charges per mile for each mile over m miles $\Rightarrow (n + 1)$ dollars per mile
Charges for miles over m miles $\Rightarrow \$(n + 1)(t - m)$
Total Charges for t miles = $mn + (n + 1)(t - m) = mn + nt - mn + t - m = nt + t - m = t(n + 1) - m$

Question #9:   A photocopy center charges for copies as follows: n cents per copy for the first 10 copies and $n - 5$ cents per copy for each copy over 10 copies. How much will it cost in cents to have 200 copies made?
     (A) $200n - 750$ (B) $100n + 750$ (C) $200n - 950$ (D) $100n + 950$ (E) $200(n - 5)$

Solution A: **Using EZ Plug-In Numbers Method:**
Pick EZ smart numbers for $n \Rightarrow n = 10$

Now let's substitute these numbers in the question-stem, which will yield the following:
$\Rightarrow$ 5 dollars per mile for the first 2 miles, and 6 dollars per mile for each additional mile over 2 miles
Now let's calculate price for making 150 copies:
$\Rightarrow$ Cost for the first 10 copies: $10 \times 10 = 100$ cents
$\Rightarrow$ Cost for the remaining 190 copies: $190 \times 5 = \underline{950 \text{ cents}}$
$\Rightarrow$ Total cost for 200 copies: $= 1{,}050$ cents
Now let's plug-on these numbers in all the answer choices and find out which one gives us 1,050 cents when $n = 10$.

(A) $200n - 750$ $\Rightarrow 200(10) - 750$ $= 2000 - 750$ $= 1{,}250$ ✘

(B) $100n + 750$ $\Rightarrow 100(10) + 750$ $= 1000 + 750$ $= 1{,}750$ ✘

(C) $200n - 950$ $\Rightarrow 200(10) - 950$ $= 2000 - 950$ $= 1{,}050$ ✓

(D) $100n + 950$ $\Rightarrow 100(10) + 950$ $= 1000 + 950$ $= 1{,}950$ ✘

(E) $200(n - 5)$ $\Rightarrow 200(10 - 5)$ $= 200(5)$ $= 1{,}000$ ✘

Therefore, the correct answer is (C), since that's the only one that yields 1,050 cents.

Solution B: **Using EZ Direct Method:**
Cost per copy for first 10 copies = n cents
Cost for first 10 copies = $10n$ cents
Cost per copy for next 190 copies = $(n - 5)$ cents
Cost for next 190 copies = $190(n - 5)$
Total Cost for 200 copies = $10n + 190(n - 5) = 10n + 190n - 950 = 200n - 950$

Question #10:   John bought n pounds of nuts at d dollars per pound. If he ate a pounds of his nuts and sold the rest to George for m dollars per pound, how much money did John spend, in dollars, on the nuts he ate himself?
(A) $nd - am$ (B) $nm - ad$ (C) $nd - nm + am$ (D) $nd + nm - na$ (E) $na - ma - mn$

Solution A: **Using EZ Plug-In Numbers Method:**
Pick EZ smart numbers $\Rightarrow$ No of pounds of nuts John bought = $n = 10$
                         $\Rightarrow$ Dollar price per pound = $d = 2$
                         $\Rightarrow$ No of pounds John ate = $a = 7$
                         $\Rightarrow$ Dollar price George paid per pound = $m = 4$
If we plug in these numbers, the problem becomes something like this:
John bought 10 pounds of nuts at \$2 per pound $\Rightarrow$ Therefore, he spent \$20.
John ate 7 pounds of his nuts and sold the rest of the nuts to George $\Rightarrow$ Therefore, John sold 3 pounds of nuts to George at \$4 per pound $\Rightarrow$ Therefore George paid \$12 for the nuts.
The question now is: How much money did John spend on the nuts that he ate himself?
$\Rightarrow$ John spent \$20 on the nuts and sold \$12 worth of nuts to George $\Rightarrow$ Therefore, John spent \$20 – \$12 = \$8 on the nuts that he ate himself.
Now let's plug-in these numbers in all the answer choices and find out which one equals 8

(A) $nd - am$ $\Rightarrow (10)(2) - (7)(4) = 20 - 28 = -8$ ✘

(B) $nm - ad$ $\Rightarrow (10)(4) - (7)(2) = 40 - 14 = 26$ ✘

(C) $nd - nm + am$ $\Rightarrow (10)(2) - (10)(4) + (7)(4) = 20 - 40 + 28 = 8$ ✓

(D) $nd + nm - na$ $\Rightarrow (10)(2) + (10)(4) - (10)((7) = 20 + 40 - 70 = -10$ ✘

(E) $na - ma - mn$ $\Rightarrow (10)(7) - (4)(7) - (4)(10) = 70 - 28 - 40 = 2$ ✘

Therefore, the correct answer is (C), since that's the only one that yields 8.

Solution B: **Using EZ Direct Method:**
No of pounds of nuts John bought = n
Purchase rate per pound = d
Purchase price of nuts for John = nd
No of pounds of nuts John ate = a
No of pounds John sold to George = $n - a$

Sale rate per pound to George = m
Sale price of nuts to George = $(n - a)m$
Price of nuts John ate $\Rightarrow$ Purchase price of nuts for John – Sale price of nuts to George
$\Rightarrow nd - (n - a)m$
$\Rightarrow nd - (nm - am)$
$\Rightarrow nd - nm + am$

Question #11: Hard cover copies of a book are sold for $\$h$ each and soft cover copies are sold for $\$s$ each. If 10,000 books are sold, and x of the books sold are hard cover books, which of the following expression gives the fraction of money made on books sold that came from selling hard cover books?

(A) $\dfrac{hx}{10,000}$ (B) $\dfrac{sx}{sx + (10,000 - x)h}$ (C) $\dfrac{hx}{hx + (10,000 - x)s}$ (D) $\dfrac{10,000}{hsx}$ (E) $\dfrac{h}{h + s}$

Solution A: **Using EZ Plug-In Numbers Method:**
Pick EZ smart numbers $\Rightarrow$ Cost of hard cover book = h = 20
$\Rightarrow$ Cost of soft cover book = s = 10
$\Rightarrow$ No of hard cover books sold = x = 2,000
$\Rightarrow$ No of soft cover books sold = 10,000 – 2,000 = 8000

If we plug in these numbers, the problem becomes something like this:
Total Sales from Hard Cover Books = 2,000 × 20 = 40,000
Total Sales from Soft Cover Books = 8,000 × 10 = 80,000
Total Sales from All Books = 40,000 + 80,000 = 120,000

Fraction of Sales made on hard cover books = $\dfrac{40,000}{120,000} = \dfrac{1}{3}$

Now let's plug-in these numbers in all the answer choices and find out which one equals 1/3.

(A) $\dfrac{hx}{10,000}$ $\Rightarrow \dfrac{20 \times 2000}{10,000} = \dfrac{40,000}{10,000} = 4$ ✘

(B) $\dfrac{sx}{sx + (10,000 - x)h}$ $\Rightarrow \dfrac{10 \times 2000}{10 \times 2000 + (10,000 - 2000)20} = \dfrac{20000}{20000 + 160000} = \dfrac{20000}{180000} = \dfrac{1}{9}$ ✘

(C) $\dfrac{hx}{hx + (10,000 - x)s}$ $\Rightarrow \dfrac{20 \times 2000}{20 \times 2000 + (10,000 - 2000)10} = \dfrac{40000}{40000 + 80000} = \dfrac{40000}{120000} = \dfrac{1}{3}$ ✔

(D) $\dfrac{10,000}{hsx}$ $\Rightarrow \dfrac{10,000}{20 \times 10 \times 2000} = \dfrac{10,000}{400,000} = \dfrac{1}{40}$ ✘

(E) $\dfrac{h}{h + s}$ $\Rightarrow \dfrac{20}{20 + 10} = \dfrac{20}{30} = \dfrac{2}{3}$ ✘

Therefore, the correct answer is (C), since that's the only one that yields 1/3.

Solution B: **Using EZ Direct Method:**
Total No of books sold = 10,000
Cost of one hard cover book = h Cost of one soft cover book = s
No of hard cover books sold = x No of soft cover books sold = 10,000 – x
Total sales from hard cover books = hx Total sales from soft cover books = $(10,000 - x)s$
Total sales from all books = $hx + (10,000 - x)s$

Fraction of sale made on hard cover book = $\dfrac{hx}{hx + (10,000 - x)s}$

EZ Plug-in For Multiple Variable Equations:

Question #12:   If $p = \dfrac{q+7}{r}$, what is the value of q in terms of p and r?

(A) $\dfrac{pr}{7}$ (B) $p(7-r)$ (C) $pr-7$ (D) $7(p-r)$ (E) $7pr$

Solution A: **Using Plug-In Numbers Method:**
Since there is an equation with three variables, we'll have to plug-in numbers for all but two of the variables.
Pick EZ smart numbers: $\Rightarrow r = 2$
                               $\Rightarrow q = 5$

$\Rightarrow p = \dfrac{q+7}{r} = \dfrac{5+7}{2} = \dfrac{12}{2} = 6$

So when $r = 2$ and $q = 5$, $p = 6$.
Now, lets plug-in $r = 2$ and $p = 6$ in each of the answer choices; and find out which answer-choice equals gives $q = 5$.

(A) $\dfrac{pr}{7}$ $\Rightarrow \dfrac{6 \times 2}{7}$ $\Rightarrow \dfrac{12}{7}$ $\Rightarrow 1.71$ ✘

(B) $p(7-r)$ $\Rightarrow 6(7-2)$ $\Rightarrow 6(5)$ $\Rightarrow 30$ ✘

(C) $pr-7$ $\Rightarrow (6)(2)-7$ $\Rightarrow 12-7$ $\Rightarrow 5$ ✔

(D) $7(p-r)$ $\Rightarrow 7(6-2)$ $\Rightarrow 7(4)$ $\Rightarrow 28$ ✘

(E) $7pr$ $\Rightarrow 7(6)(2)$ $\Rightarrow 7(12)$ $\Rightarrow 84$ ✘

Therefore, the correct answer is (C), since that's the only one that yields $q = 5$.

Solution B: **Using EZ Direct Method:**

$p = \dfrac{q+7}{r}$

$\Rightarrow pr = q + 7$ [multiply both sides of the equation by r]
$\Rightarrow q = pr - 7$ [subtract 7 from both sides of the equation]

EZ Plug-in For Special Format Answers:

"CANNOT BE" Type of Questions:

Question #13:   If $a > b$ and $b > c$, which of the following CANNOT be true?
                 (A) $2a > b + c$ (B) $a + c > b + c$ (C) $2c > a + b$ (D) $a + b > 2b + c$ (E) $ab > bc$

Solution: If $a > b$ and $b > c$, then $a > b > c$
Let's plug in numbers for a, b, and c.
Let $a = 3$ and $b = 2$ and $c = 1$
Now let's plug these numbers in the answer choice and see which one results in a false statement:

(A) $2a > b + c$ $\Rightarrow 2(3) > 2 + 1$ $\Rightarrow 6 > 3$ $\Rightarrow$ TRUE ✘

(B) $a + c > b + c$ $\Rightarrow 3 + 1 > 2 + 1$ $\Rightarrow 4 > 3$ $\Rightarrow$ TRUE ✘

(C) $2c > a + b$ $\Rightarrow 2(1) > 3 + 2$ $\Rightarrow 2 > 5$ $\Rightarrow$ FALSE ✔

(D) $a + b > 2c + b$ $\Rightarrow 3 + 2 > 2(1) + 2$ $\Rightarrow 5 > 4$ $\Rightarrow$ TRUE ✘

(E) $ab > bc$ $\Rightarrow 3(2) > 2(1)$ $\Rightarrow 6 > 2$ $\Rightarrow$ TRUE ✘

As can be clearly seen, only answer choice (C) results in a true statement, therefore, this is the correct answer.

"MUST BE" Type of Questions:

Question #14:   If a, b, and c are all positive numbers, which of the following is always true?
(A) $(a + b) \times c = a + (b \times c)$ (B) $a - b - c = c - b - a$ (C) $(a + b) + c = a + (c + b)$
(D) $(a - b) + c = (b - a) + c$ (E) $bc + a = ac + b$

Solution: According to the question: "a, b, and c are all positive integers"
First, pick three simple-easy-to-use positive integers: 1, 2, and 3.
Next, we need to find out: which of the answer choice gives us a true statement.
Now, plug in $a = 1$, $b = 2$, and $c = 3$, in all the answer choices and see which one results in a true statement:

(A) $(a + b) \times c = a + (b \times c)$ $\Rightarrow (1 + 2) \times 3 = 1 + (2 \times 3)$ $\Rightarrow 9 = 7$ ✗

(B) $a - b - c = c - b - a$ $\Rightarrow 1 - 2 - 3 = 3 - 2 - 1$ $\Rightarrow -4 = 0$ ✗

(C) $(a + b) + c = a + (c + b)$ $\Rightarrow (1 + 2) + 3 = 1 + (3 + 2)$ $\Rightarrow 6 = 6$ ✓

(D) $(a - b) + c = (b - a) + c$ $\Rightarrow (1 - 2) + 3 = (2 - 1) + 3$ $\Rightarrow 2 = 4$ ✗

(E) $bc + a = ac + b$ $\Rightarrow 2 \times 3 + 1 = 1 \times 3 + 2$ $\Rightarrow 7 = 5$ ✗

Note: You should know that the order or grouping of a set of numbers does not matter when there it only involves addition. Note that the question asks for something that is always true. The other answers could be true with certain sets of numbers but are not always true. Hence, answer choice (C) is always correct.

"COULD BE" Type of Questions:

Question #15:   If n is an integer, which of the following could be an even integer?
(A) $\dfrac{19}{n}$ (B) $\dfrac{17}{n}$ (C) $\dfrac{n}{7}$ (D) $\dfrac{13}{n}$ (E) $\dfrac{11}{n}$

Solution: Let's test each one of the answer choices and see which one could result in an even integer:

(A) $\dfrac{19}{n}$ $\Rightarrow$ The only factors of 19 are 1 & 19, and if n is any of these two, it will results in odd integer.

(B) $\dfrac{17}{n}$ $\Rightarrow$ The only factors of 17 are 1 & 17, and if n is any of these two, it will results in odd integer.

(C) $\dfrac{n}{7}$ $\Rightarrow$ The multiples of 7 are many, such as, 14, 21, 28, etc, and if n is 14, it will results in 2, which is an even integer.

(D) $\dfrac{13}{n}$ $\Rightarrow$ The only factors of 13 are 1 & 13, and if n is any of these two, it will results in odd integer.

(E) $\dfrac{11}{n}$ $\Rightarrow$ The only factors of 11 are 1 & 11, and if n is any of these two, it will results in odd integer.

Therefore, the only answer choice which could be an even integer is answer choice (C).

"NOT ENOUGH INFORMATION GIVEN" Type of Questions:

Question #16:   The area of a right triangle is 25. What is its perimeter?
(A) 5   (B) 10   (C) 15   (D) 20   (E) Not enough information is given

Solution: Area of triangle = ½ × base × height = 25
$\Rightarrow$ base × height = 25 × 2 = 50
Since base and height could have infinite number of values, it's impossible to find its area, and the question cannot be answered; therefore, there is not enough information given. So the correct answer is answer choice (E)

"ROMAN NUMERAL" Type of Questions:

Question #17:   If n is negative, which of the following must be true?

I. $n^3 < n^2$

II. $n + \dfrac{1}{n} < 0$

III. $n = \sqrt{n^2}$

   (A) I only   (B) II only   (C) III only   (D) I, II, and III   (E) I and II only

Solution: You can use the picking-numbers technique to evaluate the truth of these statement; however, in this case there is no need to do that, we can prove the validity of each statement simply by evaluating them.

     Statement I: $n^3 < n^2$ $\Rightarrow$ If n is negative, then n^3 must be negative (cube of any negative number is negative) and n^2 must be positive (square of any negative number is positive)

                      Therefore $n^3 < n^2$

                      $\Rightarrow$ True ✔

     Statement II: $n + \dfrac{1}{n} < 0$ $\Rightarrow$ If n is negative, then $\dfrac{1}{n}$ is also negative; and sum of negative numbers is always negative

                      Therefore $n + \dfrac{1}{n} < 0$

                      $\Rightarrow$ True ✔

     Statement III: $n = \sqrt{n^2}$ $\Rightarrow$ If n is negative, then n^2 must be positive (square of any negative number is negative) and its square root must be positive (square root of any positive number is positive)

                      Therefore $n \neq \sqrt{n^2}$

                      $\Rightarrow$ False ✘

   Only statement I and II are true, so the correct answer is answer choice (E).

CHAPTER 9.0: EZ MISCELLANEOUS STRATEGIES

HIGHLIGHTS:
9.1 EZ Consistent Units Strategy
9.2 EZ Approximation & Estimation Strategy
9.3 EZ Systematic List Strategy
9.4 EZ Interpretation Strategy
9.5 EZ Equivalency Strategy
9.6 EZ Comparison Strategy
9.7 EZ Computation Strategy
9.8 EZ Special Symbol Strategy
▪ Practice Exercise with Detailed Explanations

9.1 EZ CONSISTENT UNITS STRATEGY

WORK IN CONSISTENT UNITS & GET THE ANSWER IN THE UNITS ASKED:
If a problem involves units, keep track of the units and make sure your answer has the correct units.

EZ STEP-BY-STEP METHOD: While working in Consistent Units, apply the following steps:
STEP 1: First, make sure to convert all the measurements involved into one consistent unit.
STEP 2: Next, apply the appropriate formula and get the answer in that consistent unit.
STEP 3: Finally, convert your answer in the units asked.

DIFFERENT UNITS FOR DIFFERENT MEASURES:
▪ To find the Perimeter   ⇒ units should be in linear units (unit).   ⇒ Examples: meters, feet
▪ To find the Circumference   ⇒ units should be in linear units (unit).   ⇒ Examples: meters, feet
▪ To find the Surface Area   ⇒ units should be in square units (unit^2)   ⇒ Examples: square meters, square feet
▪ To find the Volume   ⇒ units should be in cubic units (unit^3)   ⇒ Examples: cubic meters, cubic feet
▪ To find the Rate   ⇒ units should be in rate format (*a* per *b*) ⇒ Examples: miles per hour, feet per minute

Most Commonly Used Units on the Test: dollars or cents; hours or minutes or seconds; feet or inches; meters or centimeters; pounds or ounces; kilometer or mile; kilogram or pound; etc.

EZ TIP: Often the answer to a question is usually in units different from the units used in the question. As you read the question, make a note on your scratch paper and/or <u>underline</u> the units in which the answer is been asked.

EZ WARNING: Be very careful, on the multiple-choice questions, an answer with the wrong units is almost always given as one of the answer choices. So be careful of not falling in the trap.

EZ REFERENCE: To learn more about Measurement units, refer to our Content-Knowledge Review-Module on Measurements.

9.1.1: WORK IN CONSISTENT UNITS:
Make sure to work in consistent units. It is very important to work in consistent units before doing any calculations or applying any formulas.

Example #1:   If the length and width of a rectangle are 5 feet and 24 inches respectively, what is its area?
              Note: First, convert either the 5 feet into 60 inches or the 24 inches into 2 feet before calculating the area or the perimeter of the rectangle.

Solution: **Method #1:** First, convert the 24 inches to 2 feet so that both the units are consistently in inches.
                       ⇒ Area of Rectangle = 5 feet × 2 feet = 10 sq feet

                       Method #2: First, convert the 5 feet to 60 inches so that both the units are consistently in feet.
                       ⇒ Area of Rectangle = 60 inches × 24 inches = 1440 sq inches.

                       Wrong: Never make the mistake of working in different units.
                       ⇒ Area of Rectangle = 5 feet × 24 inches = 120   ⇒ This clearly wrong!

9.1.2: GET THE ANSWER IN THE UNITS ASKED:

Make sure to get the answer in the units asked. It is recommended that you underline or circle the units in which the answer is being asked, this would remind you to convert your answer to the appropriate units.

Example #2:   If the length of and width of a rectangle are 2 feet and 5 feet respectively, what is the perimeter of the rectangle in inches?
                      Note: First, convert either the 2 feet into 24 inches, and the 5 feet into 60 inches before calculating the area; or calculate the answer, and then convert it to inches.

Solution A: **Method #1:** First, find the perimeter and then convert the answer into inches.
                      ⇒ Perimeter of Rectangle = 2(2 + 5) = 2 × 7 = 14 feet = 14 × 12 = 168 inches

                      Method #2: First, convert the 2 feet to 24 inches and 5 feet to 60 inches.
                      There is no need to do any conversions, as the answer will automatically be in inches.
                      ⇒ Perimeter of Rectangle = 2(24 + 60) = 2 × 84 = 168 inches

9.2   EZ APPROXIMATION & ESTIMATION STRATEGY

As we have already mentioned in the beginning of this book, the primary purpose of your test is not to test your computational skills; nevertheless, you will still need to do some calculations. If a math problem involves some complex calculations that are either too tedious and/or time consuming, it may be a good idea to round-off or approximate the numbers involved and then do the calculation. In most cases, you only need to find an approximate solution in order to answer a question. Moreover, some questions don't even ask for an exact value, instead they ask for an approximate answer.

You can make the computations easier and faster, by avoiding any unnecessary long calculations. So try to estimate whenever you can to save time, and simplify the calculations. Since time is limited, you shouldn't waste it when you can avoid it. The time you spend in approximations is significantly shorter than getting the exact answer. The time that you save, can instead be used to check your answer, or to answer other questions. There is almost always a way where you can answer the question by either estimating or doing an approximate calculation rather than by figuring out the exact answer. First, try to approach a question on very simple terms and try to get a rough estimate of the answer. Whenever you see a calculation that looks complex, try to round off the numbers to something more manageable.

OTHER ADVANTAGES OF EZ APPROXIMATION AND ESTIMATION:

(i)   **Guessing and Eliminating:** Approximation can also be used to help you narrow down the answer choices by eliminating out-of-range answer choices in multiple-choice problems. This may or may not lead you to the correct answer, but it will definitely help you narrow down the possible answer choices before you make a guess. You should try to answer every question where you can estimate the answer, even if you don't know how to answer it or are not sure about it.

(ii) **Checking:** Approximation can also be useful to quickly check and re-check your calculations.

(iii) **Traps:** Approximation can also prevent you from picking a trap answer if you already eliminated it through approximation. Moreover, it will save you from choosing the wrong answer by mistake.

(iv) **Geometry:** Approximation can also be very useful on geometry problems that include a figure or a diagram. Even if you don't know how to solve the question, you can still make a rough estimate of the answer.

Therefore, approximation and estimation can help you answer the question easily, quickly, and correctly, and save you some valuable time.

EZ REFERENCE: To learn more about using EZ Approximation and Estimation Strategy on geometry questions, refer to our Content-Knowledge Review-Module on Geometry.

Degree of Approximation: While using approximation, make sure to first scan the answer choices and see how spread-out they are, and that will indicate the degree of approximation.

*   If the answer choices are quite spread-out and are not closely clustered, such as, 5, 25, 50, 100, and 500, then you can use approximation more liberally.
*   If the answer choices are not very spread-out and are closely clustered, such as, 5, 6.25, 7.5, 8.75, and 9, then you have to use approximation more conservatively.

EZ STEP-BY-STEP METHOD: While using EZ Approximation & Estimation Strategy, apply the following steps:

STEP 1: First, make the appropriate approximations and rewrite the problem.

STEP 2: Next, solve the problem using those approximations.

STEP 3: Next, eliminate answers that aren't very close to your answer.

STEP 4: Finally, pick the answer-choice that is closest to your approximate answer.

    (A) If there's only one reasonably close answer, you don't need to calculate the exact answer.

    (B) If there's more than one reasonably close answer, you'll need to go back and redo the calculation with a lesser degree of approximation to find the closest one.

EZ STANDARD NUMBERS: COMMON APPROXIMATIONS:

When you deal with a variety of numbers of different sizes, it's always useful to have some standard numbers that can be used as a benchmark or a yardstick or a point-of-reference. These are simple numbers, fractions, and percents with which you are already familiar. If you ever get thrown off or get confused when working with percents, decimals and/or fractions, think about EZ Standard or Smart Numbers as a way to approximate numbers.

Following are some EZ Smart Numbers:

$\Rightarrow 200\%$ $\Rightarrow 2.00$ $\Rightarrow \dfrac{200}{100} = \dfrac{2}{1}$

$\Rightarrow 100\%$ $\Rightarrow 1.00$ $\Rightarrow \dfrac{100}{100} = \dfrac{1}{1}$

$\Rightarrow 75\%$ $\Rightarrow 0.75$ $\Rightarrow \dfrac{75}{100} = \dfrac{3}{4}$

$\Rightarrow 66.6\%$ $\Rightarrow 0.67$ $\Rightarrow \dfrac{66.6}{100} = \dfrac{2}{3}$

$\Rightarrow 50\%$ $\Rightarrow 0.50$ $\Rightarrow \dfrac{50}{100} = \dfrac{1}{2}$

$\Rightarrow 33.3\%$ $\Rightarrow 0.34$ $\Rightarrow \dfrac{33.3}{100} = \dfrac{1}{3}$

$\Rightarrow 25\%$ $\Rightarrow 0.25$ $\Rightarrow \dfrac{25}{100} = \dfrac{1}{4}$

$\Rightarrow 10\%$ $\Rightarrow 0.10$ $\Rightarrow \dfrac{10}{100} = \dfrac{1}{10}$

$\Rightarrow 1\%$ $\Rightarrow 0.01$ $\Rightarrow \dfrac{1}{100}$

Following are some of the other most common approximations that you must try to memorize:
- Value of π $\Rightarrow 3.14$ (or just slightly more than 3)
- Value of $\sqrt{2}$ $\Rightarrow 1.41$ (or just about slightly less than 1.5)
- Value of $\sqrt{3}$ $\Rightarrow 1.73$ (or just about slightly less than 1.75)

EZ Standard Numbers can be used to estimate fractions, decimals, and percents.

For instance: To estimate the value of $\dfrac{52}{210}$ $\Rightarrow \dfrac{52}{210} \approx \dfrac{1}{4} \approx 0.25 \approx 25\%$

EZ Standard Numbers can also be used as an important estimation strategy to compare and compute fractions, decimals, and percents. It can be used to first estimate numbers, and then use it for comparisons and computations.

For Comparisons: Using EZ Standard Numbers to compare fractions, decimals, and percents

For instance: To compare $\dfrac{139}{275}$ & $\dfrac{261}{525}$ $\Rightarrow \dfrac{139}{275}$ is slightly more than ½ & $\dfrac{261}{525}$ is slightly less than ½

$\Rightarrow$ Therefore, $\dfrac{139}{275} > \dfrac{261}{525}$

For Computations: Using EZ Standard Numbers to compute with fractions, decimals, and percents

For instance: To find the value of $\dfrac{55}{210}$ of $\dfrac{79}{105}$ of 8000 $\Rightarrow \dfrac{55}{210} \approx \dfrac{1}{4}$ & $\dfrac{79}{105} \approx \dfrac{3}{4}$

$\Rightarrow \dfrac{1}{4}$ of $\dfrac{3}{4}$ of 8000 = 1,500

EZ REFERENCE: To learn more about computing and comparing fractions and decimals, refer to our Content-Knowledge Review-Module on Arithmetic.

9.2.1: WHEN A QUESTION ASKS FOR AN EXACT ANSWER:

Example #1: What is the exact value of (9.972 × 5.19) ÷ 2.06?
(A) 10.268   (B) 15.678   (C) 17.269   (D) 20.579   (E) 25.123

Solution: We can estimate an answer by rounding-off the values and doing the calculations, and then checking it against the answer-choice that is closest to our estimate.
First make approximations and re-write the problem as: $(10 \times 5) \div 2$
Then, solve the problem: $(10 \times 5) \div 2 = 50 \div 2 = 25$.
Finally, pick the answer-choice that is closest to 25.
Therefore, the correct answer is (E)
Note: The exact answer to the calculation above is 25.123, which is very close to what we got without doing any tedious calculations and by using approximation strategy.

Example #2:   What is the exact value of $(9.98 \times 9.96 \times 2.08 \times 5.07) \div 199.66$?
(A) 5.25   (B) 7.75   (C) 10.8   (D) 25.25   (E) 50.5

Solution: We can estimate an answer by rounding-off the values and doing the calculations, and then checking it against the answer-choice that is closest to our estimate.
First make approximations and re-write the problem as: $(10 \times 10 \times 2 \times 5) \div 200$
Next, solve the problem: $(10 \times 10 \times 2 \times 5) \div 200 = 1000 \div 200 = 5$.
Finally, pick the answer-choice that is closest to 5.
Therefore, the correct answer is (A)
Note: The exact answer to the calculation above is 5.25, which is very close to what we got without doing any tedious calculations and by using approximation strategy.

9.2.2: WHEN A QUESTION ASKS FOR AN APPROXIMATE ANSWER:

Example #3:   Which of the following is closest to $(24 \times 989) \div 10$?
(A) 1,200   (B) 2,000   (C) 2,400   (D) 3,000   (E) 5,000

Solution: We can estimate an answer by rounding-off the values and doing the calculations, and then checking it against the answer-choice that is closest to our estimate.
First make approximations and re-write the problem as: $(24 \times 1,000) \div 10 = 24,000 \div 10 = 2,400$
Therefore, the correct answer is (C)
Note: The exact answer to the calculation above is 2373.6, which is very close to what we got without doing any tedious calculations and by using approximation strategy.

Example #4:   What is the closest estimate for: $124 \times \dfrac{51}{24}$?
(A) 50   (B) 100   (C) 250   (D) 500   (E) 1,250

Solution: We can estimate an answer by rounding-off the values and doing the calculations, and then checking it against the answer-choice that is closest to our estimate.
First make approximations and re-write the problem as: $125 \times \dfrac{50}{25}$
Solve the problem: $125 \times \dfrac{50}{25} = 125 \times 2 = 250$
Therefore, the correct answer is (E)
Note: The exact answer to the calculation above is 263.5, which is very close to what we got without doing any tedious calculations and by using approximation strategy.

9.3 EZ SYSTEMATIC LIST STRATEGY

MAKE EZ SYSTEMATIC LISTS:
Sometimes, when a question asks for "how many" or involves some kind of counting, often the best strategy is to make a systematic list of all the possibilities. It's important to make the list in a systematic and organized manner so that you don't accidentally leave anything out or count something twice. Oftentimes, shortly after starting the list, you may see a pattern developing, and will be able to predict the remaining possibilities without actually listing them all down.

EZ TIP: Even if the question does not specifically ask you to count, you may need to count some items in order to answer it; so in this case as well, the best way is to make a systematic list.

EZ NOTE: If the problem uses very big or complex numbers, or the list is too long and you are not able to spot any sort of pattern, in such cases you may have to take aid of some formulas. Counting problems related to Permutation & Combination are reviewed separately in our module on Logical Reasoning. However, a few problems can only be solved by making a systematic list, such as the ones given below.

EZ REFERENCE: To learn more about Counting problems including Permutation and Combination, refer to our Content-Knowledge Review-Module on Word Problems.

Following examples are solved by making EZ systematic lists so that you can understand its benefits.

Example #1:   How many odd prime numbers are there between 0 and 20?
(A) 5   (B) 6   (C) 7   (D) 8   (E) 9

Solution: Let's make a systematic list of all the prime numbers between 0 and 20.
1st Prime Number   2 $\Rightarrow$ Even
2nd Prime Number   3 $\Rightarrow$ Odd
3rd Prime Number   5 $\Rightarrow$ Odd
4th Prime Number   7 $\Rightarrow$ Odd
5th Prime Number   11 $\Rightarrow$ Odd
6th Prime Number   13 $\Rightarrow$ Odd
7th Prime Number   17 $\Rightarrow$ Odd
8th Prime Number   19 $\Rightarrow$ Odd
It's clear from the above list that there are 7 odd prime numbers that are between 0 and 20. Therefore, the correct answer is (C).

Example #2:   How many even prime numbers are there between 0 and 100?
(A) 1   (B) 5   (C) 10   (D) 20   (E) 25

Solution: Let's make a systematic list of all the prime numbers between 0 and 100.
1st Prime Number   2 $\Rightarrow$ Even
2nd Prime Number   3 $\Rightarrow$ Odd
3rd Prime Number   5 $\Rightarrow$ Odd
4th Prime Number   7 $\Rightarrow$ Odd
5th Prime Number   11 $\Rightarrow$ Odd
6th Prime Number   13 $\Rightarrow$ Odd
7th Prime Number   17 $\Rightarrow$ Odd
8th Prime Number   19 $\Rightarrow$ Odd
9th Prime Number   23 $\Rightarrow$ Odd
10th Prime Number   29 $\Rightarrow$ Odd
Stop and see for some kind of a pattern. Shortly after starting the list, you must realize that all the prime numbers but the first one are all odd numbers. Based on this pattern, you can easily predict that there is only one prime number between 0 and 100, which is even.
Therefore, the correct answer is (A).

Example #3: During a seven-day trade exhibition, the number of visitors doubled each day. The exhibit opened on Monday and closed on the following Sunday. If the attendance on the closing day was 6,400, what was the attendance on the opening day?

(A) 100   (B) 200   (C) 400   (D) 800   (E) 1,600

Solution: Let's make a systematic list of attendance on each day, starting from the closing day:

Closing Day: Sunday $\Rightarrow$ 6,400
                   Saturday $\Rightarrow$ 3,200
                   Friday $\Rightarrow$ 1,600
                   Thursday $\Rightarrow$ 800
                   Wednesday $\Rightarrow$ 400
                   Tuesday $\Rightarrow$ 200
Opening Day: Monday $\Rightarrow$ 100

It's clear from the above list that the attendance on the opening day was 100.
Therefore, the correct answer is (A).

Example #4: A man took a 1,500-mile trip in 5 days. Each day, he drove 25 miles more than the previous day. How many miles did he cover on the first day?

(A) 100   (B) 200   (C) 250   (D) 500   (E) 1,000

Solution: Let's make a systematic list of miles covered on each day, starting from the first day:

Number of miles covered on 1st Day $\Rightarrow n$
Number of miles covered on 2nd Day $\Rightarrow n + 25$
Number of miles covered on 3rd Day $\Rightarrow n + 25 + 25$
Number of miles covered on 4th Day $\Rightarrow n + 25 + 25 + 25$
Number of miles covered on 5th Day $\Rightarrow n + 25 + 25 + 25 + 25$

Total Number of miles covered on all 5 Day:
$\Rightarrow 5n + 25(10) = 1,500$
$\Rightarrow 5n + 250 = 1,500$
$\Rightarrow 5n = 1,500 - 250$
$\Rightarrow 5n = 1,250$
$\Rightarrow n = 1,250 \div 5 = 250$

It's clear from the above list that the miles covered on the first day were 250 miles.
Therefore, the correct answer is (C).

9.4 EZ INTERPRETATION STRATEGY

DIFFERENT INTERPRETATION OF SAME COMPUTATION IS REQUIRED FOR DIFFERENT SITUATIONS:

Sometimes a different interpretation of the same computation is required under different situations, and we need to adjust our computations accordingly.

For instance, note that the computation (72 ÷ 10) is appropriate for each of the following examples; however, based on the situation given in the question, we may need to adjust our computation accordingly.

Example #1:   How many 10-foot length segments of rope can be cut from a rope that is 72 feet long?
  (A) 5   (B) 6   (C) 7   (D) 8   (E) 9
Solution: $\Rightarrow$ 72 ÷ 10 = 7.2 = 7 + 0.2
  $\Rightarrow$ At most 7 pieces of length segments 10-foot long can be cut from a 72-foot rope length.
  Note: there will be a waste of 2 feet of rope.

Example #2:   How many boxes are needed to ship 72 books if no more than 10 books can be placed in a box?
  (A) 6   (B) 7   (C) 8   (D) 9   (E) 10
Solution: $\Rightarrow$ 72 ÷ 10 = 7.2 = 7 + 0.2
  $\Rightarrow$ At least 8 boxes are needed to ship the 72 books if no more than 10 books can be placed in a box.
  Note: since each box can contain a maximum of 10 books, the eighth box will contain only 2 books.

Example #3:   If 10 people share equally in the profit, what is each person's share for a net profit of $72?
  (A) $2.7   (B) $7.1   (C) $7.2   (D) $7.5   (E) $8
Solution: $\Rightarrow$ 72 ÷ 10 = 7.2
  $\Rightarrow$ Each of 10 people should get a share of $7.20 in the total net profit of a $72.
  Note: in this case, the profit can be divided equally to the last decimal point.

Example #4:   If a 72-foot length of rope is cut into 10 pieces of equal length, how long is each of the pieces?

  (A) $7\frac{1}{10}$ (B) $7\frac{1}{7}$ (C) $7\frac{1}{5}$ (D) $7\frac{1}{4}$ (E) $7\frac{1}{2}$

Solution: $\Rightarrow$ 72 ÷ 10 = 7.2 = 7 + 1/5

  $\Rightarrow$ Each of the 10 pieces of rope cut from a 72 -foot length would be $7\frac{1}{5}$ feet long.

  Note: in this case, the rope can be divided in fractions.

EZ TIP: As you can see, the above examples illustrate the fact that in a real-life situation, the "answer" to "72 ÷ 10" may be 7 or 8 or 7.20 or $7\frac{1}{5}$, depending on the context.

Example #5:   If it takes exactly one minute per cut, how long will it take to cut a 10-foot long timber into 10 equal pieces?
  (A) 1   (B) 5   (C) 9   (D) 10   (E) 11
Solution: 1st cut $\Rightarrow$ 1 minute $\Rightarrow$ 2 pieces
  2nd cut $\Rightarrow$ 2 minutes $\Rightarrow$ 3 pieces
  3rd cut $\Rightarrow$ 3 minutes $\Rightarrow$ 4 pieces
  4th cut $\Rightarrow$ 4 minutes $\Rightarrow$ 5 pieces
  5th cut $\Rightarrow$ 5 minutes $\Rightarrow$ 6 pieces
  As you can see, each cut results in 1 additional piece; therefore, to get 10 pieces, we only need to make 9 cuts and that will take only 9 minutes.

EZ WARNING: These are very simple problems and it's very easy to make a silly mistake on them.

9.5 EZ EQUIVALENCIES STRATEGY

FIND EQUIVALENT FORMS OF NUMBERS:
It is important to know equivalent forms of numbers given in the same or different forms. It is very common to find questions that may ask you to find an answer-choice that is either equivalent or not equivalent to others. You should be able to determine equivalency in numbers given in the form of fractions, decimals, exponents, scientific notations, percents, place value notations, equations, inequalities, and mixed numbers.

EZ REFERENCE: To learn more about Equivalence of different forms of numbers, refer to our Content-Knowledge Review-Module on Arithmetic.

9.5.1: EQUIVALENCY FOR FRACTIONS:
Example #1: Which of the following expressions is NOT equivalent to the others?

    (A) $\dfrac{7}{9}$ (B) $\dfrac{77}{99}$ (C) $\dfrac{707}{999}$ (D) $\dfrac{707}{909}$ (E) $\dfrac{7007}{9009}$

Solution: The best way to compare all five answer choices is by expressing them in the same form.

    (A) $\dfrac{7}{9}$ $\Rightarrow 0.77777.......$ ✓

    (B) $\dfrac{77}{99}$ $\Rightarrow 0.77777.......$ ✓

    (C) $\dfrac{707}{999}$ $\Rightarrow 0.7077077.......$ ✗

    (D) $\dfrac{707}{909}$ $\Rightarrow 0.77777.......$ ✓

    (E) $\dfrac{7007}{9009}$ $\Rightarrow 0.77777.......$ ✓

Therefore, the correct answer is (C), since that's the only choice, which is different from others.

9.5.2: EQUIVALENCY FOR DECIMALS:
Example #2: Which of the following expressions is NOT equivalent to the others?
    (A) $(0.2 + 0.9) \times 2.5$ (B) $(0.2 \times 2.5) + (0.9 \times 2.5)$ (C) $2.5 + (0.2 \times 0.9)$
    (D) $2.5 \times (0.2 + 0.9)$ (E) 1.1×2.5

Solution: The best way to compare all five answer choices is by expressing them in the same form.

    (A) $(0.2 + 0.9) \times 2.5$ $\Rightarrow 2.75$ ✓

    (B) $(0.2 \times 2.5) + (0.9 \times 2.5)$ $\Rightarrow 2.75$ ✓

    (C) $2.5 + (0.2 \times 0.9)$ $\Rightarrow 2.68$ ✗

    (D) $2.5 \times (0.2 + 0.9)$ $\Rightarrow 2.75$ ✓

    (E) 1.1×2.5 $\Rightarrow 2.75$ ✓

Therefore, the correct answer is (C), since that's the only choice, which is different from others.

9.5.3: EQUIVALENCY FOR EXPONENTS:
Example #3: Which of the following expressions is NOT equivalent to the others?
    (A) $2^2 \times 10 \times 16$ (B) $2^3 \times 10 \times 12$ (C) $2^4 \times 5 \times 12$ (D) $2^5 \times 5 \times 6$ (E) $2^6 \times 3 \times 5$

Solution: The best way to compare all five answer choices is by expressing them in the same form.
    Method #1: One way to solve is by factoring-out all of the answer choices:

        (A) $2^2 \times 10 \times 16$ $\Rightarrow 2^2 \times 2 \times 5 \times 2 \times 2 \times 2 \times 2$ $\Rightarrow 2^6 \times 2 \times 5$ ✗

(B) $2^3 \times 10 \times 12$	$\Rightarrow 2^3 \times 2 \times 5 \times 2 \times 2 \times 3$	$\Rightarrow 2^6 \times 3 \times 5$	✓
(C) $2^4 \times 5 \times 12$	$\Rightarrow 2^4 \times 5 \times 2 \times 2 \times 3$	$\Rightarrow 2^6 \times 3 \times 5$	✓
(D) $2^5 \times 5 \times 6$	$\Rightarrow 2^5 \times 5 \times 2 \times 3$	$\Rightarrow 2^6 \times 3 \times 5$	✓
(E) $2^6 \times 3 \times 5$	$\Rightarrow 2^6 \times 3 \times 5$	$\Rightarrow 2^6 \times 3 \times 5$	✓

Method #2: Another way to solve is by multiplying-out all of the answer choices:

(A) $2^2 \times 10 \times 16$	$\Rightarrow 4 \times 10 \times 16$	$\Rightarrow 640$	✗
(B) $2^3 \times 10 \times 12$	$\Rightarrow 8 \times 10 \times 12$	$\Rightarrow 960$	✓
(C) $2^4 \times 5 \times 12$	$\Rightarrow 16 \times 5 \times 12$	$\Rightarrow 960$	✓
(D) $2^5 \times 5 \times 6$	$\Rightarrow 32 \times 5 \times 6$	$\Rightarrow 960$	✓
(E) $2^6 \times 3 \times 5$	$\Rightarrow 64 \times 3 \times 5$	$\Rightarrow 960$	✓

Therefore, the correct answer is (A), since that's the only choice, which is different from others.

9.5.4: EQUIVALENCY FOR SCIENTIFIC NOTATIONS:

Example 4: Which of the following is not equal to 0.00695?
(A) 695×10^{-5} (B) 6.95×10^{-3} (C) 0.00695×10^0 (D) 0.0000695×10^2 (E) 0.0000695×10^1

Solution: The best way to compare all five answer choices is by expressing them in the same form.

(A) 695×10^{-5}	$\Rightarrow 0.00695$	✓
(B) 6.95×10^{-3}	$\Rightarrow 0.00695$	✓
(C) 0.00695×10^0	$\Rightarrow 0.00695$	✓
(D) 0.0000695×10^2	$\Rightarrow 0.00695$	✓
(E) 0.0000695×10^1	$\Rightarrow 0.000695$	✗

Therefore, the correct answer is (E), since that's the only choice, which is different from others.

9.5.5: EQUIVALENCY FOR PERCENTS:

Example #5: Which of the following expressions is NOT equivalent to the others?
(A) 1% of 2,000   (B) 5% of 400   (C) 10% of 200   (D) 25% of 80   (E) 50% of 50

Solution: The best way to compare all five answer-choices is by expressing them in the same form.

(A) 1% of 2,000	$\Rightarrow 20$	✓
(B) 5% of 400	$\Rightarrow 20$	✓
(C) 10% of 200	$\Rightarrow 20$	✓
(D) 25% of 80	$\Rightarrow 20$	✓
(E) 50% of 50	$\Rightarrow 25$	✗

Therefore, the correct answer is (E), since that's the only choice, which is different from others.

9.5.6: EQUIVALENCY FOR PLACE VALUE NOTATIONS:

Example #6: Which of the following numbers is NOT equivalent to the others?
(A.) 10 million   (B.) 100 ten thousands   (C.) 1,000 thousands
(D.) 10,000 hundreds   (E.) 100,000 tens

Solution: The best way to compare all five answer-choices is by expressing them in the same form.

(A.) 10 million	$\Rightarrow 10,000,000$	✗
(B.) 100 ten thousands	$\Rightarrow 100 \times 10,000 = 1,000,000$	✓
(C.) 1,000 thousands	$\Rightarrow 1,000 \times 1,000 = 1,000,000$	✓

(D.) 10,000 hundred $\Rightarrow$ 10,000 × 100 = 1,000,000 ✔

(E.) 100,000 tens $\Rightarrow$ 100,000 × 10 = 1,000,000 ✔

Therefore, the correct answer is (A), since that's the only choice, which is different from others.

9.5.7: EQUIVALENCY FOR EQUATIONS:

Example #7:   Which of the following expressions is NOT equivalent to the others?

(A) $2x + 5 = 10y + 17$ (B) $2x - 2 = 10y + 10$ (C) $2x - 10y = 12$

(D) $x - 5y = 6$ (E) $x = 5y + 7$

Solution: The best way to compare all five answer-choices is by expressing them in the same form.

(A) $2x + 5 = 10y + 17$ $\Rightarrow x = 5y + 6$ ✔

(B) $2x - 2 = 10y + 10$ $\Rightarrow x = 5y + 6$ ✔

(C) $2x - 10y = 12$ $\Rightarrow x = 5y + 6$ ✔

(D) $x - 5y = 6$ $\Rightarrow x = 5y + 6$ ✔

(E) $x = 5y + 7$ $\Rightarrow x = 5y + 7$ ✘

Therefore, the correct answer is (E), since that's the only choice, which is different from others.

9.5.8: EQUIVALENCY FOR INEQUALITIES:

Example #8:   Which of the following expressions is NOT equivalent to the others?

(A) $2x + 5 > 10y + 17$ (B) $2x - 2 > 10y + 10$ (C) $2x - 10y > 12$

(D) $x - 5y > 6$ (E) $x > 5y + 7$

Solution: The best way to compare all five answer-choices is by expressing them in the same form.

(A) $2x + 5 > 10y + 17$ $\Rightarrow x > 5y + 6$ ✔

(B) $2x - 2 > 10y + 10$ $\Rightarrow x > 5y + 6$ ✔

(C) $2x - 10y > 12$ $\Rightarrow x > 5y + 6$ ✔

(D) $x - 5y > 6$ $\Rightarrow x > 5y + 6$ ✔

(E) $x > 5y + 7$ $\Rightarrow x > 5y + 7$ ✘

Therefore, the correct answer is (E), since that's the only choice, which is different from others.

9.5.9: EQUIVALENCY FOR MIXED NUMBERS:

Example #9:   Which of the following is not equal to the others?

(A) $\sqrt{64}$ (B) 2^3 (C) $\dfrac{512}{64}$ (D) $1.9 + 6.1$ (E) 2% of 800

Solution: The best way to compare all five answer-choices is by expressing them in the same form.

(A) $\sqrt{64}$ $\Rightarrow 8$ ✔

(B) 2^3 $\Rightarrow 8$ ✔

(C) $\dfrac{512}{64}$ $\Rightarrow 8$ ✔

(D) $1.9 + 6.1$ $\Rightarrow 8$ ✔

(E) 2% of 800 $\Rightarrow 16$ ✘

Therefore, the correct answer is (E), since that's the only choice, which is different from others.

9.5.10: SPECIAL CASES:

On a multiple-choice question, if your answer is not among the given five answer choices – check to see whether it is equivalent to one of the answer choices. In other words, your answer may not be exactly given as one of the answer choices; however, it may be equivalent to one of the answer choices. The following is one such example:

Example 10: If $a = b(c + x)$, what is the value of x in terms of a, b, and c?

(A) $\dfrac{a}{c} - b$ (B) $\dfrac{a - b}{c}$ (C) $\dfrac{b}{c} - a$ (D) $\dfrac{b - c}{a}$ (E) $\dfrac{a}{b} - c$

Solution:

$\Rightarrow a = b(c + x)$

$\Rightarrow a = bc + bx$ [apply distributive property]

$\Rightarrow a - bc = bx$ [subtract both sides of the equation by bc]

$\Rightarrow x = \dfrac{a - bc}{b}$ [divide both sides of the equation by b]

As you can see, we have successfully been able to find what we were asked – the value of x in terms of a, b, and c.

$\Rightarrow x = \dfrac{a - bc}{b}$

Unfortunately, our answer is not even listed as one of the answer choices. Nevertheless, it may be equivalent to one of the answer choices. Now, what we need to do is manipulate and convert our answer to one of the given answer choices. One way to do so is by using the distributive property, and splitting-up the fraction into two fractions and canceling the common terms. If we use the distributive law to divide a by b and bc by b, we see that our answer is just like choice (E) but in another form.

$\Rightarrow x = \dfrac{a}{b} - \dfrac{bc}{b} = \dfrac{a}{b} - c$

Therefore, the correct answer-choice is (E)

9.6 EZ COMPARISON STRATEGY

It is important to compare numbers given in the same or different forms. You should be able to compare and find the smallest or the largest quantity in numbers given in the form of fractions, decimals, scientific notations, and percents. It is very common to find questions that may ask you to compare the given numbers and find an answer-choice that is the smallest or the largest.

A few questions on the math section will ask you to compare different things. Before you compare any two or more items, make sure that they are comparable. Don't compare apples with oranges. For instance, if a question asks you to compare two or more values that are in different forms, first you must convert all the values into fractions, decimals, or percent, and then compare the numbers. A question may also ask you to compare two or more fractions, in which case first make sure that all the denominators are common, and then compare the numerators. A question may also ask you to compare decimals, in which case first make sure that all the decimals have equal number of digits to the left and right of the decimal point, and then compare them.

(i) Never assume that a variable can only have positive values.
Always remember that variables, such as, x or y, could be positive or negative, especially when you are comparing them, and you need to know which one is larger and which one is smaller.
For Example: If $x = 5y$, this does not imply that since x is five time y, hence x is greater than y
$\Rightarrow$ If $y = 1$,   then $x = 5$ $\Rightarrow$ in this case, since $5 > 1$, it mean x is greater than y
$\Rightarrow$ If $y = -1$, then $x = -5$ $\Rightarrow$ in this case, since $-5 < -1$, it means x is less than y

(ii) Never assume that the whole of the parts is the largest number in the problem.
The whole of the parts is the original value, but it is not necessarily the largest number in the problem.
For Example: If a quarter of the 100 members admitted every year into a certain club are Hispanics, how many Hispanic members will there be after five years?
$\Rightarrow$ Whole = 100
$\Rightarrow$ Parts (Number of Hispanic members each year) = ¼ of 100 = 25
$\Rightarrow$ Total Number of Hispanic members in five years = 5 × 25 = 125
Therefore, as you can see, 125 > 100 $\Rightarrow$ the whole is not the biggest number in this problem

EZ REFERENCE: To learn more about Comparison of fractions and decimals, refer to our Content-Knowledge Review-Module on Arithmetic.

Example #1:   Which of the following quantity is the smallest and largest?

(A) 10^{-5} (B) $\sqrt{10,000}$ (C) $\dfrac{1,000,000}{100,000}$ (D) 10.1 + 100.01   (E) 0.10% of 1,000,000

Solution: The best way to compare all five answer-choices is by expressing them in the same form.

(A) 10^{-5} $\Rightarrow$ 0.00001 ✔ (Smallest)

(B) $\sqrt{10,000}$ $\Rightarrow$ 100   ✘

(C) $\dfrac{1,000,000}{100,000}$ $\Rightarrow$ 10   ✘

(D) 10.1 + 100.01 $\Rightarrow$ 110.11   ✘

(E) 0.10% of 1,000,000 $\Rightarrow$ 1,000   ✔ (Largest)

Therefore, answer-choice (A) is the smallest, and answer-choice (E) is the largest.

9.7 EZ COMPUTATION STRATEGY

COMPUTE ARITHMETIC EXPRESSIONS IN DIFFERENT FORMS:

It is very common to find questions that may ask you to compute a given operation and find an answer-choice that expresses that computation correctly. To solve such types of problems, it is important to know how to compute an arithmetic expression in different forms using the "Order of Operations" and "Laws of Operations". You should be able to determine the correct computation of the given arithmetic expression.

EZ REFERENCE: To learn more about Laws of Operations and Order of Operations, refer to our Content-Knowledge Review-Module on Arithmetic.

Example #1:   Which of the following may be used to accurately compute $16 \times 5\frac{1}{2}$?
(A) $(10 \times 5) + (6 \times \frac{1}{2})$ (B) $(10 \times 6) + (6 \times 5) + (6 \times \frac{1}{2})$ (C) $(10 \times 5) + (6 \times 5) + (10 \times \frac{1}{2}) + (6 \times \frac{1}{2})$
(D) $(10 \times 6) + (6 \times 5) + (16 \times \frac{1}{2})$ (E) $(10 \times \frac{1}{2}) + (6 \times 5)$

Solution: We are asked to find the computation of $16 \times 5\frac{1}{2} = 88$
Let's evaluate each answer-choice and see which one results in 88:

(A) $(10 \times 5) + (6 \times \frac{1}{2})$	$\Rightarrow 50 + 3 = 53$	✘
(B) $(10 \times 6) + (6 \times 5) + (6 \times \frac{1}{2})$	$\Rightarrow 60 + 30 + 3 = 93$	✘
(C) $(10 \times 5) + (6 \times 5) + (10 \times \frac{1}{2}) + (6 \times \frac{1}{2})$	$\Rightarrow 50 + 30 + 5 + 3 = 88$	✓
(D) $(10 \times 6) + (6 \times 5) + (16 \times \frac{1}{2})$	$\Rightarrow 60 + 30 + 8 = 98$	✘
(E) $(10 \times \frac{1}{2}) + (6 \times 5)$	$\Rightarrow 5 + 30 = 35$	✘

Therefore, the correct answer is (C), since that's the only choice, which resulted in 88.
Note: answer-choice (C) is nothing but expansion of the distributive law.

Example #2:   Which of the following has the smallest and largest value?
(A) $8 \times 8 - 8 \times 8$ (B) $8 \div 8 \times 8 + 8$ (C) $8 \times 8 \div 8 + 8$ (D) $8 + 8 \times 8 - 8$ (E) $8 \div 8 + 8 \times 8$

Solution: Let's evaluate each answer-choice and see which one has the smallest and the largest value:

(A) $8 \times 8 - 8 \times 8 \Rightarrow 64 - 8 \times 8 = 64 - 64 = 0$ ✓ (Smallest)

(B) $8 \div 8 \times 8 + 8 \Rightarrow 1 \times 8 + 8 = 8 + 8 = 16$ ✘

(C) $8 \times 8 \div 8 + 8 \Rightarrow 64 \div 8 + 8 = 8 + 8 = 16$ ✘

(D) $8 + 8 \times 8 - 8 \Rightarrow 8 + 64 - 8 = 64$ ✘

(E) $8 \div 8 + 8 \times 8 \Rightarrow 1 + 8 \times 8 = 1 + 64 = 65$ ✓ (Largest)

Therefore, answer-choice (A) is the smallest value, and answer-choice (E) is the largest value.
Note: Make sure to remember to apply PEMDAS.

Example #3:   Which of the following accurately expresses ten to the fifth power?
(A) 10×5 (B) $10^{10} \div 10^2$ (C) $10 \times 10 \times 10 \times 10 \times 10$ (D) $5\sqrt{10}$ (E) 5^{10}

Solution: The best way to compare all five answer choices is by expressing them in the same form.

(A) 10×5	$\Rightarrow 50$	✘
(B) $10^{10} \div 10^2$	$\Rightarrow 10^8$	✘
(C) $10 \times 10 \times 10 \times 10 \times 10$	$\Rightarrow 10^5$	✓
(D) $5\sqrt{10}$	$\Rightarrow 1.5$ (approx)	✘
(E) 5^{10}	$\Rightarrow 25^5$	✘

Therefore, the correct answer is (C), since that's the only choice, which accurately expresses ten to the fifth power

GREATEST POSSIBLE VALUE OF AN EXPRESSION:

Example #4:   If x, y, and z are different positive integers less than 10, what is the greatest possible value of $\dfrac{x^2 - y}{z}$?

(A) 10   (B) 12   (C) 79   (D) 99   (E) 100

Solution: To make a fraction larger, the numerator should be the largest possible and the denominator should be the smallest possible.

The greatest possible value of $x^2 - y \Rightarrow 9^2 - 1 = 81 - 1 = 80$

The smallest possible value of $z \Rightarrow 2$

Value of Fraction = $\dfrac{80}{2} = 40$

Now let's try to interchange y and z:

The greatest possible value of $x^2 - y \Rightarrow 9^2 - 2 = 81 - 2 = 79$

The smallest possible value of $z \Rightarrow 1$

Value of Fraction = $\dfrac{79}{1} = 79$

Therefore, the correct answer is (C), since the greatest possible value of the given expression is 79.

9.8 EZ SPECIAL SYMBOLS STRATEGY

INTERPRET SPECIAL SYMBOLS PROPERLY & ACCURATELY:
To test your ability to learn, understand, and effectively apply mathematical concepts, a special symbol is sometimes introduced and defined. So be prepared, you may see a few math questions that involve the use of special symbols that are strange or unfamiliar to you.

You are already familiar with common arithmetical symbols such as +, −, ×, and ÷. For instance, finding the value of 10 + 2, or 10 − 2, or 10 × 2, or 10 ÷ 2 is quite simple. However, you may come across some strange, weird, or bizarre symbols on your test that defines a certain procedure. For instance, you may be asked to find the value of 10 ⊗ 2, or 10 ✪ 2, or 10 ◆ 2, or 10 ★ 2.

Most Commonly Used Special Symbols: θ, ⊗, ⊕, ∅, ☉, ◎, ✪, ✚, ☐, ▲, ▼, ◀, ▶, △, ▽, ◁, ▷, ◆, ◆, ✫, ★, ✦, ✿, ❖, Ω, Ψ, ∈, ←, ↑, →, ↓, ↔

You can usually predict that you've come across a function problem when you get completely blank after seeing a strange symbol, and you think to yourself, after preparing for your test so vigorously, how you could miss this part of the test that deals with such strange symbols. Well, **the good news is that after you review this section, a strange symbol will no longer be strange to you**!

In some questions, the test-makers insert some arbitrary symbols to either confuse or frighten you. Don't let them succeed in their mission to scare you away. These problems may look confusing because of the unfamiliar symbols, which may puzzle you; however, the question-stem in each of these problems always tells you what a strange symbol means or does. The symbol is irrelevant; the important thing is that you carefully follow each step in the procedure that the symbol directs. These types of problems may seem weird or difficult, but in actuality, it's nothing more than an extension of the substitution process and an exercise in plugging-in numbers. Hence, don't get intimidated by these strange looking symbols or let them throw you off; you will always be told what they mean.

Generally, the special symbols are unusual looking signs so that you don't confuse them with standard mathematical symbols. These symbols typically represent a function, that is, a mathematical operation or a combination of multiple mathematical operations with which you are already familiar. A function is just a set of directions. The question will always define what these strange symbols mean. All you have to do is to read the definition carefully and use it as your instruction to work out the answer. In other words, simply follow the directions carefully in order to answer the question correctly, and take one step at a time.

Therefore, if you ever see a strange or special symbol you have never seen before, don't panic, or freak out. Relax; chances are that it's simply a made-up symbol, which actually has no mathematical meaning. Remember, any strange-looking symbol on a question is just a function with a set of directions. Everything you need to know about the symbols will be in the question-stem.

For the purpose of your test, functions are relatively simple, and it's easy to solve such problems as long as you correctly follow the given directions. Hence, the key to answering these types of questions is to make sure that you read and understand the definition carefully, and you are able to follow the directions or instructions properly.

Some of the more challenging strange symbol problems require you to use the given procedure more than once. The important thing to remember in such cases is to always perform the procedure inside the parentheses first, and work your way out, just like PEMDAS.

Some questions may ask you to apply the definition of the special symbols to more complex situations, for instance:
- You may be asked to compare two values, each of which requires the use of special symbols.
- You may be asked to evaluate an expression that involves adding, subtracting, multiplying, dividing, or squaring terms that contain special symbols.
- You may be asked to solve or evaluate an equation that involves the use of special symbols.
- You may find a special symbol as part of a Data Sufficiency question.

EZ REFERENCE: To learn more about functions, refer to our Content-Knowledge Review-Module on Algebra.

Following are a few typical examples that involve special symbols. They will help you understand the concept of special symbols, and the best way to approach such problems.

9.8.1: SINGLE FUNCTION:

Example #1:　　Let x^* be defined by the equation: $x^* = \dfrac{x^2}{1-x^2}$. Evaluate $\left(\dfrac{1}{2}\right)^*$

(A) $\dfrac{1}{9}$　　　　　(B) $\dfrac{1}{8}$　　　　　(C) $\dfrac{1}{6}$　　　　　(D) $\dfrac{1}{4}$　　　　　(E) $\dfrac{1}{3}$

Solution:　　$\Rightarrow \left(\dfrac{1}{2}\right)^* = \dfrac{\left(\dfrac{1}{2}\right)^2}{1-\left(\dfrac{1}{2}\right)^2} = \dfrac{\dfrac{1}{4}}{1-\dfrac{1}{4}} = \dfrac{\dfrac{1}{4}}{\dfrac{3}{4}} = \dfrac{1}{4} \div \dfrac{3}{4} = \dfrac{1}{4} \times \dfrac{4}{3} = \dfrac{1}{3}$

Example #2:　　Let $\Delta x = 5x$ if x is positive, or $2x$ if x is negative, what is the value of $\left(\dfrac{\Delta 20}{\Delta -5}\right)$

(A) –10　　　　　(B) –1　　　　　(C) 1　　　　　(D) 10　　　　　(E) 100

Solution:　　According to the directions given in the problem:
If x is positive, then the function of any number x is $5x$
If x is negative, then the function of any number x is $2x$
Now, evaluate the given expression according to the given directions:
$\Rightarrow \left(\dfrac{\Delta 20}{\Delta -5}\right) = \dfrac{20(5)}{-5(2)} = \dfrac{100}{-10} = -10$

Example #3:　　If $x \text{ ✦ } y = 9x - y$, then what is $8 \text{ ✦ } 2$?
(A) 10　　　　　(B) 30　　　　　(C) 50　　　　　(D) 70　　　　　(E) 90

Solution:　　First half of this problem gives the directions: whenever there is a ✦ in between two numbers $\Rightarrow$ it means to first multiply the number on the left by 9 and then subtract the number on the right.
Second half of problem asks you to apply these directions with two specific numbers: $8 \text{ ✦ } 2$
Now, to solve the problem, all we need to do is plug-in the specific numbers in the given expression according to the given directions:
$\Rightarrow x \text{ ✦ } y = 9x - y$
$\Rightarrow 8 \text{ ✦ } 2 = 8(9) - (2) = 72 - 2 = 70$

Example #4:　　For any real number p and q, if $p \text{ ✪ } q = p^q + q^p$, what is the value of $2 \text{ ✪ } 7$?
(A) 128　　　　　(B) 177　　　　　(C) 181　　　　　(D) 187　　　　　(E) 256

Solution:　　First half of this problem gives the directions: whenever there is a ✪ in between two numbers $\Rightarrow$ it means to raise the first number to the power of the second number, and raise the second number to the power of the first number, and then finally add the resulting two numbers.
Second half of problem asks you to apply these directions with two specific numbers: $2 \text{ ✪ } 7$
Now, to solve the problem, all we need to do is plug-in the specific numbers in the given expression according to the given directions:
$\Rightarrow p \text{ ✪ } q = p^q + q^p$
$\Rightarrow 2 \text{ ✪ } 7 = 2^7 + 7^2 = 128 + 49 = 177$

9.8.2: MULTIPLE FUNCTIONS:

Example #5: If $x \blacklozenge y = 9x - y$, then what is $(7 \blacklozenge 5) \blacklozenge 2$?
(A) 58   (B) 70   (C) 520   (D) 524   (E) 752

Solution: First half of this problem gives the directions: whenever there is a $\blacklozenge$ in between two numbers $\Rightarrow$ it means to first multiply the number on the left by 9 and then subtract the number on the right.
Second half of problem asks you to apply these directions with two specific set of numbers, twice.
Now, to solve the problem, all we need to do is plug-in the specific numbers in the given expression according to the given directions:
$\Rightarrow x \blacklozenge y = 9x - y$
First $\Rightarrow 7 \blacklozenge 5 = 7(9) - (5) = 63 - 5 = 58$
Second $\Rightarrow 58 \blacklozenge 2 = 58(9) - (2) = 522 - 2 = 520$
Therefore, $(7 \blacklozenge 5) \blacklozenge 2 = 520$
Note: Don't forget to use PEMDAS.

Example #6: For any real number p and q, if $p \odot q = p^q + q^p$, what is the value of $1 \odot (2 \odot 6)$?
(A) 99   (B) 100   (C) 101   (D) 126   (E) 202

Solution: First half of this problem gives the directions: whenever there is a $\odot$ in between two numbers $\Rightarrow$ it means to raise the first number to the power of the second number, and raise the second number to the power of the first number, and then finally add the resulting two numbers.
Second half of problem asks you to apply these directions with two specific set of numbers, twice.
Now, to solve the problem, all we need to do is plug-in the specific numbers in the given expression according to the given directions:
$\Rightarrow p \odot q = p^q + q^p$
First $\Rightarrow 2 \odot 6 = 2^6 + 6^2 = 64 + 36 = 100$
Second $\Rightarrow 1 \odot 100 = 1^{100} + 100^1 = 1 + 100 = 101$
Therefore, $1 \odot (2 \odot 6) = 101$
Note: Don't forget to use PEMDAS.

.PRACTICE EXERCISE WITH DETAILED EXPLANATIONS

EZ Consistent Units Strategy:

Work in Consistent Units:

Question #1: If the length and width of a rectangle are 2 feet and 60 inches respectively, what is its area?
Note: First, convert either the 5 feet into 60 inches or the 24 inches into 2 feet before calculating the area or the perimeter of the rectangle.

Solution: **Method #1:** First, convert the 60 inches to 5 feet so that both the units are consistently in inches.
$\Rightarrow$ Area of Rectangle = 2 feet × 5 feet = 10 sq feet
Method #2: First, convert the 2 feet to 24 inches so that both the units are consistently in feet.
$\Rightarrow$ Area of Rectangle = 24 inches × 60 inches = 1440 sq inches.
Wrong: Never make the mistake of working in different units.
$\Rightarrow$ Area of Rectangle = 2 feet × 60 inches = 120 $\Rightarrow$ This clearly wrong!

Get the Answer in the Units Asked:

Question #2: If the length and width of a rectangle is 24 inches and 60 inches respectively, what is the perimeter of the rectangle in feet?
Note: First, convert either the 24 inches into 2 feet, and the 60 inches into 5 feet before calculating the area; or calculate the answer, and then convert it to feet.

Solution: **Method #1:** First, find the perimeter and then convert the answer into inches.
$\Rightarrow$ Perimeter of Rectangle = 2(24 + 60) = 2 × 84 = 168 inches = 14 feet
Method #2: First, convert the 24 inches to 2 feet and 60 inches to 5 feet.
There will be no need to do any conversions, as the answer will automatically be in feet.
$\Rightarrow$ Perimeter of Rectangle = 2(2 + 5) = 2 × 7 = 14 feet

EZ Approximation & Estimation Strategy:

When a Question Asks for an Exact Answer:

Question #3: What is the value of (19.976 × 15.17) ÷ 12.09?
(A) 10.056   (B) 15.876   (C) 17.296   (D) 20.597   (E) 25.065

Solution: We can estimate an answer by rounding-off the values and doing the calculations, and then checking it against the answer choice that is closest to our estimate.
First make approximations and re-write the problem as: (20 × 15) ÷ 12
Solve the problem: (20 × 15) ÷ 12 = 300 ÷ 12 = 25.
Next, pick the answer choice that is closest to 25.
Therefore, the correct answer is (E)
Note: The exact answer to the calculation above is 25.065, which is very close to what we got by using approximation strategy.

Question #4: What is the value of (9.99 × 9.97 × 2.06 × 5.09) ÷ 99.22?
(A) 10.52   (B) 17.75   (C) 25.95   (D) 50.25   (E) 100.5

Solution: You can estimate an answer by rounding-off the values and doing the calculations, and then checking it against the answer choice that is closest to our estimate.
First make approximations and re-write the problem as: (10 × 10 × 2 × 5) ÷ 100
Solve the problem: (10 × 10 × 2 × 5) ÷ 100 = 1000 ÷ 100 = 10.
Next, pick the answer choice that is closest to 10.
Therefore, the correct answer is (A)
Note: The exact answer to the calculation above is 10.51, which is very close to what we got by using approximation strategy.

When a Question Asks For an Approximate Answer:

Question #5:   Which of the following is closest to (74 × 989) ÷ 10?
(A) 1,200   (B) 7,000   (C) 7,400   (D) 8,000   (E) 8,500

Solution: We can estimate an answer by rounding-off the values and doing the calculations, and then checking it against the answer choice that is closest to our estimate.
First make approximations and re-write the problem as: (74 × 1,000) ÷ 10 = 74,000 ÷ 10 = 7,400
Therefore, the correct answer is (C)

Question #6:   What is the closest estimate for: $251 \times \dfrac{99}{51}$?

(A) 50   (B) 100   (C) 250   (D) 500   (E) 1,250

Solution: We can estimate an answer by rounding-off the values and doing the calculations, and then checking it against the answer choice that is closest to our estimate.

First make approximations and re-write the problem as: $251 \times \dfrac{99}{51}$

Solve the problem: $250 \times \dfrac{100}{50} = 250 \times 2 = 500$

Therefore, the correct answer is (D)
Note: The exact answer to the calculation above is 487.2, which is very close to what we got by using approximation strategy.

Question #7:   Approximately what is the total score of five test series if a person's scores are 121, 129, 122, 128, and 120?
(A) 275   (B) 500   (C) 525   (D) 550   (E) 625

Solution: Since the problem asks for approximation, we don't have to find the exact number and we can easily estimate our answer.
Notice that all five scores are close to 125, so round-off all the score to 125.
Multiply the approximate score (125) in each test by 5 to find the approx total score of all five tests.
⇒ 125 × 5 = 625
Therefore, the correct answer is (E)
Note: If we were to find the exact value, simply add all the scores ⇒ 121+129+122+128+120 = 620
(The exact answer to the calculation is 620, which is very close to what we got by using approximation strategy)

Question #8:   If a person's annual mortgage payment is $12,252, approximately how much should be the monthly payment?
(A) $1,000   (B) $1,100   (C) $1,200   (D) $1,300   (E) $1,400

Solution: Since the problem asks for approximation, we don't have to find the exact number and we can easily estimate our answer.
Since 1 year = 12 months, therefore, there should be 12 equal installments.
Divide the total amount by 12 to find how many equal parts are there in the total money to be paid.
Now, round off $12,252 to $12,000 so that it can be easily divided by 12.
Next, divide $12,000 by 12 to find the monthly installment.
⇒ $12,000 ÷ 12 = $1,000
Therefore, the correct answer is (A)
Note: If we were to find the exact value, simply divide $12,252 by 12 ⇒$12,252 ÷ 12 = $1,021
(The exact answer to the calculation is $1,021, which is very close to what we got by using approximation strategy)

EZ Systematic List Strategy:

Question #9:   During a seven-day trade exhibition, the number of visitors doubled each day. The exhibit opened on Monday and closed on the following Sunday. If the attendance on the closing day was 8,000, what was the attendance on the opening day?
(A) 125   (B) 250   (C) 500   (D) 1,000   (E) 2,000

Solution: Let's make a systematic list of attendance on each day, starting from the closing day:
Opening Day: Monday $\Rightarrow$ 125
                  Tuesday $\Rightarrow$ 250
                  Wednesday $\Rightarrow$ 500
                  Thursday $\Rightarrow$ 1000
                  Friday $\Rightarrow$ 2,000
                  Saturday $\Rightarrow$ 4,000
Closing Day: Sunday $\Rightarrow$ 8,000
It's clear from the above list that the attendance on the opening day was 125.
Therefore, the correct answer is (A).

Question #10:   A man took a 1,200-mile trip in 5 days. Each day, he drove 20 miles more than the previous day. How many miles did he cover on the first day?
(A) 50   (B) 100   (C) 200   (D) 400   (E) 800

Solution: Let's make a systematic list of miles covered on each day, starting from the first day:
Number of miles covered on 1st Day $\Rightarrow n$
Number of miles covered on 2nd Day $\Rightarrow n + 20$
Number of miles covered on 3rd Day $\Rightarrow n + 20 + 20$
Number of miles covered on 4th Day $\Rightarrow n + 20 + 20 + 20$
Number of miles covered on 5th Day $\Rightarrow n + 20 + 20 + 20 + 20$
Total Number of miles covered on all 5 Day:
$\Rightarrow 5n + 20(10) = 1,200$
$\Rightarrow 5n + 200 = 1,200$
$\Rightarrow 5n = 1,200 - 200$
$\Rightarrow 5n = 1,000$
$\Rightarrow n = 1,000 \div 5 = 200$
It's clear from the above list that the miles covered on the first day were 200 miles.
Therefore, the correct answer is (C).

Question #11:   The product of three positive integers is 120. If one of them is 2, what is the least possible value of the sum of the other two?
(A) 8   (B) 10   (C) 12   (D) 14   (E) 16

Solution: Since the product of three positive integers is 120 and one of them is 2, the product of the other two integers = $120 \div 2 = 60$
Now, let's systematically list all possible factor pairs, (a, b), of positive integers whose product is 60, and look for the smallest sum:

a	+	b	=	$a + b$
1	+	60	=	61
2	+	30	=	32
3	+	20	=	23
4	+	15	=	19
5	+	12	=	17
6	+	10	=	16

It's clear from the above list that 16 is the least possible value of the sum of the other two integers.
Therefore, the correct answer is (E).
Note: This problem can become very difficult and confusing without making a systematic.

Question #12: If n is a number generated by multiplying a number from Set-A by a number from Set-B, how many distinct possible values of n are greater than 5?
Set-A: {1, 2, 3, 4, 5}
Set-B: {1, 2, 3}
(A) 2   (B) 5   (C) 6   (D) 9   (E) 15

Solution: First, let's make a systematic list of all the possibilities paring off each number in the first set with each number in the second set, so that every combination is included only once. Make sure to write down the possibilities in a systematic manner as you organize them, so that you can count them accurately and don't count the same combination more than once.

$1 \times 1 = 1$	$2 \times 1 = 2$	$3 \times 1 = 3$	$4 \times 1 = 4$	$5 \times 1 = 5$
$1 \times 2 = 2$	$2 \times 2 = 4$	$3 \times 2 = 6$	$4 \times 2 = 8$	$5 \times 2 = 10$
$1 \times 3 = 3$	$2 \times 3 = 6$	$3 \times 3 = 9$	$4 \times 3 = 12$	$5 \times 3 = 15$

Now, let's count the number of value of n that are greater than 5:
$\Rightarrow$ 6, 6, 9, 8, 12, 10, and 15 $\Rightarrow$ that's a total of 7 values
Although there are seven values for n that are greater than 5, two of them are the same (6, 6).
It's clear from the above list that there are 6 different values of n that are greater than 5, not seven.
Therefore, the correct answer is (C).
Note: In this problem, it's very easy to pick 7 as the correct answer and not pay attention to the fact that these values have to be distinct. So make sure that you read the question carefully and make a systematic list before picking your answer.

EZ Interpretation Strategy:

Question #13: How many 10-foot length segments of rope can be cut from a rope that is 82 feet long?
(A) 6   (B) 7   (C) 8   (D) 9   (E) 10

Solution: $\Rightarrow 82 \div 10 = 8.2 = 8 + 0.2$
$\Rightarrow$ At most 8 pieces of length segments 10-foot long can be cut from a 82-foot rope length.
Note: there will be a waste of 2 feet of rope.

Question #14: How many boxes are needed to ship 82 books if no more than 10 books can be placed in a box?
(A) 7   (B) 8   (C) 9   (D) 10   (E) 11

Solution: $\Rightarrow 82 \div 10 = 8.2 = = 8 + 0.2$
$\Rightarrow$ At least 9 boxes are needed to ship the 82 books if no more than 10 books can be placed in a box.
Note: since each box can contain a maximum of 10 books, the ninth box will contain only 2 books.

Question #15: If 10 people share equally in the profit, what is each person's share for a net profit of $82?
(A) $2.8   (B) $8.1   (C) $8.2   (D) $8.5   (E) $9

Solution: $\Rightarrow 82 \div 10 = 8.2$
$\Rightarrow$ Each of 10 people should get a share of $8.20 in the total net profit of a $82.
Note: in this case, the profit can be divided equally to the last decimal point.

Question #16: If a 82-foot length of rope is cut into 10 pieces of equal length, how long is each of the pieces?
(A) $8\dfrac{1}{10}$ (B) $8\dfrac{1}{7}$ (C) $8\dfrac{1}{5}$ (D) $8\dfrac{1}{4}$ (E) $8\dfrac{1}{2}$

Solution: $\Rightarrow 82 \div 10 = 8.2 = 8 + 1/5$
$\Rightarrow$ Each of the 10 pieces of rope cut from a 82-foot length would be $8\dfrac{1}{5}$ feet long.
Note: in this case, the rope can be divided in fractions.

Question #17: If it takes exactly one minute per cut, how long will it take to cut a 20-foot long timber into 20 equal pieces?
(A) 5   (B) 10   (C) 19   (D) 20   (E) 21

Solution: 1st cut $\Rightarrow$ 1 minute $\Rightarrow$ 2 pieces
2nd cut $\Rightarrow$ 2 minutes$\Rightarrow$ 3 pieces
3rd cut $\Rightarrow$ 3 minutes$\Rightarrow$ 4 pieces
4th cut $\Rightarrow$ 4 minutes$\Rightarrow$ 5 pieces
5th cut $\Rightarrow$ 5 minutes$\Rightarrow$ 6 pieces
As you can see, each cut results in 1 additional piece; therefore, to get 20 pieces, we only need to make 19 cuts and that will take 19 minutes.

EZ Equivalency Strategy:

Equivalency for Fractions:

Question #18:   Which of the following expressions is NOT equivalent to the others?

(A) $\dfrac{5}{9}$ (B) $\dfrac{55}{99}$ (C) $\dfrac{505}{999}$ (D) $\dfrac{505}{909}$ (E) $\dfrac{5005}{9009}$

Solution: The best way to compare all five answer-choices is by expressing them in the same form.

(A) $\dfrac{5}{9}$ $\Rightarrow$ 0.55555.......   ✓

(B) $\dfrac{55}{99}$ $\Rightarrow$ 0.55555.......   ✓

(C) $\dfrac{505}{999}$ $\Rightarrow$ 0.5055055.......   ✗

(D) $\dfrac{505}{909}$ $\Rightarrow$ 0.55555.......   ✓

(E) $\dfrac{5005}{9009}$ $\Rightarrow$ 0.55555.......   ✓

Therefore, the correct answer is (C), since that's the only choice, which is different from others.

Equivalency for Decimals:

Question #19:   Which of the following expressions is NOT equivalent to the others?
(A) (0.5 + 0.7) × 6.5   (B) (0.5 × 6.5) + (0.7 × 6.5)   (C) 6.5 + (0.5 × 0.7)
(D) 6.5 × (0.5 + 0.7)   (E) 1.2 × 6.5

Solution: The best way to compare all five answer-choices is by expressing them in the same form.

(A) (0.5 + 0.7) × 6.5 $\Rightarrow$ 7.80 ✓

(B) (0.5 × 6.5) + (0.7 × 6.5) $\Rightarrow$ 7.80 ✓

(C) 6.5 + (0.5 × 0.7) $\Rightarrow$ 6.85 ✗

(D) 6.5 × (0.5 + 0.7) $\Rightarrow$ 7.80 ✓

(E) 1.2 × 6.5 $\Rightarrow$ 7.80 ✓

Therefore, the correct answer is (C), since that's the only choice, which is different from others.

Equivalency for Exponents:

Question #20:   Which of the following expressions is NOT equivalent to the others?
(A) 2^2 × 20 × 16   (B) 2^3 × 10 × 24   (C) 2^4 × 5 × 24   (D) 2^5 × 5 × 12   (E) 2^6 × 6 × 5

Solution: The best way to compare all five answer-choices is by expressing them in the same form.
Method #1: One way to solve is by factoring all of the answer choices:

(A) 2^2 × 20 × 16 $\Rightarrow 2^2$ × 2 × 2 × 5 × 2 × 2 × 2 × 2 $\Rightarrow 2^7$ × 2 × 5   ✗

(B) $2^3 \times 10 \times 24$ $\Rightarrow 2^3 \times 2 \times 5 \times 2 \times 2 \times 2 \times 3$ $\Rightarrow 2^7 \times 3 \times 5$ ✓

(C) $2^4 \times 5 \times 24$ $\Rightarrow 2^4 \times 5 \times 2 \times 2 \times 2 \times 3$ $\Rightarrow 2^7 \times 3 \times 5$ ✓

(D) $2^5 \times 5 \times 12$ $\Rightarrow 2^5 \times 5 \times 2 \times 2 \times 3$ $\Rightarrow 2^7 \times 3 \times 5$ ✓

(E) $2^6 \times 6 \times 5$ $\Rightarrow 2^6 \times 2 \times 3 \times 5$ $\Rightarrow 2^7 \times 3 \times 5$ ✓

Method #2: Another way to solve is by factoring all of the answer choices:

(A) $2^2 \times 20 \times 16$ $\Rightarrow 4 \times 20 \times 16$ $\Rightarrow 1,280$ ✗

(B) $2^3 \times 10 \times 24$ $\Rightarrow 8 \times 10 \times 24$ $\Rightarrow 1,920$ ✓

(C) $2^4 \times 5 \times 24$ $\Rightarrow 16 \times 5 \times 24$ $\Rightarrow 1,920$ ✓

(D) $2^5 \times 5 \times 12$ $\Rightarrow 32 \times 5 \times 12$ $\Rightarrow 1,920$ ✓

(E) $2^6 \times 6 \times 5$ $\Rightarrow 64 \times 6 \times 5$ $\Rightarrow 1,920$ ✓

Therefore, the correct answer is (A), since that's the only choice, which is different from others.

Equivalency for Scientific Notation:

Example 21: Which of the following is not equal to 0.00965?
(A) 965×10^{-5} (B) 9.65×10^{-3} (C) 0.00965×10^0 (D) 0.0000965×10^2 (E) 0.0000965×10^1

Solution: The best way to compare all five answer-choices is by expressing them in the same form.

(A) 965×10^{-5} $\Rightarrow 0.00965$ ✓

(B) 9.65×10^{-3} $\Rightarrow 0.00965$ ✓

(C) 0.00965×10^0 $\Rightarrow 0.00965$ ✓

(D) 0.0000965×10^2 $\Rightarrow 0.00965$ ✓

(E) 0.0000965×10^1 $\Rightarrow 0.000965$ ✗

Therefore, the correct answer is (E), since that's the only choice, which is different from others.

Equivalency for Percents:

Question #22: Which of the following expressions is NOT equivalent to the others?
(A) 1% of 2,500   (B) 5% of 500   (C) 10% of 250   (D) 25% of 100   (E) 50% of 20

Solution: The best way to compare all five answer-choices is by expressing them in the same form.

(A) 1% of 2,500 $\Rightarrow 25$ ✓

(B) 5% of 500 $\Rightarrow 25$ ✓

(C) 10% of 250 $\Rightarrow 25$ ✓

(D) 25% of 100 $\Rightarrow 25$ ✓

(E) 50% of 20 $\Rightarrow 10$ ✗

Therefore, the correct answer is (E), since that's the only choice, which is different from others.

Equivalency for Place Value Notation:

Question #23: Which of the following numbers, if any, are the same?
(A.) 1 million   (B.) 100 ten thousands   (C.) 1,000 thousands
(D.) 10,000 hundreds   (E.) 10,000 tens

Solution: The best way to compare all five answer-choices is by expressing them in the same form.

(A.) 1 million $\Rightarrow 1,000,000$ ✓

(B.) 100 ten thousands $\Rightarrow 100 \times 10,000 = 1,000,000$ ✓

(C.) 1,000 thousands $\Rightarrow 1{,}000 \times 1{,}000 = 1{,}000{,}000$ ✓

(D.) 10,000 hundred $\Rightarrow 10{,}000 \times 100 = 1{,}000{,}000$ ✓

(E.) 10,000 tens $\Rightarrow 10{,}000 \times 10 = 100{,}000$ ✗

Therefore, the correct answer is (E), since that's the only choice, which is different from others.

Equivalency for Equations:

Question #24:   Which of the following expressions is NOT equivalent to the others?
        (A) $20x + 50 = 100y + 170$ (B) $20x - 20 = 100y + 100$ (C) $20x - 100y = 120$
        (D) $10x - 50y = 60$ (E) $10x = 50y + 70$

Solution: The best way to compare all five answer-choices is by expressing them in the same form.

        (A) $20x + 50 = 100y + 170$ $\Rightarrow x = 5y + 6$ ✓

        (B) $20x - 20 = 100y + 100$ $\Rightarrow x = 5y + 6$ ✓

        (C) $20x - 100y = 120$ $\Rightarrow x = 5y + 6$ ✓

        (D) $10x - 50y = 60$ $\Rightarrow x = 5y + 6$ ✓

        (E) $10x = 50y + 70$ $\Rightarrow x = 5y + 7$ ✗

Therefore, the correct answer is (E), since that's the only choice, which is different from others.

Equivalency for Inequalities:

Question #25:   Which of the following expressions is NOT equivalent to the others?
        (A) $20x + 50 > 100y + 170$ (B) $20x - 20 > 100y + 100$ (C) $20x - 100y > 120$
        (D) $10x - 50y > 60$ (E) $10x > 50y + 70$

Solution: The best way to compare all five answer-choices is by expressing them in the same form.

        (A) $20x + 50 > 100y + 170$ $\Rightarrow x > 5y + 6$ ✓

        (B) $20x - 20 > 100y + 100$ $\Rightarrow x > 5y + 6$ ✓

        (C) $20x - 100y > 120$ $\Rightarrow x > 5y + 6$ ✓

        (D) $10x - 50y > 60$ $\Rightarrow x > 5y + 6$ ✓

        (E) $10x > 50y + 70$ $\Rightarrow x > 5y + 7$ ✗

Therefore, the correct answer is (E), since that's the only choice, which is different from others.

Equivalency for Mixed Numbers:

Question #26:   Which of the following is not equal to the others?
        (A) $\sqrt{256}$ (B) 2^4 (C) $\dfrac{1024}{64}$ D) $6.9 + 9.1$ (E) 2% of 900

Solution: The best way to compare all five answer-choices is by expressing them in the same form.

        (A) $\sqrt{256}$ $\Rightarrow 16$ ✓

        (B) 2^4 $\Rightarrow 16$ ✓

        (C) $\dfrac{1024}{64}$ $\Rightarrow 16$ ✓

        (D) $6.9 + 9.1$ $\Rightarrow 16$ ✓

        (E) 2% of 900 $\Rightarrow 18$ ✗

Therefore, the correct answer is (E), since that's the only choice, which is different from others.

EZ Comparison Strategy:

Question #27: Which of the following quantity is the smallest and largest?

(A) 2^{-6} (B) $\sqrt{81}$ (C) $\dfrac{855}{57}$ (D) $1.9 + 6.8$ (E) 2% of 600

Solution: The best way to compare all five answer-choices is by expressing them in the same form.

(A) 2^{-6} $\Rightarrow \dfrac{1}{64}$ ✓ (Smallest)

(B) $\sqrt{81}$ $\Rightarrow 9$ ✗

(C) $\dfrac{855}{57}$ $\Rightarrow 15$ ✗

(D) $1.9 + 6.8$ $\Rightarrow 8.7$ ✗

(E) 2% of 800 $\Rightarrow 16$ ✓ (Largest)

Therefore, answer-choice (A) is the smallest, and answer-choice (E) is the largest.

EZ COMPUTATION STRATEGY:

Question #28: Which of the following may be used to accurately compute $18 \times 5\frac{1}{2}$?
(A) $(10 \times 5) + (8 \times \frac{1}{2})$ (B) $(10 \times 8) + (8 \times 5) + (8 \times \frac{1}{2})$ (C) $(10 \times 5) + (8 \times 5) + (10 \times \frac{1}{2}) + (8 \times \frac{1}{2})$
(D) $(10 \times 8) + (8 \times 5) + (18 \times \frac{1}{2})$ (E) $(10 \times \frac{1}{2}) + (8 \times 5)$

Solution: We are asked to find the computation of $18 \times 5\frac{1}{2} = 99$
Let's evaluate each answer choice and see which one results in 88:

(A) $(10 \times 5) + (8 \times \frac{1}{2})$ $\Rightarrow 50 + 4 = 54$ ✗

(B) $(10 \times 8) + (8 \times 5) + (8 \times \frac{1}{2})$ $\Rightarrow 80 + 40 + 4 = 124$ ✗

(C) $(10 \times 5) + (8 \times 5) + (10 \times \frac{1}{2}) + (8 \times \frac{1}{2})$ $\Rightarrow 50 + 40 + 5 + 4 = 99$ ✓

(D) $(10 \times 8) + (8 \times 5) + (18 \times \frac{1}{2})$ $\Rightarrow 80 + 40 + 9 = 129$ ✗

(E) $(10 \times \frac{1}{2}) + (8 \times 5)$ $\Rightarrow 5 + 40 = 45$ ✗

Therefore, the correct answer is (C), since that's the only choice, which resulted in 99.
Note: answer choice (C) is nothing but expansion of the distributive law.

Question #29: Which of the following has the smallest and largest value?
(A) $9 \times 9 - 9 \times 9$ (B) $9 \div 9 \times 9 + 9$ (C) $9 \times 9 \div 9 + 9$ (D) $9 + 9 \times 9 - 9$ (E) $9 \div 9 + 9 \times 9$

Solution: Let's evaluate each answer-choice and see which one has the smallest and the largest value:

(A) $9 \times 9 - 9 \times 9 \Rightarrow 81 - 9 \times 9 = 81 - 81 = 0$ ✓ (Smallest)

(B) $9 \div 9 \times 9 + 9 \Rightarrow 1 \times 9 + 9 = 9 + 9 = 18$ ✗

(C) $9 \times 9 \div 9 + 9 \Rightarrow 81 \div 9 + 9 = 9 + 9 = 18$ ✗

(D) $9 + 9 \times 9 - 9 \Rightarrow 9 + 81 - 9 = 81$ ✗

(E) $9 \div 9 + 9 \times 9 \Rightarrow 1 + 9 \times 9 = 1 + 81 = 82$ ✓ (Largest)

Therefore, answer-choice (A) is the smallest value, and answer-choice (E) is the greatest value.
Note: Make sure to remember to apply PEMDAS.

Question #30: Which of the following accurately expresses twenty to the fifth power?
(A) 20×5 (B) $20^{10} \div 20^2$ (C) $20 \times 20 \times 20 \times 20 \times 20$ (D) $5\sqrt{20}$ (E) 5^{20}

Solution: The best way to compare all five answer choices is by expressing them in the same form.

(A) 20×5 $\Rightarrow 100$ ✗

(B) $20^{10} \div 20^2$ $\Rightarrow 20^8$ ✗

(C) $20 \times 20 \times 20 \times 20 \times 20$ $\Rightarrow 20^5$ ✓

(D) $5\sqrt{20}$ $\Rightarrow 22.5$ (approx) ✗

(E) 5^{20} $\Rightarrow 25^{10}$ ✗

Therefore, the correct answer is (C), since that's the only choice, which accurately expresses twenty to the fifth power.

EZ Special Symbols Strategy:

Single Functions:

Question #31: Let x^* be defined by the equation: $x^* = \dfrac{x^2}{1-x^2}$. Evaluate $\left(\dfrac{1}{3}\right)^*$

   (A) $\dfrac{1}{2}$ (B) $\dfrac{1}{3}$ (C) $\dfrac{1}{4}$ (D) $\dfrac{1}{6}$ (E) $\dfrac{1}{8}$

Solution: $\Rightarrow \left(\dfrac{1}{3}\right)^* = \dfrac{\left(\dfrac{1}{3}\right)^2}{1-\left(\dfrac{1}{3}\right)^2} = \dfrac{\dfrac{1}{9}}{1-\dfrac{1}{9}} = \dfrac{\dfrac{1}{9}}{\dfrac{8}{9}} = \dfrac{1}{9} \div \dfrac{8}{9} = \dfrac{1}{9} \times \dfrac{9}{8} = \dfrac{1}{8}$

Question #32: If $\Delta x = 5x$ if x is positive, or $2x$ if x is negative, what is the value of $\left(\dfrac{\Delta 100}{\Delta - 50}\right)$

   (A) -5 (B) -1 (C) 1 (D) 5 (E) 500

Solution: According to the directions given in the problem:
If x is positive, then the function of any number x is $5x$
If x is negative, then the function of any number x is $2x$
Now, evaluate the given expression according to the given directions:
$\Rightarrow \left(\dfrac{\Delta 100}{\Delta - 50}\right) = \dfrac{100(5)}{-50(2)} = \dfrac{500}{-100} = -5$

Question #33: If $x + y = 9x - y$, then what is $7 + 2$?
   (A) 9   (B) 31   (C) 52   (D) 61   (E) 65

Solution: First half of this problem gives the directions: whenever there is a $+$ in between two numbers $\Rightarrow$ it means to first multiply the number on the left by 9 and then subtract the number on the right.
Second half of problem asks you to apply these directions with two specific numbers: $7 + 2$
Now, to solve the problem, all we need to do is plug-in the specific numbers in the given expression according to the given directions:
$\Rightarrow x + y = 9x - y$
$\Rightarrow 7 + 2 = 7(9) - (2) = 63 - 2 = 61$

Question #34: For any real number p and q, if $p \circledcirc q = p^q + q^p$, what is the value of $2 \circledcirc 9$?
   (A) 512   (B) 593   (C) 595   (D) 1024   (E) 1105

Solution: First half of this problem gives the directions: whenever there is a $\circledcirc$ in between two numbers $\Rightarrow$ it means to raise the first number to the power of the second number, and raise the second number to the power of the first number, and then finally add the resulting two numbers.
Second half of problem asks you to apply these directions with two specific numbers: $2 \circledcirc 9$

Now, to solve the problem, all we need to do is plug-in the specific numbers in the given expression according to the given directions:

$\Rightarrow p \otimes q = p^q + q^p$

$\Rightarrow 2 \otimes 9 = 2^9 + 9^2 = 512 + 81 = 593$

Multiple Functions:

Question #35: If $x \blacklozenge y = 9x - y$, then what is $(8 \blacklozenge 6) \blacklozenge 2$?
(A) 66   (B) 96   (C) 592   (D) 596   (E) 862

Solution: First half of this problem gives the directions: whenever there is a $\blacklozenge$ in between two numbers $\Rightarrow$ it means to first multiply the number on the left by 9 and then subtract the number on the right.
Second half of problem asks you to apply these directions with two specific set of numbers, twice.
Now, to solve the problem, all we need to do is plug-in the specific numbers in the given expression according to the given directions:
$\Rightarrow x \blacklozenge y = 9x - y$
First $\Rightarrow 8 \blacklozenge 6 = 8(9) - (6) = 72 - 6 = 66$
Second $\Rightarrow 66 \blacklozenge 2 = 66(9) - (2) = 594 - 2 = 592$
Therefore, $(8 \blacklozenge 6) \blacklozenge 2 = 592$
Note: Don't forget to use PEMDAS.

Question #36: For any real number p and q, if $p \odot q = p^q + q^p$, what is the value of $1 \odot (2 \odot 3)$?
(A) 6   (B) 17   (C) 18   (D) 123   (E) 125

Solution: First half of this problem gives the directions: whenever there is a $\odot$ in between two numbers $\Rightarrow$ it means to raise the first number to the power of the second number, and raise the second number to the power of the first number, and then finally add the resulting two numbers.
Second half of problem asks you to apply these directions with two specific set of numbers, twice.
Now, to solve the problem, all we need to do is plug-in the specific numbers in the given expression according to the given directions:
$\Rightarrow p \odot q = p^q + q^p$
First $\Rightarrow 2 \odot 3 = 2^3 + 3^2 = 8 + 9 = 17$
Second $\Rightarrow 1 \odot 17 = 1^{17} + 17^1 = 1 + 17 = 18$
Therefore, $1 \odot (2 \odot 3) = 18$
Note: Don't forget to use PEMDAS.

CHAPTER 10.0: EZ GRID-IN STRATEGIES

HIGHLIGHTS:
10.1 Introduction to Grid-Ins
10.2 Instructions for Grid-Ins
10.3 How to Record Grid-Ins
10.4 Gridding Strategies for Different Formats
10.5 Range of Answers in Grind-Ins
10.6 EZ Gridding Facts
▪ Practice Exercise with Detailed Explanations

SAT GRID-IN SECTION: STUDENT-PRODUCED RESPONSE QUESTIONS:

This section is exclusively dedicated to the Grid-In questions.

10.1 INTRODUCTION TO GRID-INS:

Grid-In or Student-Produced Response questions, which appear in the Math section, is a special section of the SAT. It is designed to measure your ability to solve mathematical problems when no answer choices are provided.

About one-fifth (10 questions) of the questions on the math sections of the SAT, are Grid-In questions. The rest of the math questions are multiple-choice questions.

Grid-In questions are a lot different from the usual multiple-choice questions that you are more used to. In Grid-In questions, you have to grid in your actual answer instead of picking from multiple-choices. The Grid-In questions resemble more closely the math tests you're used to taking in school. These questions are just like any regular math problem, with which you are already familiar. However, the rules and guidelines for entering the Grid-In answers are fairly unique for the SAT.

In this section, you will learn all the necessary tools to excel on Grid-In questions on the SAT, from the instructions to testing strategies. At first, most people find Grid-In questions harder than the usual multiple-choice questions. However, in reality, as you go through this section properly, soon you'll realize that Grid-In questions can be answered as easily and quickly as most multiple-choice questions. In fact, many students find them to be just like any other multiple-choice math questions on the SAT. All it takes is practice to become comfortable with the format.

10.1.1: GRID-INS VERSUS MULTIPLE-CHOICES:

Grid-In and multiple-choice questions have certain similarities and differences; while the similarities make them quite alike, the differences make them rather different, in ways more than one.

SIMILARITIES:

Grid-In questions require the same math skills and reasoning abilities as the multiple-choice math questions. They test and cover the same math concepts and topics as multiple-choice questions, from very easy to very hard. They also consist of the same type of standard math questions, such as, arithmetic, algebra, and geometry questions, just like multiple-choice questions. In fact, the question-stems of many Grid-In questions are very similar to multiple-choice questions. The same question can be given to you in a Grid-In or multiple-choice format.

DIFFERENCES:
The major differences between Grid-In and multiple-choice questions can be further bifurcated based on their disadvantages and advantages.

DISADVANTAGES:

- **No Multiple-Choice Answers:** One of the most important reasons why Grid-In questions are more challenging than the multiple-choice questions is due to the fact that Grid-Ins don't provide any multiple answer-choices from where you can pick-and-choose your answer, like in the multiple-choice questions. Instead of picking your answer from five choices, you have to work through and solve each problem yourself and then enter the answer you come up with onto a special math grid box on the answer sheet that can be read by a computer. Therefore, on Grid-Ins, you are completely on your own in this voyage of ascertaining the correct answer without any clues given to you.

- **No Back-Solving:** The other main drawback of Grid-Ins is that it's not possible to work backwards on Grid-In questions, like in the multiple-choice questions. One of the basic requirements of back-solving are the answer-choices. Since there aren't any answer choices provided for Grid-Ins, it's not possible to work backwards. Therefore, on Grid-Ins, you must know the math concepts, and the direct way to solve them.

ADVANTAGES:

- **No Penalty for Wrong Answers on Grid-Ins:** The major advantage of Grid-In questions is the way how wrong answers are scored, or in fact, not scored. On Grid-In questions, unlike multiple-choice questions, there is no penalty for wrong answers, that is, no points are subtracted for wrong answers. A wrong multiple-choice answer takes away ¼ point, but a wrong Grid-In answer costs you nothing. Therefore, on Grid-Ins, if you get a wrong answer, you don't gain any points, but you don't lose any points either.

- **No Need to Change Your Answer Format:** Another main advantage of the Grid-In format is that it allows you to enter your answer in the format in which you obtain it, as long as it's griddable. On Grid-In questions, unlike multiple-choice questions, you have the ability to grid your answer in whichever form you get it, whether it's a whole number, decimal, or fraction, without changing its format. In a multiple-choice question, you may have to convert your answer to one of given choices. For instance: On a Grid-In question, if the answer to your solution is 2/10, you can grid 2/10, if your answer is .2, you can grid .2. On a multiple-choice question, if your answer to your solution is 2/10 or .2, you may have to change its format depending on the types of choices that are given. Therefore, on Grid-Ins, there is no need to change your answer format.

- **No Distracters:** Lastly, one more advantage of the Grid-In format is that there are fewer chances of you being tricked into picking a wrong answer, simply because there aren't any options given. On Grid-In questions, unlike multiple-choice questions, there are no multiple choices given and you are required to come up with your own answer. In multiple-choice questions, the five options are given in a way that is confusing and many students are tempted to pick the wrong one, just because some of the options seem to be correct but they are nothing more than a hoax. Therefore, on Grid-Ins, there is no way that you will be tricked into picking one of the distracting answer choices.

10.1.2: GUESSING ON GRID-INS:
On Grid-Ins, there are no answer choices to eliminate or pick, but you won't lose points for guessing. Since there's no wrong-answer penalty on Grid-Ins, if you make a guess and get it wrong, you won't lose any points. Even if you have no idea how to solve a problem, you might as well try your luck by guessing without any apprehension. The worst that can happen is that you get zero points for the questions on which you guessed. However, if you get just a couple of guesses correct, you are looking at gaining a few extra bonus points for guessing.

So feel comfortable gridding whatever answer you get without the fear of losing any points or of the thought that it may subtract from your final score if it is wrong. Therefore, given that there is no scope of losing any points, we recommend that you always enter a response for every Grid-In and never leave them blank.

THE DOWNSIDE IN GRID-IN GUESSING: In the absence of multiple-choices, the odds of randomly guessing the right answer on Grid-Ins are very slim. Even without the wrong-answer penalty, the likelihood of guessing the right answer on a Grid-In is so low that if you have no idea what the answer to a Grid-In question is, it doesn't make much sense in taking a wild or random guess. It's almost like throwing an arrow in the dark in the hope of hitting the bull's-eye!

THE UPSIDE IN GRID-IN GUESSING: However, it doesn't necessarily mean that guessing is a bad idea on Grid-Ins. If you have worked out a Grid-In problem, and have an answer, make sure to grid it in. Even if you're unsure of the answer, gridding it can't hurt your score. Moreover, if you have done some work on a Grid-In question but don't quite have an answer, try to estimate the general range of the answer and make a guess. That is, if you are stuck in the middle of a problem you'll be in a position to make an intelligent guess. You never know, you may just get lucky.

10.2 INSTRUCTIONS FOR GRID-INS

At the beginning of the set of Grid-In questions, you will see the following instructions, describing the directions for Grid-In questions.

DIRECTIONS:

On the SAT, you will find 10 Grid-In questions for which no choices will be given. The answer sheet for this section will have 10 blank grids, one for each question. Each Grid-In question provides a Grid-In table. Each Grid-In table contains four blank boxes or spaces where you can write your answer and underneath each blank box or space is the column of ovals or bubbles, where you must grid your answer. Each grid will look exactly like the grid shown below:

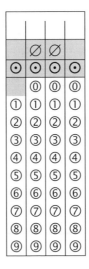

The answer grid for Grid-In questions is somewhat similar to the grid for your zip code on the personal information section of your answer sheet, other than the fact that this one also has options for decimals and fraction slashes.

PARTS OF GRID BOX:

The grid box is made up of 4 columns and 13 rows.

First Row: The first row of the grid box contains open spaces for you to write in the numerical value of your answer.

Second Row: The second row of the grid box contains ovals with a slash "/", and has only two ovals in the middle, in the second and third column. These allow you to enter numbers in fractional format.
Note: Since a fraction must have both a numerator and a denominator, it is not possible that the leftmost or rightmost columns could have a "/". Just to save yourself from making the reckless error of gridding a slash in the first or fourth column, there are no options for "/" in those positions.

Third Row: The third row of the grid box contains ovals with decimal points in all four columns. These allow you to enter numbers in decimal format.
Note: Try not to grid a decimal in the last column, as there is no good reason to do so.

Fourth Row: The fourth row of the grid box contains ovals with zeros in the second, third and fourth column, there is no zero option in the first column.

Fifth thru Thirteenth Row: The fifth through thirteenth row of the grid box contains digits in all four columns where you can grid your numerical answer.

Note: The horizontal bar separates the first three rows with the open spaces, fraction slashes, and decimal points from the digits 0 to 9.

CHARACTERS AND SYMBOLS ALLOWED FOR GRID-INS:

Characters: The only characters that are allowed and appear in the grid are digits 0 to 9.

Symbols: The only symbols that are allowed and appear in the grid are the decimal point (.), which is used to enter decimal answers, and the slash (/), which is used to enter fractional answers.

Note: Unless a problem indicates otherwise, that is, it gives you specific instructions, you can grid your answer either as a decimal (by using a decimal point symbol), or as a fraction (by using a slash symbol).

LEARN THE RULES BEFORE YOU PLAY THE GAME:
As you can see, the directions for Grid-In questions are quite simple, but you have to spend a fair amount of time trying to understand how to record your answers on the special grid. There are certain guidelines and rules for recording your answers to Grid-In questions. You can study these directions either when you get your first Grid-In question on the test, which means wasting precious testing time that could be utilized to answer other questions or you could understand the format and the directions right NOW, which is much before you take the test.

Since the directions for Grid-In questions never change, it's a good idea to become familiar with them now, so you can save time, minimize errors, and improve your confidence by knowing the rules before the test. When you take the actual SAT, dismiss the instructions for these questions immediately – do not spend even one second reading the directions or looking at the sample problems. You should be completely conversant with these instructions in advance, much before you take the test. In fact, you should familiarize yourself with these instructions at the beginning, when you first start preparing for the SAT math section. Whenever you do your practice for Grid-In problems, it would be a good idea to actually grid in the answers in the grid boxes.

UNDERSTAND THE DIRECTIONS TO GRID-INS CORRECTLY:
Read and reread the directions for Grid-Ins until you completely understand them as they are absolutely essential to your understanding of these questions. The last thing you would want to happen is that you know the math concept that a question is testing, you solve the problem correctly, get the correct answer, but still not get credit for all your hard work, just because you didn't grid it properly, as per the rules and guidelines specified for the SAT.

Gridding your answer for the Grid-Ins is not difficult; however, there are some special rules and guidelines concerning Grid-In questions. There are limitations to what you may grid and how you may grid and what will be counted and what won't be counted. Therefore, it's imperative that you understand the directions to Grid-In questions. If needed, reread the directions and the explanations repeatedly. Make sure you know what is being asked, and what you need to do. Since you have never experienced the special way of gridding your answers before, make sure you spend enough time comprehending the whole mechanism behind recoding your answers for the Grid-In problems. In the beginning, these questions may seem difficult, but once you have gone through this section, you will start to feel more comfortable with them. The directions to Grid-In questions may look a bit overwhelming at first; nevertheless, the good news is that with a bit of practice, you won't have to think consciously about how to record your answers; they will work more like a reflex action.

AFTER SOLVING, BEFORE GRIDDING:
Before gridding your final answer, be absolutely certain of your response. If you wish to erase your answer to grid in a different one, do so completely. Incomplete erasures may be picked up by the scoring machines as errors or intended answers. Also, be very careful to mark no more than one oval in any column because answer sheets are machine-scored and you will receive credit only if the circles are filled in correctly. All these conventions are similar to the ones for regular multiple-choice questions.

PRACTICE GRID-INS:
Like any other math questions, practice will make you better at Grid-In questions. Moreover, since most people have not had much experience with SAT type of Grid-In questions, practice will definitely make you more comfortable and conversant with such types of questions. The more examples and practice questions you work out, the better you will perform on this section of the test. By the time you finish the solved examples and practice questions, you should feel confident about your ability to answer Grid-In questions.

10.3 HOW TO RECORD GRID-INS

Each Grid-In question consists of a mathematical question-stem. You are required to solve the given problem, find the correct answer, and then grid it on a special grid.

EZ STEP-BY-STEP METHOD: After solving a problem and obtaining your final answer, to Grid-In your answer, apply the following steps:

STEP 1: Write your Answer in Number Boxes: First, write all the elements of your answer, that is, the digits, decimal points, or fraction signs, in the four boxes at the top of the grid, each piece in a separate box.

STEP 2: Mark your Answer in the Grid: Next, shade or blacken the appropriate bubble or oval that corresponds to the numbers you entered in the boxes at the top of the column, underneath each box so that they match the value of the box at the top of the column.

EZ NOTE: Writing your answer in the number boxes doesn't get you any points by itself, so you really don't have to write your answer in the boxes above the grid. Hence, you may think that gridding directly will save time; however, first writing, then gridding, helps maximize accuracy and minimize errors.

10.3.1: PLACEMENT OF ANSWERS ON THE GRID:

It needs to be noted that you will receive credit for a correct answer no matter where you grid it. You can start gridding your answer in any column you choose, if space permits. Don't worry about which column to use when you begin writing the answer. As long as the answer is gridded completely, you will receive credit.

EZ Method #1: We suggest that you always start your answer from the first column box. So at all times, go in order from left to right to avoid any confusion or errors, that is, consistently start all your answers in the first far left box, with blank spaces on the right. If you always start with the first column, it will ensure that your answers always fit in, even if your answers have only one or two figures. This will also eliminate any unwarranted confusion as to where to grid your answer on each question. Moreover, by doing so you'll also be less encouraged to round off numbers or grid in impartial answers.

EZ Method #2: As an alternate way, if you like, you can also apply the standard format of writing numbers; that is, consistently write all your answers the way numbers are usually displayed – to the right, with blank spaces on the left.

Which Method to Apply? Whichever way you choose to apply, try to have a consistent approach for all Grid-In problems. Before you take your test, you must decide in advance, in which column you want to begin gridding your answers. This will save you time and confusion. We suggest that you either left-align or right-align your answers; it's not at all a good idea to center-align your answers.

EZ NOTE: Be careful, there is no oval for 0 (zero) in the first column, so you will need to grid a zero answer in any column other than the first one, that is, in the second, third, or fourth column. Zero has been omitted from the first column to encourage you to grid the most accurate values for rounded decimals.

EZ CAUTION: Any unused columns should be left blank – do not put in zeros or decimals!

For Example: The answer 127 could be gridded in any of the of the following two ways as shown below; both answers are correct.

Option #1   **Option #2**

OR

10.3.2: ONLY GRIDDED ANSWERS WILL BE SCORED:

Be careful to grid every answer very carefully. The machine that grades the test does not have the ability to read what you have written in the boxes; it reads only the answers in the grid. So, always remember that only the answers you shade in the ovals will be scored, not the ones you write in the boxes. If you just write your answers in the boxes without filling in the ovals, you won't get any credit. Merely entering your answer in the top boxes is not enough. Also, make sure to mark only one bubble per column. If you solve a problem and get the correct answer but misgrid the answer, you will not get any credit.

⇒   If you write the correct answer in the open boxes, but forget to grid it in the ovals or accidentally grid in something else in the ovals – you will get no credit.

⇒   If you grid in the correct answer in the ovals, but forget to write it in the open boxes or accidentally write something else in the open boxes – you will get full credit.

GRIDDING ANSWERS DIRECTLY WITHOUT WRITING IN THE OPEN BOX:
If the computer reads only the gridded bubbles, why bother writing in the answer?
Yes, you can mark your answer directly in the grid without bothering to write it in the boxes on the top. You will get full credit if you do that. However, you will get no credit if you write your answer in the boxes on the top and not mark it on the grid. Some SAT books and guides recommend that you shouldn't waste time writing the answer in the boxes on the top. This is the most atrocious advice you can get for the Grid-In section. We highly recommend that you first write your answer in the boxes on the top and then mark it in the grid.

For instance: If your answer to a question is 1257, first write 1257 at the top of the grid in the blank boxes, one digit in each box, and then in each column blacken the oval that contains the number you wrote at the top of the column.

Officially – you are not required to do this. Logically – it does have its benefits. It gives you something to follow as you fill in the ovals. It's true that you won't be awarded any extra points if you write the answer before you grid it; however, you're more likely to make mistakes if you don't. Writing your answer first can help ensure that you grid the correct value in each column. It only takes a second per answer to fill in the spaces at the top, and it definitely eliminates any careless errors while gridding. Moreover, if you go back to check your work or the answer, it is a lot easier to read what's written in the boxes on top than what's shaded in the grid.

10.4 GRIDDING STRATEGIES FOR DIFFERENT FORMATS

MULTIPLE CORRECT ANSWER FORMATS:

There can be more than one correct answer for Grid-In problems; in other words, the same correct answer can be expressed in different formats, such as, in terms of different types of fractions or decimals. For instance: the fraction answer ¼ is the same as the decimal answer .25.

EZ TIP: In general, you should grid your answer in the form that you obtain unintentionally in solving the problem, without wasting any time in converting it into a different format. Convert your answer format only when it doesn't fit in the grid.

10.4.1: INTEGER ANSWERS:

On Grid-In questions, you can grid one-, two-, three-, or four- digit positive integers or zeros.

For Example: Some of the integer answers can be gridded in the following ways:

Zero	One Digit	Two Digit	Three Digit	Four Digit

10.4.2: FRACTION ANSWERS:

For Entering Fractional Answers, Grid-In (/) in the Correct Column: The slash sign (/) is used for the fraction bar, and therefore it separates the numerator from the denominator. It appears only in two of the four columns, in columns two and three. Basically, you can grid your answer as a fraction in any form that fits. For fraction answers, be as accurate as possible but note that you have only four spaces to work with and that a fraction-slash uses up one of the spaces.

For Example: Some of the fractional answers can be gridded in the following ways:

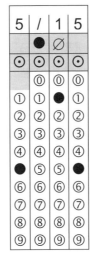

OR

NEVER REDUCE FRACTIONS:

Fractions do not have to be simplified or reduced to their simplest form unless they don't fit in the answer grid. Since full credit is given for any equivalent answer, enter your answer in the simplest way.
For instance: If your answer is 8/12, you should enter 8/12. (However, credit would be given for any of the following: 2/3, 4/6, 6/9, .666, .667.)

Case #1:   If your answer is a fraction that will fit in the grid, just enter it as is. Don't waste time reducing it or converting it to a decimal.
For Example: If your answer is a fraction, such as 2/5 or 5/25 or 8/26, quickly enter it as is.

Case #2:   If your answer is a fraction that won't fit in the grid, and can't be reduced, use your calculator to convert it to a decimal, and then enter it.
For Example: If your answer is a fraction, such as 15/19, it requires five grid-in spaces, 1 5 / 1 9 and it won't fit in a grid. The only way to grid this answer is by reducing it or converting it to a decimal. Since 15/19 can't be reduced, just convert it to a decimal by dividing it on your calculator, and enter .789.

Case #3:   If your answer is a fraction that won't fit in the grid, but can be reduced, do not attempt to reduce it; use your calculator to convert it to a decimal, and then enter it.
For Example: If your answer is a fraction, such as 24/84, it requires five spaces, 2 4 / 8 4 and it wont fit in a grid. However, it can be reduced to 12/42, which doesn't help, or to 6/21 or 2/7, both of which can be entered. But, you don't need to reduce it. Reducing a fraction takes time, and there is always a possibility that you might make a mistake. Don't waste even a few seconds trying to reduce it or take that chance of making a mistake. Just use your calculator and divide, (24 ÷ 84) and enter .285; this way you won't make a mistake.

EZ NOTE: Fractional answer with four digits can't be gridded – it won't fit and will need to be either reduced or converted to a decimal. If your fraction answer is too big to fit in the grid and can't be reduced, it doesn't necessarily mean your answer is wrong; it just means you can only enter it in the form of a decimal. So in such cases, simply reduce your fraction to a decimal and grid it.

10.4.3: Mixed Number Answers:

On Grid-In questions, you can always grid both proper and improper fractions; however, it is not possible to grid mixed numbers. Therefore, if you ever get mixed numbers as your answers, before you grid them, you must convert them to either improper fractions or decimals; it doesn't matter which one you choose, both are correct.

EZ Caution: If you ever try to Grid-In a mixed number, it will be read as a fraction and counted wrong.

For Example: If your answer is 2½, you cannot leave a space and enter your answer as 2 ½. Also, if you try to enter 2½, the scoring machine will read it as the fraction 21/2, which in mixed numbers is actually 10½, and mark it as a wrong answer, and you'll lose a point. So, first change mixed numbers to fractions or decimals, and then grid them. In this case, you must change 2½ to the improper fraction 5/2 and grid in the fraction; or change 2½ to the decimal 2.5 and grid in the decimal. The answer 2½ could be gridded in any of the following two ways; both answers are correct.

✘ WRONG   ✔ RIGHT   ✔ RIGHT

10.4.4: DECIMAL ANSWERS:

For Entering Decimal Answers, Grid-In (.) in the Correct Column: The decimal sign (.) is used for the decimal point, and therefore it separates the integer part from the decimal fractional part. It appears in all four columns. Basically, you can grid your answer as a decimal in any form that fits. For decimal answers, be as accurate as possible but note that you have only four spaces to work with and that a decimal point uses up one of the spaces.

Where to Put the Decimal Point: You must be careful and watch where you place your decimal points.
⇒ For a decimal number less than 1, such as .127, enter the decimal point in the first box.
⇒ For a decimal point greater than 1, such as 1.27, or 12.7, enter the decimal point at the appropriate spot.

For Example: Some of the decimal answers can be gridded in the following ways:

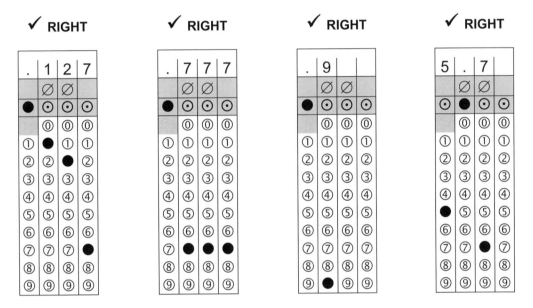

NEVER WRITE A ZERO BEFORE THE DECIMAL POINT:
Do not grid zeros before the decimal point for decimals that are less than 1. The first column of the grid doesn't even have a 0 in it. If the correct answer is 0, you can grid it in column 2, 3, or 4. Zero has been deliberately omitted from column one to promote you to grid the most accurate value for rounded numbers. If you write zero before the decimal point, you'd have to start gridding in the second column, and you might end up running out of space.
For instance: If the correct answer is .25, you don't need to grid 0.25. A simple .25 is enough.
Note: Put a zero before the decimal point only if it is part of the answer, such as, 10.5, 90.1, etc.

NEVER ROUND-OFF YOUR ANSWERS: Truncating is better than Rounding-Off:
When gridding decimals, don't shorten or round-up your decimals. Simply write out the longest version of the answer that fits in the grid. Generally, it's safer to truncate than to round-off. If the correct answer has more than two decimal digits, you must use all four columns of the grid.

Case #1:   If a decimal answer will fit in the grid and you round it off to make it shorter, your answer will be marked wrong.
For Example: If your answer is .125:
⇒ ✔ You should grid it as .125

⇒ ✘ If you truncate and make it shorter, such as, .12 or .1, it would be marked wrong and you will receive no credit.

⇒ ✘ If you correctly round it off to the nearest hundredths place and enter .13, it would be marked wrong and you will receive no credit.

⇒ ✘ If you correctly round it off to the nearest tenths place and enter .1, it would be marked wrong and you will receive no credit.

Case #2: If a decimal answer will not fit in the grid, enter a decimal point in the first column, followed by the first three digits. As a thumb rule, if you obtain a decimal answer with more digits than the grid can accommodate, it may be either rounded or truncated, but it must fill the entire grid. It is recommended that you grid-in only the first three digits, insert the decimal point where it belongs, and truncate the rest of the digits, without rounding-off.

For Example: If your answer is 1.57962:

⇒ ✔ You should grid it as 1.57

⇒ ✘ If you truncate and make it shorter, such as, 1.5 or 1, it would be marked wrong and you will receive no credit.

⇒ ✘ If you correctly round it off to the nearest tenths place and enter 1.6, it would be marked wrong and you will receive no credit.

⇒ ✔ If you correctly round it off to the nearest hundredths place and enter 1.58, it would be marked right and you will receive full credit, but it's not at all required, and you could make a mistake while rounding-off.

EZ NOTE: It's possible that you may occasionally make a mistake in rounding-off, whereas it's impossible to make a mistake if you just copy the first three digits and truncate the rest. Hence, truncating is better than rounding off.

EZ CAUTION: Rounding to a shorter answer may lead to a wrong answer:

FOR LONG REPEATING DECIMALS:
If your answer is an infinite repeating decimal, you must grid the most accurate possible decimal. The easiest rule to follow for gridding long repeating decimals is to completely fill the grid with the answer.

Example #1: If your answer is 0.177777 ⇒ ✔ Grid .177

⇒ ✔ Gridding .178 would also be correct

⇒ ✘ Gridding .1, .17, .18 would be incorrect as these are less accurate

Example #2: If your answer is .78787878 ⇒ ✔ Grid .787

⇒ ✔ Gridding .788 would also be correct

⇒ ✘ Gridding .7, .8 or .78 would be incorrect as these are less accurate

FOR LONG NON-REPEATING DECIMALS:
If your answer is an infinite but non-repeating decimal, you must grid the most accurate possible decimal. The easiest rule to follow for gridding long non-repeating decimals is to completely fill the grid with the answer.

Example #1: If your answer is 1.179286 ⇒ ✔ Grid 1.17

⇒ ✔ Gridding 1.18 would also be correct

⇒ ✘ Gridding 1.1 or 1.2 would be incorrect as these are less accurate

Example #2: If your answer is 96.75218 ⇒ ✔ Grid 96.7

⇒ ✔ Gridding 96.8 would also be correct

⇒ ✘ Gridding 96 or 97 would be incorrect as these are less accurate

10.5 RANGE OF ANSWERS ON GRID-INS

Usually every math problem has only one correct answer; however, that is not always the case with Grid-In questions. Some Grid-In questions only have one correct answer, whereas others have several correct answers. Sometimes Grid-In questions have multiple correct answers, that is, they have a range of possible correct answers. All you have to do is find the range and then pick one value that falls within that range, and grid in only one of the acceptable answers. Whichever one you grid would be right, pick the one that strikes you first. Therefore, whenever there is a range of possible correct answers, simply choose any one answer that lies within the range and grid it.

These types of questions may say something like, "What is one possible value of x?" This phrase indicates that there may be more than one value of x that is correct, which means there are multiple values of x. Under these conditions, simply pick one of the possible answers to grid on your answer sheet.

EZ CAUTION: Don't panic if there seems to be more than one right answer. This doesn't imply that your answer is wrong. In such cases, the grading computer is already configured to accept multiple correct answers.

(i)   If a question asks for a positive number less than 100 that is divisible by both 5 and 7, and there's more that one right answer, such as, 35 or 70 – you could enter either one of them, but not both.

(ii) If a question asks for a positive number less than 100 that is divisible by both 2 and 9, and there's more that one right answer such as, 18, 36, 54, 72, or 90 – you could enter any one of them, but not all.

(iii) If a question asks for a two-digit integer that is a multiple of 2, 3, and 7, and there's more that one right answer, such as, 42 or 84 – you could enter either one of them, but not both.

(iv) If a question asks for a two-digit integer that is a multiple of 2, 3, and 5, and there's more that one right answer, such as, 30, 60, or 90 – you could enter any one of them, but not all.

(v)   If a question asks for a prime number between 5 and 12, and there's more that one right answer, such as, 7 or 11 – you could enter either one of them, but not both.

IN RANGE OF VALUES, DECIMALS ARE EASIER THAN FRACTIONS:
When the answer to a question leads to a range of values, it's often easier to work with decimals than fractions.

(i)   If a question asks for a number between 2/9 and 7/8, and there's more that one right answer – you could enter any one of the hundreds of possibilities.
      Option #1: Find any fraction between 2/9 and 7/8, such as 1/4, 1/2, 3/4, 5/7, 6/11, etc., and grid it.
      Option #2: Find any decimal between 0.222 and 0.875, such as 0.25, 0.5, 0.75, 0.789, 0.815, etc., and grid it.

(ii) If a question asks for a value of n where $6n - 1 > n$ and $5n - 2 < n$
      Solve for n in the first inequality $\Rightarrow 6n - 1 > n \Rightarrow n > 1/5$
      Solve for n in the second inequality $\Rightarrow 5n - 2 < n \Rightarrow n < 1/2$
      The range of correct answer is $1/5 < n < 1/2$, so simply grid in any value that is within this range.
      Option #1: Find any fraction that is in the range: $1/5 < n < 1/2$, such as 1/3, 1/4, 2/5, 2/7, 5/11, etc., and grid it.
      Option #2: Find any decimal that is in the range: $0.2 < n < 0.5$, such as .25, .3, .35, .4, .45, etc., and grid it.
      Note: Gridding in 1/5 or 1/2; .2 or .5 would be considered wrong.

EZ TIP: Finding a fraction within a range may be difficult, it's a lot easier to first convert the fractions to decimals and then find a number in that range.

ROUNDING-OFF IN RANGE OF ANSWERS:
Be careful while rounding-off when there is a range of correct answers.
For Example: If the correct answer to a problem is a number between 7 and 9, exclusive. In this case, even though 7.00001 is within the acceptable range ($7 < n < 9$), its rounded value 7.00 is not within the range and therefore would not be considered a correct answer to the problem.

10.6 EZ GRIDDING FACTS

SMALLEST & LARGEST GRIDDABLE NUMBERS:
- The smallest number that can be gridded is 0.
- The largest number that can be gridded is 9999.
- The smallest number greater than 100 that can be gridded is 101.
- The largest number less than 100 that can be gridded is 99.9.

WHAT YOU CANNOT GRID:
The grid cannot accommodate the following types of answers:
- Negative Answers – answers that are negative, such as, –5, –½, –0.25, etc
- Long Answers – answers that are longer than four digits. i.e., greater than 9999, such as, 10000, 12345, etc
- Variable Answers – answers that have variables, such as, x, y, z, etc

The grid can accommodate only positive numbers and zeros. It's not possible to grid negative numbers of any type in any form. Since there's no option for a negative sign, the answer to every Grid-In question is a positive number or zero.

WHAT DOES THIS IMPLY?
If the answer to a Grid-In question that you come up with is:
- a negative number, or
- greater than 9999, or
- has a variable in it

Then your answer is wrong, and it won't fit in the grid!
Therefore, if you ever obtain any such answer for a Grid-In question, you should automatically know that you have made a mistake. Rework the problem and check your work for errors.

Additionally, you can't grid the following answers; you'll need to modify them into something that can fit in the grid:
- Fraction answers that include more than three numbers, such as, 12/25, 11/27, etc., must be either reduced or converted to decimals.
- Decimal answers that include more than three numbers, such as, .1234, .0025, etc., must be either truncated or rounded off.
- Mixed Number answers, such as, 1¼, 2½, etc., must be converted to either improper fractions or decimals.
- No number greater than 100 can have a decimal point, because any decimal number greater than 100 will require at least five boxes to grid and we only have four available boxes.
  For instance: To grid 100.1 or 150.7, you need more than four empty spaces to grid.
- Answers with commas – for instance, write 1234, and not 1,234.

OTHER GRIDDING STRATEGIES:
Some of the test-taking strategies that can be used on multiple-choice questions don't apply to Grid-Ins. Since Grid-Ins don't have any multiple answer choices, you can't use EZ Smart Guessing Strategy by using POE or apply EZ Back-Solving Strategy.

However, most of the other test taking strategies that we have listed in this book can also be applied to Grid-In problems. For instance, you can still apply estimation strategy, systematic list strategy, plug-in number strategy, most of the miscellaneous strategies, etc. Moreover, some strategies can be modified for Grid-In problems.

As a thumb rule, you can apply all or any of our test-taking strategies that don't take aid of the multiple choices.

CALCULATORS ARE RECOMMENDED ON GRID-IN QUESTIONS:
While calculating the answer on a Grid-In problem, be extra careful with your calculations, and always check your work. Since you won't be getting any feedback from multiple-choice options, and without any answer choices to choose from, you may make careless mistakes. Hence, it may be a good idea to use a calculator for this section to avoid unnecessary errors. However, use your calculator only when it's needed. Read the next chapter to learn how to use your calculator effectively on the SAT.

.PRACTICE EXERCISE WITH DETAILED EXPLANATIONS

After you have a firm understanding of Grid-In guidelines and techniques, it is very important that you check your knowledge by practicing. So before the test, make sure to practice completing a few grids.

Assume that the following 10 numbers are your answers to a set of Grid-In questions. Use the sample empty numbered grids that follow to enter your answers.

Grid-In #1: 0
Grid-In #2: 69
Grid-In #3: 157
Grid-In #4: 1269
Grid-In #5: 7/11

Grid-In #6: 8/40
Grid-In #7: 19/15
Grid-In #8: 77/100
Grid-In #9: 2 ¾
Grid-In #10: 7.7777777

Grid-In #1 | Grid-In #2 | Grid-In #3 | Grid-In #4 | Grid-In #5

Grid-In #6 | Grid-In #7 | Grid-In #8 | Grid-In #9 | Grid-In #10

Answers are on the following page. Each answer grid contains the answer we recommend and other acceptable answers, if there are any.

Grid-In #1:   0

⇒ 0 can be gridded as is without any modifications.
Following are the options to grid the answer:
Option #1:   0   (by gridding it in the second column)
Option #2:   0   (by gridding it in the third column)
Option #3:   0   (by gridding it in the fourth column)
The above option(s) can be gridded in the following position(s):
Note: zero can't be gridded in the first column because it doesn't exist there.

Option #1		Option #2		Option #3
0 in 2nd column	OR	0 in 3rd column	OR	0 in 4th column

Grid-In #2:   69

⇒ 69 can be gridded as is without any modifications.
Following are the options to grid the answer:
Option #1:   69   (by aligning it to the left)
Option #2:   69   (by aligning it to the center)
Option #3:   69   (by aligning it to the right)
The above option(s) can be gridded in the following position(s):

Option #1		Option #2		Option #3
69 aligned left	OR	69 aligned center	OR	69 aligned right

Grid-In #3:   157

⇒ 157 can be gridded as is without any modifications.
Following are the options to grid the answer:
Option #1:   157   (by aligning it to the left)
Option #2:   157   (by aligning it to the right)
The above option(s) can be gridded in the following position(s):

Option #1   **Option #2**

OR

Grid-In #4:   1269

⇒ 1269 can be gridded as is without any modifications.
Following are the options to grid the answer:
Option #1:   1269   (by gridding it as is)
The above option(s) can be gridded in the following position(s):

Option #1

Grid-In #5:   7/11

⇒ 7/11 can be gridded as is without any modifications or in its other equivalents.

Following are the options to grid the answer:

Option #1:   7/11   (by gridding it as is)

Option #2:   .636   (by converting it to its decimal equivalent and truncating the extra digits)

The above option(s) can be gridded in the following position(s):

Option #1   **Option #2**

(grid: Option #1 = 7 / 1 1   OR   Option #2 = . 6 3 6)

Grid-In #6:   8/40

⇒ 8/40 can be gridded as is without any modifications or in its other equivalents.

Following are the options to grid the answer:

Option #1:   8/40   (by gridding it as is)

Option #2:   4/20   (by reducing it to its fractional equivalent)

Option #3:   2/10   (by reducing it to its fractional equivalent)

Option #4:   1/5   (by reducing it to its fractional equivalent)

Option #5:   .2   (by converting it to its decimal equivalent)

The above option(s) can be gridded in the following position(s):

Option #1   **Option #2**   **Option #3**   **Option #4**   **Option #5**

(grid: Option #1 = 8 / 4 0   OR   Option #2 = 4 / 2 0   OR   Option #3 = 2 / 1 0   OR   Option #4 = 1 / 5   OR   Option #5 = . 2)

Grid-In #7:   19/15

⇒ 19/15 can't be gridded as is since it needs five spaces, so it has to be first modified to something that can fit in the grid.

Since 19/15 can't be reduced, the only way is to convert it to its decimal equivalent 1.2666666

Following are the options to grid the answer:

Option #1:   1.26   (by converting to its decimal equivalent and truncating the extra digits)
Option #2:   1.27   (by rounding-off its decimal equivalent)

The above option(s) can be gridded in the following position(s):

Option #1   **Option #2**

OR

Grid-In #8:   77/100

⇒ 77/1000 can't be gridded as is since it needs six spaces, so it has to be first modified to something that can fit in the grid.

Since 77/100 can't be reduced, the only way is to convert it to its decimal equivalent .77

Following are the options to grid the answer:

Option #1:   .77   (by aligning it to the left)
Option #2:   .77   (by aligning it to the right)

The above option(s) can be gridded in the following position(s):

Option #1   **Option #2**

OR

Grid-In #9: 2¾

⇒ 2¾ can't be gridded as is since it's a mixed number, so it has to be first modified to something that can be gridded.

Following are the options to grid the answer:

Option #1: 11/4 (by converting to an improper fraction)

Option #2: 2.75 (by converting to its decimal equivalent)

The above option(s) can be gridded in the following position(s):

Option #1   **Option #2**

OR

Grid-In #10: 7.7777777

⇒ 7.7777777 can't be gridded as is since it's a recurring decimal that won't fit in the grid, so it has to be first modified to something that can fit in the grid.

Following are the options to grid the answer:

Option #1: 7.77 (by truncating)

Option #2: 7.78 (by rounding-off)

Option #3: 70/9 (by converting to its fractional equivalent)

The above option(s) can be gridded in the following position(s):

Option #1   **Option #2**   **Option #3**

OR   OR

CHAPTER 11.0: EZ CALCULATOR STRATEGIES

HIGHLIGHTS:
11.1 Basics About Calculator Use
11.2 Who Should Use Calculator
11.3 When to Use Calculator
11.4 How to Use Calculator
11.5 Most Common Calculator Mistakes
▪ Practice Exercise with Detailed Explanations

You have read and learned all of our EZ strategies/techniques for finding the correct answers to math questions just by using your pencil and your brain and without using a calculator. However, at times it won't hurt to have a calculator handy and get some extra help as-and-when needed. If you are not very comfortable doing the calculation with a pencil or in your mind, it can definitely make your life a lot easier.

As you begin to go through this book, it is suggested that you have available the calculator you plan to take to the test, and you should use it whenever you think it is appropriate. However, you will probably use it more at the beginning of your review than later, because, as you go through this book, you will learn more and more strategies to help you solve problems easily without doing tedious calculations, and your dependency on the calculator will reduce significantly. You'll see more and more ways of how to bypass the use of a calculator.

11.1 BASICS ABOUT CALCULATOR USE

CALCULATORS ARE ALLOWED ON THE SAT:
Yes, you are allowed to bring and use a calculator on the SAT. However, you don't really need it to solve any SAT math question, and it doesn't mean that you should always use your calculator on every problem. Of course, a calculator can do computations faster, much faster than any human brain, but unnecessary use of the calculator may lead to careless mistakes and waste of time.

CALCULATORS ARE NOT REQUIRED ON THE SAT:
Using a calculator will not always make problem solving easier. SAT goes far beyond just testing your ability to do computations. Always remember, each and every math problem on the SAT can be solved within a reasonable amount of time without using a calculator. None of the SAT questions ever requires complicated or tedious calculations. As a matter of fact, there isn't a single question on any section of the SAT for which a calculator is essential. If you ever find yourself doing any extensive or elaborative calculations; i.e., long multiplications or long drawn-out divisions – stop right away, go back and check if you are on the right track. You probably either are on the wrong track or missed a shortcut. However, if you don't see how to avoid the calculations, just go ahead and do it.

You never really need a calculator to solve any SAT problem. In fact, calculators are completely useless on most math problems, especially on algebra questions involving variables or even some of the geometry problems. Even most of the arithmetic problems can be done more easily and quickly without using a calculator. So don't get tempted into blindly using your calculator at every opportunity you get. Calculators may prove to be useful only for questions that involve complex arithmetic computations.

ACCEPTABLE AND UNACCEPTABLE CALCULATORS FOR THE SAT:

Even though you are allowed to bring a calculator to the SAT, there are certain guidelines that are specified for the types of calculators that are permissible and prohibited for the SAT.

ACCEPTABLE CALCULATORS ON THE SAT:

The following are the types of calculators that you are allowed to bring to your exam.
- Four-Function calculators (able to simply add, subtract, multiply, and divide).
- Scientific calculators (able to perform somewhat complex operations, such as, radicals, exponents, etc).
- Graphing calculators (able to perform and display graphing functions).

Note: Some, but not all calculators have the same features and capability; some features depend on the model and make.

Recommended Calculator: Although any four-function, scientific, or graphic calculator is acceptable, we recommend that you use a scientific calculator. Occasionally, it is useful to have a scientific calculator on some questions. Hence, there are some clear advantages to having a scientific graphing calculator.

You should pick a scientific calculator that has the following features:
- Parentheses keys ( ) – You can use this function to do operations within the parentheses.
- Reciprocal key $1/x$ – You can use this function to find the reciprocal of any number.
- Exponent key x^y or $\wedge$ – You can use this function to find any power of any number.
- Ability to do fractional arithmetic – You can use this function to add, subtract, multiply, or divide fractions; for instance, if you want to add 1/2 and 1/9, you can do so by entering 1 / 2 + 1 / 9; the readout will be 11/18, not the decimal 0.611111. You can also reduce fractions; for instance, if you want to reduce 7/56, the calculator will automatically reduce it to 1/8.
  Note: If you are not very comfortable working with fractions, you should definitely get a calculator that can do fractional arithmetic.

Above all, we recommend you use a calculator with which you're already comfortable and thoroughly familiar, probably the one you have used for a long time, in your math classes or at home. The last thing you want to see is to find yourself wasting your precious time exploring and experimenting your new calculator's features or capabilities, and what each button does. This is especially the case if you have a graphing calculator, which has more buttons and operations than the number of hair on your head. Hence, trying to use a calculator that you are not very comfortable or familiar with can have devastating results. If you don't use a calculator regularly, practice on the calculator you plan to use before you take the actual test.

EZ CAUTION: Do not buy a new calculator right before you take the SAT. In case you don't own a calculator already or you want to have a different one, get one immediately and get enough practice using it between now and the day of the test. Do all your practice in this book with the same calculator you plan to take to the test. It takes a while to get accustomed to a calculator and if you get a different one right before you take the SAT, you may not be as quick as you should be using it while taking the actual SAT.

UNACCEPTABLE CALCULATORS ON THE SAT:

The following are the types of calculators that you are NOT allowed to bring to your exam:
- Calculators with typewriter-style keypads (known as "QWERTY")
- Calculators with paper tapes or printers and have the ability to take print outs of the calculations
- Calculators that "talk" or make unusual noises
- Calculators with electronic writing pads or pen-input devices
- Calculators that require an electrical wall outlet
- Pocket organizers PDA's
- Notebook computers, laptop computers, tablet computers, or hand-held minicomputers
- Calculators with an angled read-out screen
- Calculators that have an inbuilt cell-phone or internet connection
- Portable devices that are blue-tooth enabled with a wireless internet connection or otherwise have the ability to transmit two-way audio or video, and which can be used to ask someone the answer to a test question

Note: All of the above types of calculators are strictly prohibited and banned.

11.2 WHO SHOULD USE CALCULATOR

WHO SHOULD & SHOULDN'T USE CALCULATORS:

WHO SHOULDN'T:
If you happen to be one of the students who has strong math skills and is a good test-taker, you will probably use your calculator infrequently, or maybe not at all. The first reason is that strong math students can do a lot of basic arithmetic much more accurately and quickly in their heads, or on paper, than with the help of a calculator. The second reason is that students who are good test-takers will realize that many problems can be solved with very few calculations or even without doing any calculations at all (mental, written, or with a calculator); they will be able to solve these problems in less time than it takes to pick up a calculator and punch-in the numbers.

WHO SHOULD:
On the other hand, if you happen to be one of the students who is not very confident about your arithmetical ability or your test-taking skills, you will probably find your calculator a valuable tool.

CALCULATORS ARE RECOMMENDED:
Never make the mistake of leaving your calculator at home; bring it with you when you go to take the SAT, even if you're not sure if you will use it. As you'll realize, especially in the new SAT, there are several questions on which a calculator could prove to be a useful tool. Moreover, since calculators are permitted, you should definitely make use of this benefit and bring one with you when you take the actual SAT. In short, it is recommended that you bring a calculator to use on the mathematics sections of the SAT.

You are expected to bring your own calculator; the test administrator or the testing center will not provide any calculators. If for any reason you forget to bring a calculator to the actual test, you will not be able to use one. In addition, you will not be allowed to share one with a friend or your neighbor.

Use a Calculator that is Operational: Make sure your calculator is in good working condition and that it has new batteries. It may also be a good idea to bring a spare battery, just in case you run out of it. Also, make sure your calculator is not the one that runs only on solar energy. It is possible that you may not have enough light and your calculator may not function properly. If for any reason your calculator fails during the test, you'll have to complete the test without it.

11.3 When to Use Calculator

When You Should & Shouldn't Use Your Calculator:

As you will see, it's hard to say, this opinion is very subjective, and it varies. If you see the best approach, that is, the shortcut, sometimes a question can be answered in a few seconds, with none or some calculations. In that case, the use of a calculator is not at all recommended. However, if you are not able see the easy way, and have to do some calculations, you may prefer to take the help of a calculator. In such cases, it's better to deal straight away with the calculations than to spend a lot of time looking for a shortcut that may result in wasting more time. For some questions, a calculator may be helpful, while for others it may be completely inappropriate. Calculators may sometimes help you speed up the arithmetic. However, you must develop an understanding of when it will speed-up and when it will slow-down. The trick is to be able to determine when to use the calculator and when not to use it. You'll get better at making this call with some practice. First, try to understand whether the question involves any complex calculations, for which you require the use of a calculator, and then decide between your no. 2 pencil or your electronic machete.

Simply because you've got an amazing glittery sword doesn't mean you should try to use it to slay the ants. Your calculator is a remarkable tool which will help you on the SAT, but only if you use it wisely.

A good combination of using a calculator with the understanding and ability to determine when and how to use it can help you tremendously in solving your math questions much more easily and quickly, and that will improve your overall performance and score on the SAT.

Use Your Calculator for the Following:

- Use your calculator only when you need to use it, and on questions that require the use of a calculator.
- Use your calculator to do complex calculations that would take more time to calculate on your own, and less time if you use your calculator.

For Example: Use your calculator for calculating:

$\Rightarrow$ (157 × 961)   = 150,877
$\Rightarrow$ (2.25 × 6.75)   = 15.1875
$\Rightarrow$ (7.19 × 9.68)   = 69.5992
$\Rightarrow$ (0.725 × 0.975)   = 0.706875
$\Rightarrow$ (0.2769 × 0.5698)   = 0.1577776

Use Calculators on Grid-In Problems: Calculators are particularly useful on Grid-In problems. Since Grid-Ins don't give multiple answer choices to choose from, it's important to be sure about your answer. Moreover, calculators can help you check your calculations quickly and minimize careless errors.

Don't Use Your Calculator for the Following:

Avoid using your calculator too much. Since many problems can be solved more easily and quickly without a calculator, learn to use your calculator only when you need it. You may be tempted to use your calculator on every calculation in every problem; however, you must realize that it's much easier to solve many questions without it.

- Do not use the calculator when you don't need to, and on questions that do not require the use of a calculator.
- Do not use your calculator to do easy calculations that would take less time to calculate on your own, and more time if you use your calculator.

For Example: Don't use your calculator for calculating:

$\Rightarrow$ (25 × 5)   = 125
$\Rightarrow$ (75 × 2)   = 150
$\Rightarrow$ (50 × 10,000)   = 500,000
$\Rightarrow$ (90 × 200)   = 18,000
$\Rightarrow$ (0.125 × 10,000)   = 1,250

11.4 HOW TO USE CALCULATOR

USE, DON'T MISUSE YOUR CALCULATOR:
Use but don't abuse your calculator. Using a calculator on every math problem can be more harmful than useful. Inappropriate use of a calculator can really make things worse. Often times, trying to use a calculator on questions where a non-calculator approach would be better may result in wasting time. Most students tend to use calculators more than they should; however, if you can solve a problem with a calculator that you might otherwise miss, by all means, go ahead and use the calculator.

USE YOUR CALCULATOR WISELY, ONLY WHEN NEEDED:
Be selective while using your calculator. A calculator is most beneficial when it's used selectively and strategically. Not all problems and every part of a problem will necessarily be easier with a calculator. So use it only when you think you need it. First, reason through the question and then look for the easiest and quickest way to solve it, and then finally use a calculator, if it is needed. By segregating the parts of problems that require heavy calculations, you can maximize your score and minimize any careless mistake and your time on the SAT by using your calculator.

Use common sense – the calculator is meant to aid you in problem solving, not to get in the way. Do not get into the habit of using your calculator on every problem that involves arithmetic. Instead of intuitively reaching out for your calculator every time you see a math question, you should think through on how you will solve the problem, come up with a problem-solving plan based on what's given in the beginning of this book, and then decide whether you need to use the calculator. As a rule of thumb, use a calculator only to save time, not because you feel lazy to work out a calculation.

CALCULATIONS IN YOUR HEAD OR BY HAND:
You are allowed to write anything in your test booklet. This means you can use your test booklet like a scratch paper for doing all your calculations and work. Don't overuse your calculator; you should be able to do simple calculations in your head or by hand in your test booklet in order to get your thoughts down on paper before you start punching numbers on your calculator.

CALCULATORS ARE USEFUL:
Sometimes, the use of the calculator enables you to do arithmetic more quickly and more accurately than solving by hand or in your head. You should use your calculator to get the right answers to questions that you do not know how to solve or you are unable to solve without a calculator.

Research shows that students who use calculators on the SAT do slightly better than students who do not. Using a calculator helps ensure that you won't miss a question because of computational errors. Although math scores may improve on an average with the use of calculators, there is no way to generalize the effect of calculator use on an individual student's score. You should be fine if you follow the tips and advice given in this section.

USE YOUR CALCULATOR CAREFULLY, NOT CARELESSLY:
You should use your calculator carefully, not carelessly. It is very easy to make a mistake on the calculator by accidentally hitting the wrong button without even realizing it since the calculator will just give you the answer to your calculation and not show your work or the numbers you punched in. So there is no way to look at your work or to find out if you made any mistake. This is one more reason to limit the use of a calculator to only when it is required.

DO YOUR CALCULATIONS TWICE:
Don't blindly trust everything that your calculator does, it's possible that you punched in wrong numbers or did something other than what should have been done. So, always make sure that the result it displays makes sense. You should do the calculation twice on the calculator to make sure you didn't make a mistake, but only if you have extra time.

THE WRONG AND RIGHT APPROACH:

When it comes to using a calculator on the SAT math problems, there's always a wrong and right approach. Generally, if you're just punching keys in place of thinking, you're approaching the problem in a wrong way.

THE WRONG APPROACH:

⇒ ✖ Get hold of your calculator

    ⇒ ✖ Start punching all the numbers that you see in the problem

        ⇒ ✖ Mark your answer and wish that you didn't make any mistakes or hit any wrong buttons

THE RIGHT APPROACH:

⇒ ✓ First, think of the best method to approach the problem

    ⇒ ✓ Then, work out the problem on your scratch paper

        ⇒ ✓ Finally, use your calculator only on the parts that involve complex calculations

CALCULATOR MYTH:

CALCULATORS CAN DO THE ARITHMETIC BUT NOT THE MATHEMATICS:

The calculator is only a machine, not a human, and has a limited value on the SAT – but some students are under the misconception that they can just pop out their calculator and it will magically solve their problems. All that a calculator can do is the arithmetical calculation; no calculator can do the mathematics for you. You have to know the math (formulas and concepts) involved and the right way to apply them. No calculator in the world can tell you how to set up a problem or which formula to apply. A calculator can only do accurate computations; it does not have the ability to understand or set up and solve a mathematical problem.

For instance, a calculator can efficiently and accurately calculate the square of 127 or 1257^5 in less time than it would take you to do the calculation on paper. For such calculations, the calculator would save you a lot of time, but you are very unlikely to do such types of calculations on the SAT.

For Example: What is the sum of all the integers from 50 through 70, inclusive?

Solution: One way to answer to answer this question is by grabbing your calculator and start punching in all the numbers from 50 to 70, and find their sum.
This means hitting many keys and chances are that you may accidentally press the wrong key and get a wrong answer. With so many numbers to punch, you're likely to hit a wrong key and you may have to start over from scratch. Even if you don't accidentally hit a wrong key, punching in all those numbers will take too much time. Anyhow, this whole process could be very time-consuming, and in case you haven't noticed, it has a lot of scope for errors.

The other way to answer this question is by looking for a smart shortcut that doesn't depend on a calculator.
You will learn this in averages that the short-way to find the sum of integers that are consecutive is to – first find the average of the terms by adding the smallest and largest integer and dividing by two – then find the number of terms by subtracting the smallest integer from the largest one and add 1 – finally find the sum by multiplying the average of terms by the number of terms.

Here's how it works:

Average of Terms = (50 + 70) ÷ 2 = 120 ÷ 2 = 60
Number of Terms = 70 – 50 + 1 = 21
Sum = (average of terms) × (number of terms) = 60 × 21 = 1,260

If you want, the only part of this question where you should use your calculator is for the last step, that is, for multiplying 60 and 21.

11.5 MOST COMMON CALCULATOR MISTAKES

11.5.1: CALCULATING BEFORE ANALYZING:

One of the most common mistakes students make while using a calculator is to start entering numbers in their calculators without any plan of attack or giving any thought to how they should approach the problem. Some students even make the mistake of solving the entire problem just in their calculators without even touching their pencil. They just grab their calculators, start inputting all the numbers that they see in the problem, and enter their answers in the hope that they didn't make any errors by pressing any wrong buttons. This is a blunder, and you should stay away from it. Between the time you read a problem and the time you start punching numbers after numbers, there is a huge chance of losing track of the problem. So don't immediately reach for your calculator. Even if the question seems more of a straight math problem than a word problem, always first simplify it and then use the calculator if needed.

This is a common and simple error that students make while using a calculator. The right approach is to think of the shortest method to approach the problem, work out the problem on your scratch paper as much as you can, and if needed use your calculator only on the parts that involve complicated computations.

EZ TIP: The amount of calculations involved in directly solving a problem should indicate that there must be an easier way.

EZ CAUTION: Always remember, while doing large number of calculations, there's an equally large scope of margin for errors.

Following examples are solved with heavy calculator use and without calculator use so that you can see the difference between the two approaches.

Example #1: If $x \neq 1/3$ and $\dfrac{97}{6x-2} = \dfrac{97}{88}$, then what is the value of x?

Solution A: **With Heavy Calculator Use:**
Solve the given equation by cross multiplication:
$\Rightarrow \dfrac{97}{6x-2} = \dfrac{97}{88}$
$\Rightarrow 97(6x - 2) = (97)(88)$ [cross-multiply both sides of the equation]
$\Rightarrow 582x - 194 = 8536$ [apply distributive property]
$\Rightarrow 582x = 8536 + 194 = 8730$ [add 194 to both sides of the equation]
$\Rightarrow x = \dfrac{8730}{582} = 15$ [divide both sides of the equation by 582]

Solution B: **Without Calculator Use:**
If you notice, the numerators in both the fractions are the same. When two fractions are equal, and if the tops (numerators) of the fractions are equal, then the bottoms (denominators) must also be equal. So, we can simplify the equation, and all we have is the following:
$\Rightarrow 6x - 2 = 88$
$\Rightarrow 6x = 88 + 2 = 90$ [add 2 to both sides of the equation]
$\Rightarrow x = \dfrac{90}{6} = 15$ [divide both sides of the equation by 6]

Example #2: What is the value of $2(5n^2 + 6n + 8) - 5(2n^2 + n + 1)$ when $n = 1.1$?

Solution A: **With Heavy Calculator Use:**
$\Rightarrow 2(5n^2 + 6n + 8) - 5(2n^2 + n + 1)$
$\Rightarrow 2[5(1.1)^2 + 6(1.1) + 8] - 5[2(1.1)^2 + (1.1) + 1]$ [plug-in $n = 1.1$]
$\Rightarrow 2[5(1.21) + 6(1.1) + 8] - 5[2(1.21) + (1.1) + 1]$ [solve the exponents]

$\Rightarrow 2[6.05 + 6.6 + 8] - 5[2.42 + 1.1 + 1]$ [multiply using distributive property]
$\Rightarrow 2[20.65] - 5[4.52]$ [add within brackets]
$\Rightarrow 41.3 - 22.6$ [multiply]
$\Rightarrow 18.7$ [subtract]

Solution B: **Without Calculator Use:**
$\Rightarrow 2(5n^2 + 6n + 8) - 5(2n^2 + n + 1)$
$\Rightarrow 10n^2 + 12n + 16 - 10n^2 - 5n - 5$ [multiply using distributive property]
$\Rightarrow (10n^2 - 10n^2) + (12n - 5n) + (16 - 5)$ [group like-terms]
$\Rightarrow (0) + (7n) + (11)$ [combine like-terms]
$\Rightarrow 7(1.1) + 11$ [plug-in $n = 1.1$]
$\Rightarrow 7.7 + 11$ [multiply]
$\Rightarrow 18.7$ [add]

SIMPLIFY BY CANCELING OUT:

If you see a long series of numbers, don't immediately jump for your calculator; instead, look for ways to simplify by combining like-terms and canceling-out the common terms. Usually, in such situations, there will be some way to simplify.

Example #1: What is the value of n when $(5n)^2 \times 6^2 = 25 \times 36 \times 64 \times 81$?

Solution A: **With Heavy Calculator Use:**
$\Rightarrow (5n)^2 \times 6^2 = 25 \times 36 \times 64 \times 81$
$\Rightarrow 25n^2 \times 36 = 25 \times 36 \times 64 \times 81$ [solve the exponents]
$\Rightarrow 900n^2 = 4,665,600$ [multiply terms on both sides of the equation]
$\Rightarrow n^2 = 4,665,600 \div 900 = 5184$ [divide both sides of the equation by 900]
$\Rightarrow n = \sqrt{5184} = 72$ [square root both sides of the equation]

Solution B: **Without Calculator Use:**
$\Rightarrow (5n)^2 \times 6^2 = 25 \times 36 \times 64 \times 81$
$\Rightarrow (5n)^2 \times 6^2 = 5^2 \times 6^2 \times 8^2 \times 9^2$ [write all terms in exponential (square) form]
$\Rightarrow n^2 \times 5^2 \times 6^2 = 5^2 \times 6^2 \times 8^2 \times 9^2$ [cancel common terms on both sides of the equation]
$\Rightarrow n^2 = 8^2 \times 9^2$ [simplify]
$\Rightarrow n^2 = 72^2$ [multiply terms on both sides of the equation]
$\Rightarrow n = 72$ [square root both sides of the equation]

Example #2: What is the value of n when $\dfrac{(96.87)(8.11)}{n} = (0.09687)(81.1)$?

Solution A: **With Heavy Calculator Use:**
$\Rightarrow \dfrac{(96.87)(8.11)}{n} = (0.09687)(81.1)$
$\Rightarrow \dfrac{785.6157}{n} = (7.856157)$ [combine like terms on both sides of the equation]
$\Rightarrow (7.856157)n = 785.6157$ [multiply both sides of the equation by n]
$\Rightarrow n = \dfrac{785.6157}{7.856157} = 100$ [divide both sides of the equation by 7.856157]

Solution B: **Without Calculator Use:**
$\Rightarrow \dfrac{(96.87)(8.11)}{n} = (0.09687)(81.1)$
$\Rightarrow n = \dfrac{(96.87)(8.11)}{(0.09687)(81.1)}$ [cross multiple both sides of the equation]

Now you must realize that the numerator and the denominator have the same numbers; however, the numerator has 4 decimal places and the denominator has 6 decimal spaces. Hence, we can simply move the decimal places and the numerator must be multiplied by 100.
$\Rightarrow n = 100$

SIMPLIFY BY FACTORING:

If you see an expression that can be factored, try to first factor it. In most cases, factoring the given expression will simplify the calculations involved.

Example #1:   What is the value of $x^2 + 16x + 64$ when $x = 92$?

Solution A: **With Heavy Calculator Use:**

$\Rightarrow x^2 + 16x + 64$

$\Rightarrow (92)^2 + 16(92) + 64$ [plug-in $x = 92$ in the given expression]

$\Rightarrow 8464 + 1472 + 64$ [do the exponent and multiplication]

$\Rightarrow 10,000$ [add to find the final value]

Solution B: **Without Calculator Use:**

$\Rightarrow x^2 + 16x + 64$

$\Rightarrow (x + 8)^2$ [factor in the given trinomial into two binomials]

$\Rightarrow (92 + 8)^2$ [plug-in $x = 92$]

$\Rightarrow (100)^2$ [add the values with the parentheses]

$\Rightarrow 10,000$ [square to find the final value]

Example #2:   What is the value of $\dfrac{a^2 - b^2}{a - b}$ when $a = 9.7$ and $b = 8.2$?

Solution A: **With Heavy Calculator Use:**

$\Rightarrow \dfrac{a^2 - b^2}{a - b}$

$\Rightarrow \dfrac{(9.7)^2 - (8.2)^2}{9.7 - 8.2}$ [plug-in the value of a and b in the given expression]

$\Rightarrow \dfrac{(94.09) - (67.24)}{9.7 - 8.2}$ [solve the exponents]

$\Rightarrow \dfrac{26.85}{1.5}$ [subtract the numbers in numerator and denominator]

$\Rightarrow 17.9$ [divide to find the final value]

Solution B: **Without Calculator Use:**

$\Rightarrow \dfrac{a^2 - b^2}{a - b}$

$\Rightarrow \dfrac{(a + b)(a - b)}{(a - b)}$ [factor-in the numerator into two binomials]

$\Rightarrow a + b$ [cancel-out the common factors in numerator & denominator]

$\Rightarrow 9.7 + 8.2$`   [plug-in the value of a and b]

$\Rightarrow 17.9$ [add to find the final value]

11.5.2: IGNORING THE ORDER OF OPERATION:

One of the most common mistakes students make while using a calculator is to enter numbers in their calculator in the order they appear in the problem. They forget to realize that a normal calculator does not have the capability of determining the correct order of operation. Even if you are doing the calculations using a calculator, you just can't keep entering the numbers. You've got to follow the correct order of operations, just like while solving it with a pen and paper. If you just punch in the numbers in series, it doesn't guarantee a correct answer. Many students have a tendency of forgetting about this as soon as they get hold of a calculator. Although this may seem like a simple error that students make while using a calculator, it can very well cost you a few points on the SAT. Make sure to follow the correct order of operation, which is PEMDAS.

PEMDAS stands for
$\Rightarrow$ P – Parentheses
$\Rightarrow$ E – Exponents
$\Rightarrow$ M – Multiplication
$\Rightarrow$ D – Division
$\Rightarrow$ A – Addition
$\Rightarrow$ S – Subtraction

In short, do whatever is in parentheses first, then deal with exponents, then multiplications and divisions (from left to right), and finally additions and subtractions (from left to right).

EZ REFERENCE: To learn more about "Order or Operations", refer to our Content-Knowledge Review-Module on Arithmetic.

For Example: What is the value of the expression $\dfrac{x^2 - 25}{2x - 10}$ when $x = 15$?

Solution A: **The Wrong Way: Error with Using a Calculator:**
If you blindly entered the numbers in the order they appear in the problem, you would enter the following:
$\Rightarrow 15 \times 15 - 25 \div 2 \times 15 - 10 \Rightarrow$ and you will get 1490 as your answer, which is wrong!

Solution B: **The Right Way: Without Using a Calculator:**
The correct way to work this problem is to follow the order of operation, which is as follows:
$\Rightarrow (15^2 - 25) \div (2 \times 15 - 10)$
$\Rightarrow (225 - 25) \div (30 - 10)$
$\Rightarrow (200) \div (20)$
$\Rightarrow 10$

EZ NOTE: If you notice, even in the above problem you really don't need to touch your calculator!

-PRACTICE EXERCISE WITH DETAILED EXPLANATIONS

Question #1:   What is the value of $2(5n^2 + 8n + 6) - 5(2n^2 + n + 1)$ when $n = 9.9$?

Solution A: **With Heavy Calculator Use:**

$\Rightarrow 2(5n^2 + 8n + 6) - 5(2n^2 + n + 1)$

$\Rightarrow 2[5(9.9)^2 + 8(9.9) + 6] - 5[2(9.9)^2 + (9.9) + 1]$ [plug-in $n = 9.9$]

$\Rightarrow 2[5(98.01) + 8(9.9) + 6] - 5[2(98.01) + (9.9) + 1]$ [solve the exponents]

$\Rightarrow 2[490.05 + 79.2 + 6] - 5[196.02 + 9.9 + 1]$ [multiply using distributive property]

$\Rightarrow 2[575.25] - 5[206.92]$ [add within brackets]

$\Rightarrow 1150.5 - 1034.6$ [multiply]

$\Rightarrow 115.9$ [subtract]

Solution B: **Without Calculator Use:**

$\Rightarrow 2(5n^2 + 8n + 6) - 5(2n^2 + n + 1)$

$\Rightarrow 10n^2 + 16n + 12 - 10n^2 - 5n - 5$ [multiply using distributive property]

$\Rightarrow (10n^2 - 10n^2) + (16n - 5n) + (12 - 5)$ [group like-terms]

$\Rightarrow (0) + (11n) + (7)$ [combine like-terms]

$\Rightarrow 11(9.9) + 7$ [plug-in $n = 9.9$]

$\Rightarrow 108.9 + 7$ [multiply]

$\Rightarrow 115.9$ [add]

Question #2:   What is the value of $x^2 + 18x + 81$ when $x = 16$?

Solution A: **With Heavy Calculator Use:**

$\Rightarrow x^2 + 18x + 81$

$\Rightarrow (16)^2 + 16(18) + 81$ [plug-in $x = 16$ in the given expression]

$\Rightarrow 256 + 288 + 64$ [do the exponent and multiplication]

$\Rightarrow 625$ [add to find the final value]

Solution B: **Without Calculator Use:**

$\Rightarrow x^2 + 18x + 81$

$\Rightarrow (x + 9)^2$ [factor in the given trinomial into two binomials]

$\Rightarrow (16 + 9)^2$ [plug-in $x = 16$]

$\Rightarrow (25)^2$ [add the values with the parentheses]

$\Rightarrow 625$ [square to find the final value]

Question #3:   What is the value of $\dfrac{a^2 - b^2}{a - b}$ when $a = 15.2$ and $b = 12.7$?

Solution A: **With Heavy Calculator Use:**

$\Rightarrow \dfrac{a^2 - b^2}{a - b}$

$\Rightarrow \dfrac{(15.2)^2 - (12.7)^2}{15.2 - 12.7}$ [plug-in the value of a and b in the given expression]

$\Rightarrow \dfrac{(231.04) - (161.29)}{15.2 - 12.7}$ [solve the exponents]

$\Rightarrow \dfrac{69.75}{2.5}$ [subtract the numbers in numerator and denominator]

$\Rightarrow 27.9$ [divide to find the final value]

Solution B: **Without Calculator Use:**

$$\Rightarrow \frac{a^2 - b^2}{a - b}$$

$$\Rightarrow \frac{(a + b)(a - b)}{(a - b)}$$ [factor-in the numerator into two binomials]

$\Rightarrow a + b$ [cancel-out the common factors in numerator & denominator]

$\Rightarrow 15.2 + 12.7$ [plug-in the value of a and b]

$\Rightarrow 27.9$ [add to find the final value]

Question #4:   What is the value of n when $(11n)^2 \times 12^2 = 121 \times 144 \times 49 \times 64$?

Solution A: **With Heavy Calculator Use:**

$\Rightarrow (11n)^2 \times 12^2 = 121 \times 144 \times 49 \times 64$

$\Rightarrow 121n^2 \times 144 = 121 \times 144 \times 49 \times 64$ [solve the exponents]

$\Rightarrow 17424n^2 = 54{,}641{,}664$ [multiply terms on both sides of the equation]

$\Rightarrow n^2 = 54{,}641{,}664 \div 17424 = 3136$ [divide both sides of the equation by 17424]

$\Rightarrow n = \sqrt{3136} = 56$ [square root both sides of the equation]

Solution B: **Without Calculator Use:**

$\Rightarrow (11n)^2 \times 12^2 = 121 \times 144 \times 49 \times 64$

$\Rightarrow (11n)^2 \times 12^2 = 11^2 \times 12^2 \times 7^2 \times 8^2$ [write all terms in exponential (square) form]

$\Rightarrow n^2 \times \cancel{11^2} \times \cancel{12^2} = \cancel{11^2} \times \cancel{12^2} \times 7^2 \times 8^2$ [cancel common terms on both sides of the equation]

$\Rightarrow n^2 = 7^2 \times 8^2$ [simplify]

$\Rightarrow n^2 = 56^2$ [multiply terms on both sides of the equation]

$\Rightarrow n = 56$ [square root both sides of the equation]

Question #5:   What is the value of n when $\dfrac{(85.72)(9.16)}{n} = (0.8572)\,(91.6)$?

Solution A: **With Heavy Calculator Use:**

$$\Rightarrow \frac{(85.72)(9.16)}{n} = (0.8572)\,(91.6)$$

$$\Rightarrow \frac{785.1952}{n} = (78.51952)$$ [combine like terms on both sides of the equation]

$\Rightarrow (78.51952)n = 785.1952$ [multiply both sides of the equation by n]

$$\Rightarrow n = \frac{785.1952}{78.51952} = 10$$ [divide both sides of the equation by 78.51952]

Solution B: **Without Calculator Use:**

$$\Rightarrow \frac{(85.72)(9.16)}{n} = (0.8572)\,(91.6)$$

$$\Rightarrow n = \frac{(85.72)(9.16)}{(0.8572)(91.6)}$$ [cross multiple both sides of the equation]

Now you must realize that the numerator and the denominator have the same numbers; however, the numerator has 4 decimal places and the denominator has 5 decimal spaces. Hence, we can simply move the decimal places and the numerator must be multiplied by 10.

$\Rightarrow n = 10$

Question #6: What is the value of the expression $\dfrac{x^2 - 1}{2x - 12}$ when $x = 11$?

Solution A: **The Wrong Way: Error with Using a Calculator:**
If you blindly entered the numbers in the order they appear in the problem, you would enter the following:
$\Rightarrow 11 \times 11 - 1 \div 2 \times 11 - 12 \Rightarrow$ and you will get 648 as your answer, which is wrong!

Solution B: **The Right Way: Without Using a Calculator:**
The correct way to work this problem is to follow the order of operation, which is as follows:
$\Rightarrow (11^2 - 1) \div (2 \times 11 - 12)$
$\Rightarrow (121 - 1) \div (22 - 12)$
$\Rightarrow (120) \div (10)$
$\Rightarrow 12$

EZ BOOK STORE: ORDERS & SALES

ORDERS & SALES INFORMATION: Copies of this book can be ordered by one of the following EZ methods:

① 🖥 ON-LINE ORDERS:
On-line Orders can be placed 24/7 via internet by going to: www.EZmethods.com

② ✉ E-MAIL ORDERS:
E-Mail Orders can be placed 24/7 via internet by emailing: orders@EZmethods.com

③ ☎ PHONE ORDERS:
Phone Orders can be placed via telephone by calling: 301.622.9597

④ ✉ MAIL ORDERS:
Mail Orders can be placed via regular mail by writing to the address given below:
Orders Department
EZ Solutions
P.O. Box 10755
Silver Spring, MD 20914
Note: You may also purchase this book from your bookseller.

Institutional Sales: For volume/bulk sales to schools, colleges, universities, organization, and institutions, please contact us. Quantity discounts are available.

EZ BOOK LIST

EZ SAT TEST PREPARATION SERIES OF BOOKS:
Following is the complete list of all the modules for SAT Test Prep by EZ Solutions:

- EZ SAT General Test Taking Strategies
- EZ SAT Math Test Taking Strategies – Problem Solving & Data Sufficiency
- EZ SAT Math Content-Knowledge Review Modules:
  - EZ SAT Math Content Knowledge Review Module – Arithmetic Module
  - EZ SAT Math Content Knowledge Review Module – Algebra Module
  - EZ SAT Math Content Knowledge Review Module – Geometry Module
  - EZ SAT Math Content Knowledge Review Module – Word Problems Module
  - EZ SAT Math Content Knowledge Review Module – Algebra Applications Module
- EZ SAT Reading Content-Knowledge Review Modules:
  - EZ SAT Reading Content Knowledge Review Module – Reading Comprehension
  - EZ SAT Reading Content Knowledge Review Module – Sentence Completion
- EZ SAT Writing Content-Knowledge Review Modules:
  - EZ SAT Writing Content Knowledge Review Module – Essay Writing
  - EZ SAT Writing Content Knowledge Review Module – Sentence Corrections

Note: Some of these books have already been published and others will be released shortly.

LIST OF PUBLICATION BY EZ SOLUTIONS:
Following is the complete list of publication by EZ Solutions:

- EZ GMAT Test Preparation Series of Books:
- EZ GRE Test Preparation Series of Books:
- EZ SAT Test Preparation Series of Books:
- EZ PSAT Test Preparation Series of Books:
- EZ ACT Test Preparation Series of Books:
- EZ PRAXIS Test Preparation Series of Books:
- EZ POWER Test Preparation Series of Books:

Note: Some of these books have already been published and others will be released shortly.